The Open Book 🌿

Creative Misreading in the Works of Selected Modern Writers

Margaret M. Jensen

palgrave
macmillan

First published 2002 by
PALGRAVE MACMILLAN™
175 Fifth Avenue, New York, N.Y. 10010 and
Houndmills, Basingstoke, Hampshire, England RG21 6XS.
Companies and representatives throughout the world.

PALGRAVE MACMILLAN is the global academic imprint of the Palgrave
Macmillan division of St. Martin's Press, LLC and of Palgrave Macmillan
Ltd. Macmillan® is a registered trademark in the United States, United
Kingdom and other countries. Palgrave is a registered trademark in the Eu-
ropean Union and other countries.

ISBN 0–312–29353–4

Library of Congress Cataloging-in-Publication Data
Jensen, Margaret M., 1963-
The open book : creative misreading in the works of selected modern writers
/ by Margaret M. Jensen.
   p.   cm.
Includes bibliographical references and index.
ISBN 0–312–29353–4
   1. English fiction—20th century—History and criticism.   2. Hardy,
Thomas, 1840–1928—Criticism and interpretation.   3. Mansfield,
Katherine, 1888–1923—Criticism and interpretation.   4. Woolf, Virginia,
1882–1941—Criticism and interpretation.   5. Reader-response criticism.
I. Title.

PR881.J46   2002
823'.91209—dc21   2002020724

A catalogue record for this book is available from the British Library.

Design by Letra Libre, Inc.

First edition: July 2002
10 9 8 7 6 5 4 3 2 1

Printed in the United States of America.

To the lost brothers.

Acknowledgements

I acknowledge and thank The Society of Authors as the Literary Representative of the Estate of Virginia Woolf for permission to reprint from *A Room of One's Own, Jacob's Room, The Voyage Out, To the Lighthouse, Mrs. Dalloway, Collected Essays by Virginia Woolf,* and *Orlando.*

Extracts from *A Room of One's Own* by Virginia Woolf, copyright 1929 by Harcourt, Inc. and renewed 1957 by Leonard Woolf, reprinted by permission of the publisher.

Extracts from *Mrs. Dalloway* by Virginia Woolf, copyright 1925 by Harcourt, Inc. and renewed 1953 by Leonard Woolf, reprinted by permission of the publisher.

Extracts from *To the Lighthouse* by Virginia Woolf, copyright 1927 by Harcourt, Inc. and renewed 1954 by Leonard Woolf, reprinted by permission of the publisher.

Extract from "A Sketch of the Past" in *Moments of Being* by Virginia Woolf, copyright © 1976 by Quentin Bell and Angelica Garnett, reprinted by permission of Harcourt, Inc.

Extract from *Moments of Being* by Virginia Woolf, published by the Hogarth Press. Used by permission of the executors of the Virginia Woolf estate and by The Random House Group Limited.

Extracts from *The Letters of Virginia Woolf* by Virginia Woolf, published by the Hogarth Press. Used by permission of the executors of the Virginia Woolf estate and The Random House Group Limited.

Extract from "Letter to Violet Dickinson" in *The Letters of Virginia Woolf, Volume 1: 1888–1912,* copyright © 1975 by Quentin Bell and Angelica Garnett, reprinted by permission of Harcourt, Inc.

Extracts from *The Letters of Virginia Woolf, Volume 2: 1912–1922,* copyright © 1976 by Quentin Bell and Angelica Garnett, reprinted by permission of Harcourt, Inc.

Extracts from *The Letters of Virginia Woolf, Volume 3: 1923–1927,* copyright © 1977 by Quentin Bell and Angelica Garnett, reprinted by permission of Harcourt, Inc.

I acknowledge and thank The Society of Authors, as the Literary Representative of the Estate of Katherine Mansfield for their permission to reprint extracts from *Katherine Mansfield's Letters to John Middleton Murry 1913–1922* by Katherine Mansfield, J. M. Murry ed., published by Constable and Co, 1951.

I acknowledge and thank The Society of Authors, as the Literary Representative of the Estate of John Middleton Murry for their permission to reprint extracts from *The Letters of John Middleton Murry to Katherine Mansfield*, by J. M. Murry, C. A. Hankin ed., published by Constable, 1983.

I acknowledge and thank The Society of Authors, as the Literary Representative of the Estate of John Middleton Murry for their permission to reprint extracts from John Middleton Murry's letters to Thomas Hardy and the poem "To T.H." I would also like to thank and acknowledge the Trustees of the Thomas Hardy Memorial Collection at Dorset County Museum for their assistance and permission to use these extracts as well.

I acknowledge and thank The Society of Authors as the Literary Representative of the Estate of John Middleton Murry for their permission to reprint extracts from *Defending Romanticism: Selected Essays of John Middleton Murry* by J. M. Murry, Malcolm Woodfield, ed., published by Bristol Press.

Extracts from *The Anxiety of Influence* by Harold Bloom, © 1973 by Oxford University Press, are reprinted by permission of the publisher.

Extracts from *Hardy* by Martin Seymour-Smith, 1994, published by Bloomsbury Publishing are reprinted by permission of the publisher.

Extracts from *The Collected Letters of Thomas Hardy* by Thomas Hardy, Richard Purdy and Michael Millgate eds., are reprinted by permission of the Oxford University Press. Letters © Trustees of the Thomas Hardy Estate.

Extracts from *The Collected Letters of Thomas Hardy, Volume I: 1840–1892* Richard Purdy and Michael Millgate eds. 1978–88.

Letters © Trustees of the Thomas Hardy Estate, 1978, by permission of the Oxford University Press.

Extracts from *The Collected Letters of Thomas Hardy, Volume V: 1914–1919* Richard Purdy and Michael Millgate eds. 1978–88.

Letters © Trustees of the Thomas Hardy Estate, 1985, by permission of the Oxford University Press.

Extracts from *The Collected Letters of Thomas Hardy, Volume VI: 1920–1925* Richard Purdy and Michael Millgate eds. 1978–88.

Letters © Trustees of the Thomas Hardy Estate, 1987, by permission of the Oxford University Press.

.

Preface

I began this study in 1991. In the ten or so years since then, I married, moved countries, moved universities, changed jobs, and had a child. Thus, the list of people who have helped me along the way is commensurate with such a period of gestation. Firstly I would like to thank my editors, Maura Burnett and Kristi Long, for their patience and much needed guidance. Secondly my fervent thanks, respect, and admiration to my academic supervisors, Professors Suzanne Raitt and Perry Meisel, without whom there would have been no Woolf in me, and therefore, no book. My colleagues at Kingston University, Dr. David Rogers and Dr. Anne Rowe in particular, have provided me with support and perspective over the years— thank you both. I also owe an untold debt to my students, whose curiosity has aided, abetted and challenged my own.

On a personal note, I offer heartfelt gratitude to my former boss, Mr. Ardeshir Laloui, who put up with me being a bad secretary for a very long time, because he believed night school should come first. My girlfriends, I thank you for the reality checks, the babysitting, and of course the laughs that allowed me to keep working. My brothers and sisters have all offered guidance over the years; help in the field of publishing, financial assistance, emotional rescues and attitude adjustments: they alone know what it means to me to have my voice heard here. To my parents, a special note: Mom, thank you for loving books, and Dad, thank you for paying a childhood's worth of overdue fines at Hicksville Library. Finally, to Stephen and Tessa: no words of thanks are enough—it is for you I write.

Chapter One ❧

Palimpsest

Gratitude and Subterfuge:
The dynamics of (inter)textual relations

In 1919, Virginia Woolf wrote an essay entitled "Modern Novels" in which, among other things, she bemoaned the state of the novel as she then saw it. "In making any survey, even the freest and loosest, of modern fiction," Woolf began, "it is difficult not to take it for granted that the modern practice of the art is somehow an improvement upon the old" (189).[1] As Woolf soon makes clear, however, this is not her view of things at all. Instead, she argues that it is "doubtful whether in the course of the centuries [. . .] we have learnt anything about making literature. We do not come to write better" (189).

As the essay continues, Woolf details the causes for her dissatisfaction. The work of modern "materialist" fiction writers, Woolf argues, "at this moment [. . .] more often misses than secures the thing we seek" (189). Of novelist Arnold Bennett she is particularly wary, noting that "he can make a book so well constructed and solid in its craftsmanship that it is difficult for the most exacting of critics to see through what chink or crevice decay can creep in" (189). For Woolf, it seems, the perfection of form achieved by such writers induces a kind of claustrophobia on the reader: there is, she complains, no room for real, flawed life to exist in works like these.

As Woolf's argument demonstrates, she found the Edwardian novelists' emphasis on the accurate and realistic depiction of the material world to be misguided. In spite of the attempts of these writers to capture reality through their carefully detailed descriptions, Woolf believed that, effectively, they ignore the most important aspects of life. "And yet," Woolf asks, "if life should refuse to live there?" Then "[w]hat is the point of it all?" (189). In her view, despite the materialists' "magnificent apparatus," in their novels "[l]ife escapes; and perhaps without life nothing else is worthwhile" (189). Shortly after this brusque dismissal, Woolf makes another biting criticism of her contemporaries. For all the skill of these modern novelists, Woolf insists, their work "fails to compare" with the great writers of the past, "Mr. Hardy" and "Mr. Conrad" among them. It is to these novelists, and not to her contemporaries, that Woolf expresses her "unconditional gratitude" (189), though even this debt is described as partial and insecure. Woolf argues that these "classic" writers "have excited so many hopes and disappointed them so persistently that our gratitude largely takes the form of thanking them for having shown us what it is that we certainly could not do, but as certainly, perhaps, do not wish to do" (189).

This theme of gratitude, indebtedness, and the mixed blessing of literary influence reverberates throughout this essay as Woolf discusses the relative pressures upon writers past and present. As she makes clear at the opening of the piece, it is for the "historian of literature to decide" (189) the merits of the modern period and the debts it owes to the past, for those in the midst of that era have a necessarily limited view. Woolf later summed up this ambivalence toward the literature of the past when she revised the essay for *The Common Reader* in 1925. Then, she noted, "[w]e only know that certain gratitudes and hostilities inspire us; that certain paths seem to lead to fertile land, others to the dust and the desert; and of this perhaps it may be worth while to attempt some account" ("Modern Fiction" 185). I cite from the two versions of this essay in these opening pages of my book for one important reason: Woolf's words here recall my own sense of the obstacles that I encountered when researching this study. As Woolf's comments above suggest, the difficulties of tracing artistic influences among texts are considerable: by its very nature, influence study is an inexact science. Moreover, as Woolf forewarned and I soon discovered, as one searches for the "gratitudes and hostilities" that inspire and inform a given text, one is in danger of stumbling down blind alleys and trudging across the dust and desert most of the time.

It is, I have found, only very rarely that all the pieces of the influence puzzle seem to fit together, that an obscure historical fact found in some dusty old tome, or the repetition of certain unusual names, places, or tropes in two seemingly unconnected texts, strengthen one's intuitive sense of a connection between them. This is the "Eureka!" moment for the critic of literary influence, but of course when it does occur the joy of discovery must necessarily be partial, insecure, and short-lived: one is always aware that in choosing to pursue any one particular "fertile" path, countless others must be overlooked. "[A]nd of this," as Woolf wisely counsels, it may be "worth while to attempt some account" ("Modern Fiction" 185).

Just such an attempt is what I present in the pages to come. Herewith my account of the variety of social, political, aesthetic, and (inter)personal influences that have combined to inform, contaminate, and/or enhance the creation of certain literary texts. In the following chapters I will illustrate these various forces at play in the works of five writers who lived and composed, literally and figuratively, alongside one another: Sir Leslie Stephen, Thomas Hardy, Virginia Woolf, Katherine Mansfield, and John Middleton Murry. As I shall demonstrate, each of these figures had strong personal and professional associations with two or more of the others. This "cross-pollination" of influence offered me a great range of interpretive opportunities in the early stages of my research. As I soon discovered, however, it also dictated certain organizational difficulties: with so many writers and so many relationships to describe here, the tangle of connections at times becomes confusing. For the sake of clarity, therefore, the study follows these figures through a roughly chronological sequence.

I begin in the mid 1870s, by looking at the personal and professional relationship between the then aspiring young novelist, Thomas Hardy, and his editor at the *Cornhill* literary magazine, the great Victorian man of letters, Leslie Stephen. While Stephen is perhaps now known best as the father of Virginia Woolf, he was also an important figure in the London literary world in the last quarter of the nineteenth century. During his tenure at *Cornhill*, moreover, Stephen played a key role in shaping Thomas Hardy's own career. Indeed, Stephen's highly intrusive editorial style greatly affected the serialized versions of two of Hardy's earliest novels: *Far from the Madding Crowd* and *The Hand of Ethelberta*. As I shall document in the next chapter, these two men shared an intense and mutually frustrating relationship that came to have a measurable impact on Hardy's writing. In particular, I discuss their work on the serialization of Hardy's *Far from the Madding Crowd,* and the influence of this joint project on Hardy's later works. Hardy's uncomfortable relation to Stephen, I will argue, can be seen to surface in several of Hardy's most well-known texts.

The history of these five figures then progresses through the early years of the twentieth century, as in chapter three I look at the work of John Middleton Murry, the essayist, critic, and influential literary editor. Alongside Murry's essays, I also examine works by his wife, the short story writer Katherine Mansfield. Like Hardy and Stephen, Murry and Mansfield also met through their literary endeavors, when Murry edited Mansfield's submissions to his magazine, *Rhythm*. The literary and textual nature of their relationship, as I will demonstrate, greatly affected the works of both writers, as did their respective connections to another subject of this study: Thomas Hardy.

Thomas Hardy was nearly eighty by the time he got to know Murry and Mansfield in 1918. Although he had long since stopped writing novels,

Hardy continued to publish collections of poetry that became popular among the soldiers fighting in World War I. As critic Patricia Hutchins notes in her essay "Thomas Hardy and Some Younger Writers": "[t]he publication of *Satires of Circumstance,* (1914) and *Moments of Vision,* (1917), put Hardy in touch with soldier-poets who bought the books on leave and read the poems in France" (Hutchins 37). Among these were Wilfred Owen, Siegfried Sassoon, and Walter De la Mare, who all befriended Hardy soon after their return from the war. It was John Middleton Murry, however, who saw himself as chief among this new generation of Hardy fans. Moreover, due to Murry's position as the well-regarded editor of *The Athenaeum* literary magazine, his fervor for Hardy's works found a very public forum.

As I will detail in chapter three, Mansfield's own interest in Hardy appears to have begun at the same time as her husband's. Nevertheless, Katherine Mansfield related to Hardy's works in a very different way than did Murry. Whereas Murry pursued a kind of public affirmation through his affiliation with Hardy, Mansfield's interaction with Hardy's works was conducted privately. Evidence of this abounds in Mansfield's diaries, as she transcribed many of Hardy's poems, sometimes in full and other times partially, into those private pages. This truly personal negotiation of Hardy's works is thus in sharp contrast to her husband's highly public relation to Hardy. In chapter three, therefore, I examine these differing approaches to Hardy's influence and the social and critical categories into which they appear to fall. In particular, I look at the gendered distinctions implied in notions of public and private discourse and in theoretical models of literary influence and indebtedness, examining these in light of the Murry/Hardy/Mansfield triad.

At around the same period of time that Mansfield was transcribing Hardy's poems, there was another name quite frequently repeated in her journals: Virginia Woolf. Woolf and Mansfield became, over time, good friends and literary collaborators, but theirs was nevertheless a relationship fraught with tensions. Mistrustful and judgmental about each other's lifestyles and writing abilities, this highly charged friendship had, as I will demonstrate in chapter four, profound effects on the texts of both writers. As I examine the works of the two women of my study alongside one another, I consider whether the dynamics of literary influence may be seen to work differently in the texts of these female writers than in the works of Hardy, Stephen, and Murry. Is influence gendered? Did Woolf, that is, see Mansfield as a kind of female muse? Or was their relation more mutual, and therefore more complicated than such a utopian feminist model might suggest? Specifically, in chapter four I look at the images that connect Woolf's first experimental novel, *Jacob's Room,* to Mansfield's most well-known story, "Prelude," and offer a reading of these works as evidence of the personal, cultural, and historical forces at work in the texts of both writers.

As I will argue, Katherine Mansfield's tale "Prelude" came to permeate Woolf's thoughts during the years 1917–18, as she and her husband Leonard had undertaken to publish the work at their newly founded Hogarth Press. The Woolfs, though literary professionals, were relative novices to the practical world of printing presses and employee relations. The task of publishing "Prelude," therefore, was more arduous and time consuming than either they or Mansfield had anticipated. As a result of short-staffing and time constraints, Virginia herself set the type for much of Mansfield's text. This physical immersion in the words of "Prelude" was, in my view, matched by Woolf's creative immersion in the experimental aspects of Mansfield's tale. Thus, I suggest that the practical, material connections between these writers came to have a literal and literary effect upon their writing. Throughout this study, I examine the creative impact of just such circumstantial links among the works of these writers. In each case, I explore the possibilities for understanding such complicated influences among texts in critical terms. As Woolf points out in the passage I cited earlier, there is more than one path to inspiration, and her own writing demonstrates this quite effectively. While I will examine in detail the debt that Woolf's novel *Jacob's Room* (1922) owes to Mansfield's work, Mansfield was certainly not the only strong influence on Woolf's early fiction. Indeed, shortly after Katherine Mansfield's death in January 1923, Woolf seems to have become fascinated by a very different kind of literary muse, the poet and novelist Thomas Hardy.

Hardy, as I noted above, had a close relationship with Woolf's father Leslie Stephen, but after Stephen's death in 1902, the Stephen family heard little from Hardy. In 1915, however, Virginia Woolf and Thomas Hardy exchanged a series of letters, prompted by Hardy's reissue of a poem of eulogy he had written for the late Sir Leslie. A brief correspondence between them then ensued, but eventually their communications ceased. Then, suddenly, in 1924, Woolf began to make frequent references to Hardy and his works in her journals and essays. As I argue in chapter five, these numerous references culminate in Woolf's two long accounts of her visit with Hardy at his home in Dorset in May of 1926.

That Woolf's rekindled interest in Thomas Hardy corresponds with her composition of *Mrs. Dalloway* (1925) is, in many ways, the origin of this entire study. As I explain in detail later on, the first time I read *Mrs. Dalloway* I noticed several similarities between it and another novel I happened also to be reading, Hardy's *The Mayor of Casterbridge*. Later, to my great excitement, I came across an intriguing assortment of textual and biographical connections among Woolf, Stephen, and Hardy, and took note of Woolf's interest in and visit to Hardy during this period. Eventually these researches led to, and encompassed, the lives and works of Katherine Mansfield and John Middleton Murry as well.

In chapter five, then, I concentrate on texts from the mid 1920s, as I consider Virginia Woolf's textual negotiation of her relationship with Thomas Hardy. Here, I will demonstrate that Hardy's close association with Woolf's father, and Woolf's own ambivalence toward Hardy, provide several contexts through which to interpret the connections that I sense among their texts. Do Woolf's works exhibit an anxiety about debts owed to Hardy's legacy? Or does the surfacing of similar motifs in the works of both writers lend itself to an intertextual interpretation, removed from author-centered criticism? I will look at works of both writers in light of several contemporary paradigms of literary influence and intertextuality, in order to examine the kinds of readings that such formulations produce. By doing so, I hope to suggest the vital importance of Thomas Hardy to Woolf's fiction.

The final literary relationship that I examine in this study brings me full circle; in chapter six I look at the father/daughter pair, Leslie Stephen and Virginia Woolf. Here, I examine some of the earliest and the latest examples of Woolf's writing, as I consider the textual images she created of her father throughout her life. Woolf interrogated her father's influence upon her writing repeatedly in her essays and journals, perhaps most famously through the character of Mr. Ramsay in *To the Lighthouse*. What I believe has not been adequately explored in other examinations of their relationship, however, is the connection between her father's career as a biographer and essayist, and Woolf's own work in those genres.

In particular, I concentrate upon the ways in which Stephen's final project as biographer and editor of the *Dictionary of National Biography* came to affect his daughter's later career. Woolf's fictional and nonfictional renderings of her father, and her concern with the art of biography, form a large part of her oeuvre. In chapter six, then, I look at several of Woolf's texts, and consider the often-ambivalent vision of her father they provide. These same ambiguities also allow me to confront reductive readings of this father/daughter relationship: Is it more facile/difficult, important/pointless, necessary/unnecessary for a woman writer to surpass a literary father who is also a biological father? Which is a more compelling influence upon Woolf's work: gender or genre? Finally, I will conclude by considering the usefulness of such leading questions and survey the mutable nature of Woolf's lifelong personal and creative struggles with her father's legacy. By addressing these subjects here, I hope to account for many of the "paths" that led to the highly "fertile ground" of Woolf's fiction.

Creative Misreadings and Historical Contexts:
The Work of the Curious Reader

As I demonstrate in the chapters that follow, the personal associations among these writers were informed by the changing historical and cultural circumstances of their lives; their works were influenced by the dynamics of their mutual textual relations. Of course, all of these associations began, changed, and ended in different ways, and for different reasons. In this sense, each relationship I look at here provides a kind of "case study" of the means and mechanics of literary influence. As each chapter documents, the texts that these five figures produced were inflected by, among other things, their unique negotiations of the texts of other writers. The documents that emerge from these literary "case studies," therefore, are highly individual, and lend themselves to different methods of interpretation. Thus, examining the works of these writers leads me to consider a whole range of theoretical models of influence, indebtedness, and intertextuality, as I read those paradigms alongside the texts produced by Woolf, Hardy, Stephen, Mansfield, and Murry.

Let me be clear: my overriding purpose in this book is to account for the connections I sense among certain texts by highlighting my view of reading as an active and creative endeavor. To do so, I interpret and contextualize specific examples of creative misreading, and suggest how such acts might have informed and influenced the works of these writers. For the purposes of this work, therefore, I take "reading" to mean much more than the deciphering of words on a page. Throughout this project I have defined reading as a participatory sport—one in which I myself engage energetically in the pages to come. In doing so, however, I will endeavor to avoid making any claim that the readings of the texts I offer here are conclusive or definitive. It is, I know, in my nature to seek connection, to hunt for patterns, and to sometimes force readings that suggest form in the chaotic world of the curious reader. Luckily, Virginia Woolf offered a caveat for critics like me. In a late essay entitled "The Leaning Tower," Woolf cautions: "let us always remember—influences are infinitely numerous; writers are infinitely sensitive; each writer has a different sensibility" ("Tower" 163).

As Woolf argues, and my own study confirms, closed, resolved reading of literary texts lead only to the "dust and desert" of which she warned. In my view, the goal, the intent of the curious reader, is not to locate a definitive, stable meaning in our reading, but to open up and stimulate our sense of the possible: to imagine. Reading, or more specifically, re-reading, should allow one the space to consider not only the facts of the words on the page, but also the imaginary sphere in which these words were composed. Re-reading provides a location for the possible and the implausible to exist side by side.

In this sense, I would argue, it is only in the solipsism of thinking through language that we are able to taste of the sublime. The joy of working within a text, drawing our own connections, noting the dissonances we hear, is the joy of a hunger impossible to satisfy: the reader's curiosity.

Moreover, as I shall demonstrate in the following pages, reductive interpretations of literary texts are often based on gendered and cultural presumptions of a rather unsavory kind. Such oversimplified judgments about the reasons behind a given writer writing this, or avoiding writing that, are thus in my view not only specious but also fundamentally uninteresting, as is all thinking that is closed and limiting. Critics, that is, who offer singular static interpretations of a given work as symptomatic of, say, anxiety, or evidence perhaps of childhood trauma, are, I believe, missing the point: they look upon a forest and name it "tree."

While artists are certainly affected by their experiences and relationships, such influences are, as Woolf suggested, "infinitely numerous." To argue (as critics often have) that a given work of art is primarily the result of any one cause, is to limit one's "view of the sky": there are, to name one famous example, many sufferers of childhood traumas, but only one Virginia Woolf. Critical readings of texts that attempt to confine the creative process into a cause and effect dialectic, do a disservice both to the skill and originality of writers, and to the desire of the curious reader. What is the point of re-reading, that reader may ask, when Professor X has already decoded the secret meanings of the text for me? Reductive and closed readings thus evacuate the intrigue from the act of reading, by defining the reader's sense of what is possible. My aim in this study, therefore, is to question the value of definitive-sounding interpretations of literary texts, and to demonstrate the far greater power of the open, unstable reading. As I see it, the artistic sublime, the nature of the creative, can never be defined, but it can be glimpsed in the parallel process of the open creative misreading. Thus in the pages to come I will challenge repeatedly the gendered and cultural presumptions that lead to oversimplified judgments about the dynamics of influence, authorship, and textual meaning. In the end, I would argue, what influence study does best is raise questions, not resolve them.

In the following chapters, then, I examine not only texts *written* by my chosen authors, but also many of the texts that *they read*. As I do so, I will be proposing my own ideas, based on these textual sources, about the personal and cultural forces that affected how these authors read one another's writing. Because each of the five authors examined here came from different social, historical, and cultural backgrounds, this study not only investigates their creative debts, but also their culturally inflected interpretations of the texts of others. Finally, and perhaps most importantly, I will make use of this biographical and historical evidence to suggest the impact that such creative misreadings had upon each writer's own works.

A further concern is also explored in this study: the connection between literary influence and literary history. Among the writers whose works I look at here are two of the most well-known and widely read authors of the present day: Virginia Woolf and Thomas Hardy. As the cultural and historical importance of these two figures looms so large in our own time, it would be well to take note of the influence they had upon each other's works, as well as the circumstances that gave rise to their respective (current) places in the literary canon. One benefit of this approach is that it enables me to examine why and how certain texts (and, therefore, certain authors) gain high status in literary history. Thus, while I look at specific examples of influence and canonical stature in the following pages, I mean also to suggest that such instances are evidence of a much more pervasive and complex dialogue between literary influence and literary history.

Literary tradition not only influences what we read, but also how it is read and with what value it is imbued. While the writers whose works I examine here have been affected artistically by their relations to the literary past, they have been informed politically and ideologically by that past as well. It is these pressures, interacting with the artists' respective creative visions, which produce their written works. Furthermore, such social, political, and cultural forces have power beyond their impact on fiction: the same methods of culturally inflected reading have, as I suggest, also informed the eventual canonical status of authors. In order to ground my arguments in a historical context, in the following pages I explore the mechanics of canonicity via an examination of the changing cultural importance, over time, of the five authors with whom I am concerned.

Fittingly enough, the theoretical bases for the present study arose out of a tangle of (mostly) discernible influences. Here, I draw frequently on the works of Harold Bloom, as these account specifically for the mechanics of literary influence and literary history (in the guise of the canon). I cannot overstate the significance of Bloom's theory of literary influence, as outlined in *The Anxiety of Influence* (1973) and *A Map of Misreading* (1975), to my work. As I shall demonstrate in the chapters to come, however, I do not adopt his patriarchal paradigm of influence without question: like the other writers I examine here, I engage creatively rather than prescriptively with works from the past.

In *The Anxiety of Influence,* Bloom conceives of literary influence as a struggle to gain aesthetic strength: Bloom figures the process of becoming a strong poet and achieving a place in literary history, in terms of battle. The later poet of Bloom's influence paradigm must wrestle with his strong precursor "even to the death" in order to "clear imaginary space for himself" (*Anxiety* 5). For Bloom, the dilemma of the would-be "strong poet," that reader turned writer, is his need to achieve a balance between the solitude defined by canonical texts, and the debt to other writers whose legacy he has inherited through his reading. As Bloom tells it, this tightrope walk between solipsism and artistic indebtedness is so difficult to negotiate that it becomes a neurotic state: the anxiety of influence. What Bloom's reading of influence does not account for, however, is the cultural, social, and ideological pressures that are always a part of the narratives we read. "[A]nd of this," to repeat Virginia Woolf's refrain, "it may be worth while to attempt some account" ("Modern Fiction" 185).

But if we choose to account for literary influence without relying solely on Bloom's author-centered theory to guide us, we may face another critical dilemma. For what other contexts are available for interpreting such artistic, aesthetic, and/or linguistic connections among texts? Well, one important alternative to Bloom can be found in the work of the intertextual critics. This field of inquiry was first propounded by the French critic Julia Kristeva in her study of the works of Mikhail Bakhtin.[2] In Kristeva's reading, Bakhtin's sense of the "literary word" is that of "an *intersection of textual surfaces* rather than a *point* (a fixed meaning), as a dialogue among several writings" (Kristeva, *Desire* 65). Importantly, Kristeva's work turns away from traditional, humanist paradigms of literary influence such as Bloom's. Instead of concentrating on what critics Jay Clayton and Eric Rothstein refer to as "an author-centered criticism, concerned with issues of originality and genius" ("Figures" 10), Kristeva embarks on a decidedly antihumanist approach to the reading of texts.

In their study *Influence and Intertextuality in Literary History,* Clayton and Rothstein assert that Bloom's theory, through its author-centered interpretations and its reliance on history, biography, and psychology, "locate[s] a work's unity in the controlling vision of its author" ("Figures" 22). At the level of textual analysis, then, such a view would suggest that any lack of unity or tension within a text could be directly traceable to the author as the agent of the text's meaning. Bloom's reading of influence accounts for intertextual connections as symptomatic of the author's discomfort with literary debts. Kristeva, on the other hand, believes that the idea of textual unity is itself a fallacy. As Clayton and Rothstein make clear, intertextual theory maintains that "the intersection of textual surfaces in a literary word can never be circumscribed, is open to endless dissemination" ("Figures" 19). The traceable, knowable agent of meaning that Bloom's ideas promote is thus disallowed in Kristeva's intertextual model.

Despite such differences in their accounts of intertextuality, both Kristeva and Bloom are useful to this study as each examines the nature of misreading, and struggles with the possibility of determining "fixed meaning" in any text. Critic Susan Stanford Friedman has another view on textual meaning, which is that the interest of any given reading is *based on* the lack of a fixed meaning in a text. For her, it is the play of possible meanings within a text that holds the reader's interest. By "seeing all texts as 'surfaces' that intersect with other texts," Friedman posits that those "points of surface intersection [are] part of a psychic and linguistic negotiation between desire and denial— both conscious and unconscious—as these are historically constructed" (Friedman 172). Of course by making this distinction, Friedman puts herself in clear opposition to the distinctly antihumanist approaches of Kristeva and of French critic Roland Barthes. Barthes, in his influential essay "The Death of the Author," insisted upon the final anonymity of authorship, claiming that the "modern scriptor is born simultaneously with the text, is in no way equipped with a being simultaneously preceding or exceeding the writing" ("Death" 145).

In my own view, however, Barthes' account of intertextual dynamics leaves several critical questions unanswered, and it is just such questions in which I am interested. Even if I were to step away from author-centered criticism, that is, when sensing a connection among the texts I read, I am still compelled to ask: Why does this word appear in this text, and not that? Why these intersections of texts, and not those? Friedman's argument may serve to resolve this dilemma, as, for her, the "(re)birth of the author," "along with some of the biographical and historical methodologies of influence studies" (Friedman 173), provides a more useful tool for textual critics than does Barthes' model of the modern scriptor. This more complex model of influence that Friedman calls for, I would argue, offers a fuller frame of reference through which textual choices can be read.

In the following pages, then, I will employ aspects of these various accounts of intertextuality and influence, in order to explore textual negotiations of what Friedman terms "desire and denial." Specifically, as I noted above, I will examine the works of Sir Leslie Stephen, Thomas Hardy, Virginia Woolf, Katherine Mansfield, and John Middleton Murry. As I explained earlier, I have chosen to write about these particular authors of differing talents, education levels, and social backgrounds, because of the strong and traceable personal and commercial connections among them. The resulting examinations of their (textual) lives will, I hope, reveal a much more random, circumstantial, and therefore more complex, model of literary influence than either Bloom's "anxiety" paradigm or Kristeva's "endless dissemination" of meaning. What Bloom has discussed on a psychic level as the unconscious will to power of the strong poet, I plan to restore to and explore in a historical context. Similarly, while I make use of aspects of Kristeva's intertextual model, I feel it would be negligent of me to ignore the well-documented personal and textual relations among the writers with whom I am concerned. To paraphrase Albert Einstein, any theory must be as simple as it can be, but no simpler. My approach in this study heeds this advice, and I hope therefore that it will deepen and complicate the scope of influence study as a result.

Thus, the ideas of Bloom, Kristeva, Barthes, and Friedman are essential to my project here. Jay Clayton and Eric Rothstein's overview of intertextual theory was particularly helpful for contextualizing the continuing relevance of Bloom's work on literary influence.[3] Also at work in the following pages are the significant feminist alternatives to Bloom's readings of influence and the criteria for literary canonization. The theorists that I draw upon most heavily in this context include Sandra Gilbert and Susan Gubar, Jane Marcus, Annette Kolodny, and, of course, Virginia Woolf. Although each of these feminist critics propounds very different ideas, there is one concern upon which all of them have, at one point or another, focused: the notion of language as a battleground in which words become weapons of patriarchy. Some twenty years ago, critic Carolyn Burke, in her "Report from Paris," argued this idea as follows: "the very forms of the dominant mode of discourse show the mark of the dominant masculine ideology. Hence, when a woman writes or speaks herself into existence, she is forced to speak in something like a foreign tongue, a language with which she may be uncomfortable" (Burke 844). Here, Burke proposes that women writers can and do feel a constrained relation to the texts they compose, if they attempt (as it seems they must) to employ the language of the father/master. Writing herself "into existence," as Burke suggests, is an exercise in translation for the woman writer. While I address these arguments about women, writing, and language at length in later chapters, the idea of gendered constraints upon writing can also be applied, perhaps unsurprisingly, to the evolution of this book. For, from its very inception, the language of this work has been a location of interest and difficulty: *how* I wrote this study has been at least as much of a concern, at times, as *what* I wrote.

This fact became clear to me when, having submitted my book to the publisher, I was asked to rewrite the introduction. This study began its life as doctoral research, and in the time-honored tradition of academic dissertations, it opened with a scholarly (if perhaps dry) survey of current theoretical debates on language, meaning, influence, and the role of the canon. In order to open up the text to a wider audience, I was asked by the editor to drop most of this section. Instead, she suggested that I introduce the book by explaining the origins of the ideas it contains. Moreover, she requested that in this chapter I make an effort to allow my own voice to be more clearly heard above the voices of my critical sources. While I was happy to comply with these suggestions, I couldn't help but call to mind the title of one of the texts I mention later in this study: Thomas Hardy's *Life's Little Ironies*.

You see, I well remembered that when I first began writing my dissertation several years earlier, I was advised by my academic supervisors to do pretty much the opposite of what my editor now requested. My supervisors, that is, strongly suggested that I formalize the tone of my developing work. They encouraged me, for example, to make greater use of scholarly devices such as sophisticated critical terminology and exhaustively detailed footnotes in order, I supposed, to help clarify and perhaps legitimate my own formulations. I needed, as I soon discovered, to adhere to certain specific, and other merely implied, parameters of academic discourse if I wanted to make the grade.

What was clear to me then was that my own, untrained, natural voice would simply not do. As an avid and eager student, however, I was more than willing to undertake whatever was needed in order to achieve my short-term goal—a doctorate in English Literature. I did so through a pointed and determined study of the voices of other academic writers: I immersed myself in critical literature and pored over the successful dissertations of other students. I agonized over the appropriate usage of such terms as hermeneutic, epistemology, historiography, and polemic. Eventually, like most determined students, I grew more confident in my use of such language, as is evidenced by the row of letters that now follow my name. Even so, I would be lying if I said that I am now completely "at ease" with the terminology of academic discourse: it still feels like a second language.

Nevertheless, I find it so ironic as to be unsettling (getting back to Hardy and the editor's request) that my own, original voice seems to have somehow become lost in the academic process. Moreover, I begin to worry whether it will ever be possible to recuperate that natural, untrained, uncensored language I once called "me," or if it is now and forever informed and contaminated by the scholarly tone that I so eagerly adopted. Now that I am asked to let more of my own voice come through in this introduction, that is, I am forced to ask some essential new-millennium-style questions: What *is* my own voice, for a start? And how accurately does that voice represent or justify or communicate the ideas and words running around my head? Indeed, how far is the voice of any writer predicated, as was mine, upon the desire for material and/or cultural gain?

In February of 1874, one of the subjects of this book, Thomas Hardy, wrote to ask some general advice on literary matters from the editor in charge of serializing the first of his novels to reach magazine publication. In the letter, Hardy admits his inexperience to the *Cornhill* editor, the often acerbic Leslie Stephen, with a tone of anxiety and deference. Hardy wrote, "[t]he truth is that I am willing, and indeed anxious, to give up any points which may be desirable. [. . .] Perhaps I may have higher aims some day, and be a great stickler for the proper artistic balance of the completed work, but for the present circumstances lead me to wish merely to be considered a good hand at a serial" (Hardy, *CLTH* 1:28). I find the sentiments expressed in this letter intriguing as they offer a telling commentary on the spirit of Hardy's ambitions. Indeed, while Leslie Stephen has been criticized in several works as being an overbearing censor of Hardy's writing, Hardy's words here may call this view of Stephen into question.[4] Certainly Stephen was willing to dramatically alter any submission to *Cornhill* in order to avoid provoking his subscribers. Nevertheless, as the letter above illustrates, Hardy was in his own words "willing, and indeed anxious" to comply with Stephen's requests so that he could be "considered a good hand at a serial."

In this letter, Hardy envisions his future self as a "stickler for the proper artistic balance" but also shows that at the start of his career he simply wanted success. If Hardy did have this agenda in mind, he must have been aware that a powerful, if intrusive, editor like Stephen could help him to achieve his goal. In the following chapter, I look at the effect that Hardy's cooperation, or, more darkly, complicity, played in Stephen's censorship of Hardy's novel *Far from the Madding Crowd*. Hardy's desire to become " a good hand at a serial," I argue, created specific artistic compromises that came to affect Hardy's later work and his relationship with Leslie Stephen. While I maintain this as a valid critique of Hardy's negotiations of Stephen's influence, my own publishing experiences nevertheless remind me to be wary of accepting it as a criticism of Hardy's artistic integrity: like me, Hardy changed what his editor wanted him to change in order to get his first works published. Just as Hardy's early writing was thus informed by material concerns and ambitions, so too is my own.

Likewise, my academic background has also instilled in me a desire (or, fear?) to write with a voice of confidence and authority that was at first alien to me. Often I would, and still do, introduce my ideas with a "perhaps," "it may be," or that other catch-all—"one could argue." Such language, as my advisors pointed out, was sheepish, for it allowed me to preempt criticism by disowning my ideas while simultaneously apologizing for ever having them in the first place. Luckily, teachers over the years insisted that I adopt a bolder tone if I wanted my formulations to be taken seriously, and I have followed their suggestions to the very best of my (still somewhat hesitant) ability. Thoughts such as these, therefore, came into my mind when I first encountered the journals of Katherine Mansfield, another of the subjects of this book. Mansfield, like Woolf, sought to create something new in the world of fiction, and indeed she is best known for her experimental short stories. Nevertheless, as I soon discovered, Mansfield's own journals are filled with the words of other writers. Rather than using her diaries as a workshop for her experimental ideas, as many writers do, in Mansfield's personal notebooks she employed the words of well-recognized, and largely male, literary figures to communicate her feelings.

Throughout these private pages, Mansfield pieces together her own words with, for example, verses from Thomas Hardy's poems, scenes from the plays of Anton Chekov, and aphorisms from Oscar Wilde. By doing so, I suggest, Mansfield created a mosaic, fabricated language with which to speak to herself. As I argue in chapter three, Mansfield's journals seem to point to her overwhelming desire for acknowledgement, approval, and validation on both personal and professional levels. Mansfield, that is, while bold enough to experiment in her published, public fiction, nevertheless submitted her private writings to be translated, authorized, and narrated by the traditional masculine voices of literary authority.

As I write this judgment upon Mansfield's journals, however, I am also aware of the irony of my doing so. For, just as Mansfield's own private writing is thus "culturally inflected" by her apparent need for validation, this book is surely informed by an equally strong desire for approval and legitimization. Like Mansfield, I employ the works of writers from the past to communicate my vision. In the pages that follow, I also cut and paste their texts and my own words together. By doing so, moreover, I may arguably be creating the kind of hybrid discourse I sense in Mansfield's diaries: half familiar, half foreign, both public and private—this book is itself a palimpsest.

While reading Mansfield's journals in this light, I sensed a pattern of what I then called "influence" emerging. As I suggested above, Mansfield used the texts of many writers in her diaries. However, during the period of her greatest creativity, she refers most frequently to the works of Thomas Hardy. Was it possible, I wondered, to discern any likely artistic debt that Mansfield owed to Hardy? Did these extensive private references to his work have any noticeable literary influence upon Mansfield's published fiction? I consider these questions in some depth in chapter three. In that same section, I also examine the very different textual connections I uncovered between Hardy and another figure in this study: Mansfield's husband, John Middleton Murry.

As I will illustrate, the relationships among Murry, Hardy, and Mansfield are well documented, and reading these documents, I began to form certain ideas about these three writers, and the nature of their respective associations. In 1918, Murry was the newly appointed editor of a formerly influential literary magazine, *The Athenaeum*. Murry's private papers at this time suggest that he was desperate to recreate the prestigious past of the serial and to secure a solid reputation for himself. In order to do so, Murry would eventually pursue, pamper, compliment, and cajole the then elderly Thomas Hardy into submitting works to *The Athenaeum*. What their correspondence thus chronicles is the process and progression of what was to become a very public relationship between the flattered Hardy and his loyal fan, Murry. This seemingly superficial friendship of convenience, however, in fact continued until Hardy's death in early 1928. Throughout this ten-year period, Murry published essays and reviews in praise of Hardy and his works, while

Hardy's poetic contributions and general support of Murry conferred a very real public affirmation on *The Athenaeum* and its editor.

Thus, I began to believe that while Katherine Mansfield's letters and journals suggest her private, creative debt to Hardy, Murry's own relation to Hardy was a thoroughly public and commercial negotiation. The compelling differences between these respective relationships, moreover, encouraged me to look at the gendered distinctions inscribed on models of literary influence. Was Murry's public praising of Hardy, I wondered, an attempt to align himself with an important patriarchal precursor? I further questioned why New Zealander Katherine Mansfield might transcribe the poems of Hardy, the elder statesman of English poetry, into her journals? Did she also claim Hardy as a literary forefather? Or was something less clearly formulaic at work in Murry and Mansfield's very different readings of Hardy's work? These are the kinds of queries that surfaced in my initial reading of the relationships among Hardy, Mansfield, and Murry. Further exploration, moreover, has not provided me with any simple answers to these questions. In fact, as I argued earlier, it has led me to be increasingly suspicious about reductive or definitive readings of texts wherever they arise.

My own public and private negotiation of the works I look at here is itself filtered, fittingly enough, through a wide range of personal and practical considerations, most notably my academic influences. As a Master's degree student at New York University in the early nineties, I had the great fortune to be supervised by Professor Perry Meisel. Professor Meisel encouraged my passion for the works of Thomas Hardy, and later inspired my abiding love of Virginia Woolf's fiction. Moreover, during this period I began to develop a taste for returning to and re-examining literary texts: quite simply, under Professor Meisel's influence, I had learned to read.

At his suggestion, I took a class taught by the influential Professor Harold Bloom, and I benefited profoundly from his startling readings as well as his patience, insight, and kindness. Soon after completing my Master's, I was relocated to London. Sadly, this meant having to abandon my planned doctoral research in New York, and begin all over again in a new city, armed only with developing interest in intertextuality and literary influence, and my love for Woolf and Hardy. I was fortunate indeed, with such meager accomplishments, that Dr. Suzanne Raitt, at Queen Mary and Westfield College, agreed to supervise my doctoral thesis, then called "Thomas Hardy's influence on the novels of Virginia Woolf." As with Professor Meisel, Dr. Raitt's own sense of Woolf was a constant source of inspiration (and occasionally intimidation). Under her guidance I expanded my research to include the connections I found among the other figures of this study: Leslie Stephen, Thomas Hardy, John Middleton Murry, and Katherine Mansfield.

Aside from the obviously interesting biographical connections that arose from my research, however, I soon became fascinated by the over-whelmingly textual nature of these relationships. As curious but belated onlookers to Modernism, I noted, we contemporary readers receive the stories of the lives of Woolf, Hardy, and Mansfield *as stories,* as texts to be interpreted in the form of journals, letters, and essays. This very textual-ity, I was intrigued to find, was also an integral part of their relationships as they occurred: these five writers related to each other, communicated to themselves and to one another through textual means. It is therefore these written words, this plethora of fictional and nonfictional documen-tation with which my study is concerned. I am not particularly interested, for this reason, in surmising Woolf's sense of Mansfield from a given let-ter or story, or reaching reductive personal conclusions about these writ-ers from selective textual sources. Instead, in the following pages, I explore a sampling of the innumerable variety of ways that these writers chose to put their negotiations of relationships and mutual creative debts into written words.

Informed then, as my own study surely is, by influence study, and in par-ticular the works of Harold Bloom, this book nevertheless offers a more ran-dom and therefore more complex model of literary influence than Bloom's original paradigm provides. Here, I ground theories of indebtedness and in-tertextuality in the historical, textual records of the lives of the writers with whom I am concerned. By doing so, I provide a reading of influence not as an unusual defense mechanism available only to the "strong poet," as Bloom would have it, but rather as the unavoidable consequence of a life steeped in literature. If through his model of literary influence Bloom reads connec-tions among texts as a symptom of anxiety, I sense a much wider array of possible interpretations in intertextual moments.

For me then, as for Hardy and Murry, practical, commercial, and random forces most certainly influenced my writing. What if I had never attended Professor Meisel's class? Might I now be examining, say, the role of the nar-rator in George Eliot's novels? Or analyzing representations of the body in *Vanity Fair?* Perhaps. Then again, if I had not worked with Dr. Raitt, I might not be writing at all—for if New York University and Professor Meisel taught me to read, Dr. Raitt taught me to write. Hard work it was, too, but as students or aspiring writers, it is natural, and it seems even advisable, to defer to the wisdom of your editors. I examine the nature of just such a re-lationship in the next chapter, as I look at the impact of Leslie Stephen's ed-itorship upon Thomas Hardy's early works. Before I begin, though, I think it would be timely to pause for a moment to consider another, less interper-sonal influence on the writing process, then and now.

Biography and the Western Canon

Over the past ten years, I have taken on a wide variety of occupations in order to, quite literally, pay the rent. Like any employee, however, I have found that whether I am hired as a secretary, receptionist, researcher, or lecturer there are always certain formal limits imposed by the powers that be upon any job. Some rules are tougher to conform to than others, though, and some difficulties arose for me when I came to write biographical entries for the *New Dictionary of National Biography*. Doing so, I encountered what I felt to be the most frustratingly static parameters surrounding my work that I had ever known. There were, naturally, very good reasons for these parameters.

The monumental work of the *New DNB* is to replace and greatly expand the original Victorian *DNB*. The *New DNB* will be a staggering collection of some 50,000 biographies, written especially for the Dictionary, of those who have shaped British history past and present. Clearly, as the central biographical reference work on noteworthy Britons throughout history, the *New DNB* must adhere to strict formal criteria in order to make this information reliable and accessible to the largest possible audience. Nonetheless, the resultant constraints upon the writers/researchers are considerable. After weeks or perhaps months investigating the life of some often obscure figure from the past, a researcher might find that their final five- or six-hundred-word biographical sketch contains little aside from the barebones essentials that the *New DNB* format allows. The results can be discouraging. But, if one is able to see the set criteria as a formal challenge rather than as a constraint, a world of possibilities arises: how then to manipulate, cajole, and stretch the form so that it may bear a trace of its author's existence? Part of my reason for mentioning this experience, of course, is that this strict and static design for *DNB* articles can be traced back to the work of its original chief editor—none other than Sir Leslie Stephen himself.

In 1882, well-known Victorian publisher George Smith had approached Leslie Stephen, then editor of the prestigious *Cornhill* magazine, to take charge of the project of a dictionary of British biography. Once he accepted the post, Stephen set about designing the format for the biographical entries. Intriguingly, then, the biographical entry format to which I owe some money, several gray hairs, and the kind of pressure that occasionally calls forth inspiration, was having an impact on the life of at least two of the people in my study (Stephen and Woolf) long before I was around.

The *DNB's* second editor, Sydney Lee, made note of Stephen's strict enforcement of these guidelines, recalling in Leslie Stephen's own posthumous *DNB* entry, "[Stephen] recognized that archaeological details within reasonably liberal limits were of primary importance to the Dictionary, and he refused mercy to contributors who offered him vague conjecture or sentimental eulogy instead of unembroidered fact" (Lee 403). Thus, Stephen's role was remembered, and continues to wield its merciless, yet efficient, power over *New DNB* contributors. More to the point, however, Leslie Stephen's career as a biographer would come to play a key role not only in my life and work, but also in his daughter Virginia's writing. As my researches led me to find, the textual relationship of these two writers, who were also father and daughter, was greatly informed by their mutual fascination with biography.

Finally, Stephen's *DNB* connection also helps me to explore another facet of the intertextual relations I examine here: the modern canon. My interest in the literary canon and the importance of being important, as it were, arose directly from my research on intertextual relations among my five chosen authors. While studying these writers and their works, that is, I noticed an anomaly: although each one of these writers enjoyed a certain degree of critical acclaim during their lifetimes, their relative statures in the canon have changed enormously over time. Leslie Stephen, for example, was a very well-known literary figure in his own day, even if many contemporary readers have never heard of him. Virginia Woolf's current widespread fame, on the other hand, would most likely be a shock to her Georgian contemporaries (if not to her). Partly, as I will argue in this study, this has to do with the ways that these various figures were portrayed in biographies after their deaths: the more flattering and worshipful the posthumous portraits, the more secure the place in the canon.

For example, despite Leslie Stephen's expertise in the field, the biographies of him that appeared after his death did nothing for his long-term literary status. His two main biographers, F. W. Maitland and Noel Annan, while admirers of Stephen, nevertheless depicted him as a throwback to an earlier time. Their biographies largely portray Stephen as an old-fashioned "Eminent Victorian." Woolf's own fictional representations of her father expanded upon this theme, and added to it a new Georgian sensibility that such Victorian "great men" were irrelevant to the modern world. In the pages to follow, I examine such changes in cultural perspectives upon the figures in this study, and consider them in the light of changes to each writer's respective canonical importance over time. Just as Stephen himself had to choose which biographies to include among the unimaginable number of possible *DNB* subjects, so too do the necessarily subjective criteria for inclusion and exclusion haunt our current thinking about biography and the literary canon. In this book, then, I examine influence and canonization in terms of the texts of these five writers and the historical events of their lives. This, I hope, will demonstrate both the usefulness and the limitations of a variety of contemporary theories on influence, intertextuality, and literary history. As the works of Harold Bloom address the concerns of canonical status and literary influence most directly, I will begin by taking a close look at his ideas. Later, I will contextualize his theories alongside other paradigms of influence, indebtedness, and canonicity.

As I noted above, Virginia Woolf's own desire to "create a new form for a novel" grew up alongside the piles of biographical entries written to the strict formal guidelines that Stephen's *DNB* required. How charming and intriguing and absolutely right then to look at both concerns, literary history and literary influence, side by side once again. On the other hand, I must remind myself of my own counsel, and remain cautious on the subject of closure or the providential fatefulness of such things. Like Woolf herself, I hope to be a strong and curious reader, but, again like her, my work is necessarily informed and influenced by conflicting desires: the need to be legitimized and the need to rebel; the quest for inspiration from the works of the past, and the passion to create something entirely new; the competitive spirit hiding within the solipsistic soul. As the title of this chapter suggests, all of the texts in this study, including of course the study itself, are intertextually contaminated: informed, influenced, inspired by other texts. Each, in this sense is a palimpsest, upon which traces of the past remain to haunt, inhabit, and compel the present, insistent, and always corruptible, text.

In *The Anxiety of Influence* Bloom writes, "[a]nd what *is* Poetic Influence anyway? Can the study of it really be anything more than the wearisome industry of source-hunting, of allusion-counting, an industry that will soon touch apocalypse anyway when it passes from scholars to computers?" (*Anxiety* 31). Surely, despite advances in computer technologies, locating influences among literary texts today is not only the exercise in "source-hunting" that Bloom gloomily predicted. The ability to sense connections is, I believe, an art in itself.

In St. Paul's first letter to the Corinthians, he explains to these newfound converts to the fledging sect of Christianity that "there are varieties of gifts, but the same Spirit." To some is "given the gift of tongues, to another the interpretation of tongues." Both gifts, according to Paul, are equally important to the manifestation of the common good, for the prophecies contained in the spiritual language of tongues are worthless without interpretation. "So with yourselves," he goes on, "if in a tongue you utter speech that is not intelligible, how will anyone know what is being said? For you will be speaking into the air" (*Corinthians* 14:9–10). As someone who writes about the words of others, I have often drawn comfort from the message of this passage. To some may be given the sublime gift of tongues, it reminds me, but to others is given the critical gift of interpretation: they are equal states of grace.

The act of interpretation, of course, is never able to fully recapture the precise meaning of the original. But perhaps it can offer something more. Indeed, the contemporary writer Salman Rushdie suggests just this in his essay "Imaginary Homelands." There, while discussing the importance of the English language to the British Indian writer, Rushdie argues that translation need not necessarily imply loss: "It is normally supposed that something always gets lost in translation; I cling obstinately to the notion that something can also be gained" (Rushdie 17). Let us hope that this is so, for here, couched in the allegory of Pauline spirituality, I offer the reader not the glossolalia, the gift of tongues, but rather my own interpretation of that unique creative language granted to a greater or lesser degree upon each of the five writers I examine. Alongside the powerful sound emerging from the texts I explore in this study, you will, I hope, still be able to discern the sound of my own tongue: the corrupted, influenced, inspired, and indebted voice of me.

Chapter Two 🌿

A Case Study

The Strange Case of Thomas Hardy and Sir Leslie Stephen

Before exploring the textual connections between the two main figures examined in this chapter, Sir Leslie Stephen and Thomas Hardy, it would be well to outline briefly the critical approaches to those texts that I will be utilizing, challenging, and interrogating: Harold Bloom's theory of literary influence, and his more recent work on the Western literary canon. Bloom's influence theory, first espoused in his 1973 text *The Anxiety of Influence,* explains his vision of the manner in which major poets gain aesthetic power. In this text, Bloom structures this struggle for artistic strength as a kind of hostile poetic takeover: the "later poet" of Bloom's paradigm misreads and overwrites the text of his literary "precursor," in order to "clear imaginative space" for himself (Bloom, *Anxiety* 5). To be a successful writer, a "major figure," Bloom tells us that a poet must possess the "persistence to wrestle with [his] strong precursor, even to the death" (5). In Bloom's reading, then, poets become "strong poets" via their engagement in psychic, agonizing combat with a literary "precursor." At the level of the text, the "later poet" must go to extraordinary lengths to cover this debt, as he claims his "imaginative space" (5). Having done so, the later poet is free to command his own voice, although the diligent reader may still be able to trace the precursor's influence upon the later figure's works.

This journey, according to Bloom, represents a terrifying ordeal for the later poet, but in order to be a "major figure," he must undergo it and emerge victorious. In Bloom's view, the rewards of such persistence are ample compensation for this struggle: success in this battle offers the later poet canonical status. "Poetic history," Bloom argues, "is to be held indistinguishable from poetic influence, since strong poets make that history by misreading one another, so as to clear imaginative space for themselves" (*Anxiety* 5). As is clear from this statement, at times Bloom conflates literary influence with literary history, seeing them as two sides of the same coin. Elsewhere, for instance, Bloom writes, "[t]here can be no strong, canonical writing without the process of literary influence" (*Canon* 8). For Bloom, then, the process of undergoing a battle with one's precursor leads a strong poet to a twofold prize: clear imaginative space, and a place in poetic history. The battleground framework that Bloom depicts in *The Anxiety of Influence,* moreover, also appears to be at work in the canon that Bloom provides in his 1994 text *The Western Canon.* Indeed, in this later text, Bloom advises, "[o]ne breaks into the canon only by aesthetic strength" (*Canon* 29). It is, then, this combative dynamic, which, according to Bloom, informs the dialogue between literary influence and poetic history, that I will be employing to approach the texts of Leslie Stephen and Thomas Hardy in this chapter.

The theory of poetry that Bloom provides in *The Anxiety of Influence* offers a much needed tool for readers: that of a critical context in which to read a given text. Indeed, while Bloom's theory is meant as a guide for understanding poetry, it can also help to explore connections among many other kinds of texts. Bloom's "Six Revisionary Ratios," as described in *The Anxiety of Influence,* allow for a range of readings directly traceable to an originating agent of influence. The "later poet" of Bloom's model misreads the poems of his "precursor," and this misreading then makes its way into the later poet's works. Used even in this simple schematic way, Bloom's formulation produces intriguing and exciting readings.

The Western Canon provides a method of choosing texts, and thus appears to solve another dilemma for the reader, that of determining the "value" of a given work. The choices Bloom makes in this study are presented as definitive, not least of all because they are *Bloom's* choices, and contained in a widely read, widely reviewed, and widely available edition.[1] Certainly, a thorough reading of even half of the texts on Bloom's lists of some thousand books would endow any reader with a breathtaking range of knowledge. From the ancient texts of Greece and Rome, to the modern works of Serbian and Croatian authors, the span of Bloom's lists is overwhelming. Despite their wide range, however, the rationale behind the creation of these lists may be disturbing to some readers. Indeed, Bloom's repeated and vehement dismissal in *The Western Canon* of the works of those he terms "feminist cheerleaders" and multiculturalist "resenters" and his grouping of them into one angry "school," indicates a subtext of hostility in his ostensibly aesthetic judgments.

There are nearly 800 writers included on the lists Bloom provides in the appendix of *The Western Canon.* Out of these authors, there are fewer than

70 women. Less than 10 percent of the greatest authors in the history of the West are female, according to Bloom's canon. Multiculturalist writers in English are similarly scarce. These are mainly represented on the final of Bloom's lists, "The Chaotic Age." Here, Bloom includes, for example, six West Indian, two African and three Indian authors. By way of explanation, Bloom notes, "The defense of the Western Canon is in no way the defense of the West or a nationalist enterprise. If multiculturalism meant Cervantes, who would quarrel with it?" (*Canon* 40).

This heated language, in my view, must cast doubt on the ingenuousness of Bloom's claim of standing outside all political and ideological concerns when choosing those authors he includes in his canon. One purpose of this chapter is thus to explore the manner in which Bloom's theory of influence, and its inherent patriarchal themes, is related to his marginalization of the works of many women and multiculturalist writers in his canon. Is Bloom's canon the result of patriarchal exclusivity, disguised as objective aesthetic judgment? Does Bloom's theory of influence enhance or limit one's under-standing of connections between texts, or the role of literary tradition upon their creation? What other contexts are there for reading intertextual con-nections and poetic history?

The concept of the author/father, and its relation to a traditional canon of the kind that Bloom has endorsed, is privileged throughout *The Western Canon*. There, Bloom's conflation of literary influence and poetic history provides the criteria for his resultant canon. As I outlined above, in *The Anx-iety of Influence*, Bloom posited a psychical mechanics of literary influence. The "Six Revisionary Ratios," which Bloom provides in this text, offer an overview of his paradigm of influence. Moreover, he argues that the canon-ical lists he compiled for *The Western Canon* give readers a digest of the most aesthetically powerful works that strong writers of the West have produced as a result of their victories over their literary precursors.

Thus, in *The Anxiety of Influence*, Bloom provides a hostile blueprint for list-making, a guide to the process of canonical entrance and elimination that is conceived as a violent incursion: it is this warlike strategy, as detailed by the Six Revisionary Ratios, that creates the hierarchy of names in Bloom's canon. In Bloom's own works, notions of influence and canonical status are both interwoven with considerations of relative power: weak versus strong, major versus minor figures, lesser talents and writers of "capable imagina-tion" (5). As I shall demonstrate in this chapter, Bloom's formulation relies on *reading* as its central defensive tactic: for Bloom a strong poet is neces-sarily a strong reader. I will illustrate here that the reductive nature of Bloom's theory of influence suggests that it cannot account for the negotia-tions at work in all relationships among writers. Nevertheless it is useful in exploring the dynamics of a certain kind of literary ambition: that in which a writer battles to achieve and/or maintain literary stature and canonical status. This confluence of reading, power, and literary tradition in Bloom's paradigm will itself be explored in this chapter. First though, I will interrogate the connections that surface between Bloom's influence theory and other, more materialist notions of reading, by applying Bloom's tenets in a slightly altered form to a specific literary pairing: that of Leslie Stephen and Thomas Hardy.

The relationship between Leslie Stephen and Thomas Hardy seems in many ways to have been informed by the type of battle that Bloom's theory best explicates: a lesser poet (here, the young Hardy) struggles with his precursor (Stephen) in order to "clear imaginative space" for himself. While Bloom's paradigm is meant to explain a process of obtaining aesthetic strength, I would argue that for both Stephen and Hardy a desire for popular success and literary immortality outweighed any longing for greater artistic power. The struggle enacted between these two writers seems less centered on aesthetics, than on their mutual ambition to achieve recognition among London's literary elite. The timing of their first acquaintance may itself have influenced their later, difficult relationship. Hardy and Stephen first came into contact in the 1870s, at which time Stephen was already a respected member of the London literary circle. Hardy, by contrast, was a struggling novelist. Interestingly, 130 years later there has clearly been a change in their relative fame and their statures as writers. Indeed, Bloom's own lists in *The Western Canon* illustrate this change, as there he makes no mention of the writings of Sir Leslie Stephen, but recommends several of Hardy's novels, as well as his collected poems.[2] How did this change in their respective reputations come about?

One explanation may be suggested by reading the Hardy/Stephen association in light of Bloom's theory of influence. If, broadly speaking, I were to assert that Stephen stood as a "precursor" to Hardy's "later poet," the difference in their current canonical statures can be understood: Hardy, in some way, overthrew Stephen, his rival and precursor, and thus usurped Stephen's place in the canon. However, I must take note that while Hardy has overtaken Stephen in terms of fame, this does not seem to have occurred in the way that Bloom's theory might predict. Hardy's struggle with Stephen, his "anxiety," was not based on the work or on the imagination of Leslie Stephen, but rather upon Hardy's envy of Stephen's greater literary status. Nevertheless, Bloom's theory of influence does help to examine the complex series of misreadings through which Hardy's material battle with Stephen was enacted.

Bloom argues that the process of slaying one's precursor occurs textually, for as he explains in *The Western Canon,* the anxiety of influence is an anxiety "achieved by and in the poem, novel or play" (8). For Bloom, all strong writing is "achieved" in this way, as "[a]ny strong literary work creatively misreads and therefore misinterprets a precursor text or texts" (*Canon* 8). While this formulation does not account fully for the association between Hardy and Stephen, an argument made years earlier by Bloom (in *The Anxiety of Influence*) *may* explicate their relationship. There, Bloom wrote, strong poets misread *"one another"* in order to "clear imaginative space" (*Anxiety* 5, my emphasis) for themselves. Let me be clear: while in both *The Western Canon* and *The Anxiety of Influence* Bloom's intended argument is that of the strong poet's need to misread the *texts* of his precursor, in fact those are not the words he used upon introducing this idea in *The Anxiety of Influence*. There, he asserted, "[p]oetic history, in this book's argument, is to be held indistinguishable from poetic influence, since strong poets make that history by *misreading one another,* so as to clear imaginative space for themselves" (*Anxiety* 5, my emphasis). "Misreading *one another,*" Bloom wrote, and it is *this* negotiation that is at the heart of the Hardy/Stephen relationship. Hardy misread and reinvented not Stephen's texts, but Stephen himself. Moreover, I suggest that this was not done by Hardy in order to "clear imaginative space," but to clear *canonical* and *historical* space for himself, to achieve his great desire to become a part of "poetic history": Thomas Hardy metaphorically slayed Stephen, his precursor, in order to assure his own canonical status.

In order to make such an argument, I will not rely on any of Hardy's creative misreadings of Stephen's *work* (for indeed they do not exist). Instead I will examine his misreadings of Stephen *himself,* those images of Stephen that Hardy created in both his fictional and nonfictional works. Bloom's theory enables me to posit that Hardy succeeded in disempowering his precursor by creating his own less than heroic portrait of Stephen. Nevertheless, Hardy's fictional images of Stephen do not appear to enact a disempowerment of Stephen's aesthetics. Although Hardy was clearly threatened by Stephen, he was unlike a typical "later poet" in Bloom's paradigm. Hardy appears to have had no desire to write like Stephen: although always insecure about his lack of formal training, Hardy seems to have been convinced of his poetic gift.

The reasons for Stephen's influence on Hardy, I suggest, had more to do with Hardy's desire for popular success than with his anxiety over Stephen's literary powers. Indeed, both Hardy and Stephen appear to have been centrally concerned not with the power of what they wrote, but rather with the powers of those who read them. Aesthetic concerns were not their main focus: both were quite willing to submit to changes in their works, if such changes were demanded by the reading public.[3] If at the outset of their relationship Hardy felt himself to be the more talented writer, Stephen, as Hardy knew, was undoubtedly the more successful man. Furthermore, Hardy's own desire for popular acclaim placed him in constrained relation to Stephen: Hardy wanted to claim Stephen's place in poetic history for himself, and yet Stephen's role as editor of the prestigious *Cornhill* magazine meant that Stephen controlled the means that could produce Hardy's success. Thus, in order to negotiate this uncomfortable relationship, Hardy misread and reinvented Leslie Stephen in his works. Hardy's literary portraits of Stephen are therefore the focus of this chapter. Before I look at the fictionalized depictions of Stephen in Hardy's works, however, I will examine a poem that Hardy himself proclaimed as his poetic portrait of Stephen.

Hardy's poem "The Schreckhorn" is a eulogizing memorial to Leslie Stephen. Curiously, however, it was written in 1897, five years before Stephen's death. Hardy's pride in the merit of this poem, his purpose in composing it, and his reasons for contributing it to the first published biography of Stephen, F. W. Maitland's *The Life and Letters of Leslie Stephen* (1906), are all important keys for interpreting Stephen's influence on Hardy. If "The Schreckhorn" ostensibly honors the memory of Stephen, it can also be read as an attempt by Hardy to diminish Stephen's literary status. Such an interpretation is strengthened by Hardy's own account of his inspiration for the poem, as it appears in Maitland's biography. Hardy begins the account by noting that at the time he wrote the poem, in 1897, he had not seen Stephen for a long time. As Hardy describes it "a ten years' chasm of silence came between us in our pilgrimage." Hardy then continues as follows:

> [. . .] in 1897, I was in the Bernese Oberland, when the opening scenery revealed the formidable peak of the Great Schreckhorn, which, as I knew, he had been the first to "conquer" (to use his own word) as an Alpine climber in 1861. [. . .] Then and there I suddenly had a vivid sense of him, as if his personality informed the mountain—gaunt and difficult, like himself. [. . .] As I lay awake that night, the more I thought of the mountain, the more permeated with him it seemed: [. . .] I felt as if the Schreckhorn were Stephen in person; and I was moved to begin a sonnet to express the fancy, which I resolved to post to him when I got home. However, thinking that he might not care for it, I did not do so (cited in Maitland 277).

As Hardy describes in this recollection, Stephen had been an avid and ambitious mountain climber in his younger days. Stephen's pioneering ascent of the Schreckhorn peak in 1861 was his most highly acclaimed climb, and thus the setting provided the inspiration for Hardy's poem.

If one looks closely at the terms that Hardy uses in his remembrance, "pilgrimage," "conquer," "formidable peak," it becomes clear that Hardy articulates his poetic inspiration with alpine terminology. Was not such language more characteristic of Stephen, the climber, than of Hardy himself? Bloom's theory of influence appears to offer an explanation for Hardy's linguistic borrowing. As he argues in *The Anxiety of Influence*, this appropriation of a precursor's words is a device often employed by a later poet in a battle for supremacy over his precursor. A Bloomian reading of this passage, then, suggests that by utilizing such mountain climbing terms, Hardy was asserting linguistic control over Stephen, his presumed precursor: Here, Hardy stakes his claim over Stephen's alpine tropes.[4] Hardy's use of this alpine language as a means of control is further suggested in his explanation of the collapse of his friendship with Stephen: Hardy describes their falling out as a "ten years' chasm."

This Bloom-inspired reading of Hardy's reminiscence also raises other possibilities about Hardy's battle with Stephen. As this passage continues, for example, Hardy depicts Stephen as metaphor. Hardy notes that: "the more I thought of the mountain the more permeated with him it seemed: I could not help remarking to my wife that I felt as if *the Schreckhorn were Stephen in person*" (cited in Maitland 277, my emphasis). By employing this turn of phrase here, Hardy reverses the expected relationship of Stephen (the conqueror) to the (conquered) mountain. He does not say that Stephen evinces traits of the Schreckhorn, but rather, that "[Stephen's] personality *informed the mountain*" (my emphasis). In this passage, then, the Schreckhorn is not a metaphor for Stephen, but rather, Stephen is a metaphor for the mountain—"gaunt and difficult, like himself." Thus, Hardy's reminiscence reduces his precursor's power by placing Stephen, the conqueror, in the service of the conquered Schreckhorn. But is this the light in which Hardy himself perceived his poetic vision?

The conclusion of this passage allows me to posit an answer. Here, Hardy recalls that having composed the poem, he "resolved to post it to [Stephen] when I got home. However, thinking that he might not care for it, I did not do so" (cited in Maitland 277). As this comment suggests, Hardy may have been aware of the dark agenda at work within his poem and that Stephen "might not care for it." In fact, both the poem and Hardy's reminiscence of its inspiration remained unknown to Stephen. "The Schreckhorn" was not published until Hardy offered it to Maitland for use in his biography, published four years after Stephen's death.[5] If Hardy *was* conscious of the implicit threat of his premature poetic epitaph for Stephen, and thus refused to post it to him, would such a concealment make sense within Bloom's paradigm? While Bloom predicts that the later poet longs to hold his poem "open to his precursor" (*Anxiety* 16), Hardy in fact did the opposite, holding the poem firmly closed until after Stephen's death. My adapted Bloomian reading of this passage thus suggests that Hardy's composition of the poem was not the result of an artistic vision, but rather of an ambitious subterfuge. "The Schreckhorn" harbors Hardy's disguised reinvention and overpowering of his precursor.

In light of this reading of Hardy's reminiscence, the poem itself can be interpreted as a further enactment of his concealed and cautious attack on

Stephen. In my examination of Hardy's inspiration for this poem, I relied on elements of Bloom's theory of influence, as it suggests poetic methods for self-empowerment and the overthrow of literary rivals. Nevertheless, in my reading, Hardy's reminiscence exhibits not a Bloomian misreading of a literary precursor's *texts* but rather a misreading of the precursor (Stephen) himself.

Hardy's poem "The Schreckhorn" similarly reinvents his precursor's literary power, his legacy, and his canonical status, by misreading Stephen's character. As Bloom's paradigm of poetic influence provides a powerful tool for examining processes of misreading, I will examine Hardy's negotiations in the poem in terms of the Six Revisionary Ratios of Bloom's theory.

THE SCHRECKHORN.
With Thoughts of L.S.
(June 1897).

Aloof, as if a thing of mood and whim,
Now that its spare and desolate figure gleams
Upon my nearing vision, less it seems
A looming Alp-height than a guise of him
Who scaled its horn with ventured life and limb,
Drawn on by vague imaginings, maybe,
Of semblance to his personality
In its quaint glooms, keen lights, and rugged trim.

—At his last change, when Life's dull coils unwind,
Will he, in old love, hitherward escape,
And the eternal essence of his mind
Enter this silent adamantine shape,
And his low voicing haunt its slipping snows
When dawn that calls the climber dyes them rose?

(Hardy, cited in Maitland 278)

"The Schreckhorn," in my adapted Bloomian reading, fulfils the six stages of poetic revision depicted by Bloom's Revisionary Ratios. The first of these is poetic misreading or what Bloom terms "Clinamen," meaning swerve. This can be seen as a "corrective movement" in the later poet's poem, which, Bloom writes, "implies that the precursor poem went accurately up to a certain point, but then should have swerved, precisely in the direction that the new poem moves" (*Anxiety* 14).

It is my contention that in this poem Hardy was attempting to overtake and undermine Stephen's canonical status, not Stephen's literary strength. If this is so, then Stephen's "status" is analogous to the "precursor poem" that Bloom describes above, and it is this that Hardy negotiates in "The Schreckhorn." Thus, the mountain climb that Hardy depicts here poeticizes his struggle to gain credibility in the world of literature. The "corrective movement" of the poem that Bloom's formulation calls for is contained in "The Schreckhorn"'s close, in which Hardy imagines Stephen's soul escaping to the mountain, silent and low-voiced. Here, Hardy portrays Stephen's climbing of the Alps and the literary world as "accurate up to a point," to use Bloom's phrase. As Hardy poeticizes that climb and reduces Stephen's conquest to an "escape," the poem enacts the "swerve" of which Bloom also writes. Hardy's poem, in this reading, "swerves" toward this conclusion: while Leslie Stephen had achieved some moments of glory in his life, the importance of his conquests is questionable, and will not be long remembered.

Bloom's next stage in these Revisionary Ratios he terms "Tessera." He explains this to mean that the poet "antithetically 'completes' his precursor, by so reading the parent-poem as to retain its terms but to mean them in another sense, as though the precursor had failed to go far enough" (*Anxiety* 14). This dynamic can be seen to function in Hardy's poem through his use of alpine tropes: Hardy retains Stephen's terms, while simultaneously overturning their meanings. Employing Stephen's climbing terminology, Hardy fuses man and mountain within the poem, leaving the reader unsure of the valor or significance of Stephen's conquest. He "who scaled its horn" is figured by the poet as ultimately subsumed by the Schreckhorn, as he enters its "silent adamantine shape." If I once again read this mountain climb as a metaphor for literary status, Hardy's poem implies that Stephen had "failed to go far enough" to ensure his future fame. Stephen's legacy is portrayed as a mere "haunt" in the snow, which will be surpassed by the feats of the next generation, of that climber at dawn—who is, perhaps, Thomas Hardy himself.

According to Bloom, "Kenosis," or "a movement towards discontinuity with the precursor" (*Anxiety* 14), is the third step in the creation of a strong poet. In this stage the later poet "seems to humble himself as though he were ceasing to be a poet, but this ebbing is so performed in relation to a precursor's poem-of-ebbing that the precursor is emptied out also" (*Anxiety* 14). If I continue to imagine Stephen himself as the "precursor poem" that Hardy misreads here, it follows that although the poem begins with Hardy's "humble" stance as he is overwhelmed by this "Aloof" Alp before him, the terms he uses to articulate that awe are equivocal. Hardy describes the mountain/man on first sight as unknowable, until he draws more closely to it: "Upon my nearing vision, less it seems/A looming Alp-height." This subtle phrasing can be read in two ways: first to mean that the nearer the "I" of the poem draws to the mountain, the smaller ("less") it seems; second, that the mountain upon closer inspection appears "less" like a formidable mountain and more like "a guise of him." Thus, in a version of Bloom's "Kenosis," Hardy appears to humble himself before Stephen's man-mountain, but in doing so also manages to evacuate some of his precursor's power. Overturning the humility exhibited earlier in the poem, Hardy empties out the awe of the mountain and reduces Stephen ("less it seems") to human proportions.

Bloom tells us that in the fourth stage, "Daemonization," the later poet "opens himself to what he believes to be a power in the parent-poem that does not belong to the parent proper, but to a range of being just beyond that precursor" (*Anxiety* 15). Hardy has "opened himself up" in the poem to the power of literary status, which he represents as a mountain climb. Hardy depicts Stephen as having attained that status, but only for a brief moment. In the first stanza, for example, Stephen is momentarily endowed with the characteristics of a poet, as he is "Drawn on by vague imaginings." Here, Hardy's words imply that Stephen himself recognizes the Schreckhorn's "semblance to his personality." This vision of Stephen as a poet is, however, quickly dismissed by Hardy's qualifying "maybe." Hardy's poem, when read in this way, denies Stephen any lasting poetic power. Instead, something unnamed within the mountain traps and silences Stephen, leaving his legacy uncertain, his voice a haunting. Thus, the poem may suggest that the immortality assured by a permanent place in the literary canon was a "range of being just beyond" Leslie Stephen, as indeed it would be.

Bloom's next stage, "Askesis," which he defines as "a movement of self-purgation which intends the attainment of solitude" (*Anxiety* 15), may be utilized to explain the hesitant language Hardy uses throughout. "As if," "less it seems," "maybe," "will he," and lastly the question mark that ends the poem: these are the ambiguous terms through which Hardy defines Stephen's legacy. In my reading, Hardy diminishes Stephen's conquest of both mountain and literature by using such qualifying phrases. Stephen's imaginings are described as "vague [. . .] maybe," while the question mark that concludes the poem suggests that Stephen's voice, now reduced to a haunt, will not be listened to in the "dawn." As Bloom's formula predicts, the poem itself suffers as it sacrifices a definitive portrait of Stephen (or of the Schreckhorn) to the darker motives of lessening Stephen's canonical stature. The poet, according to Bloom, "yields up part of his own human and imaginative endowment, so as to separate himself from others, including the precursor" (*Anxiety* 15). Through Hardy's desire to be "king of the mountain," that is, the poem in fact defines neither king nor mountain, and instead provides a hesitant, indefinite poetic portrait of Leslie Stephen.

Finally, both the poem and Hardy's reminiscences of Stephen in Maitland's biography can be viewed as enactments of Bloom's final Ratio: "Aphrodades, or the return of the dead" (*Anxiety* 15). In this stage Bloom explains that the "apprenticeship" now over, the later poet is ready to hold his poem "open to the precursor, where once it *was* open, and the uncanny effect is that the new poem's achievement makes it seem to us [. . .] as though the later poet himself had written the precursor's characteristic work" (*Anxiety* 16). Hardy, as I mentioned, did not "hold his poem open" to Stephen, as he did not publish it until after Stephen's death. Interestingly, when it did first appear it was in a *biography* of Stephen.[6] Stephen's own literary status was connected to his role as biographer, as he was most widely known as the editor of the *Dictionary of National Biography*. Bearing this in mind, Hardy's poem and his reflections in Maitland's *Life* of Stephen seem to function as Bloom's sixth Ratio predicts: Hardy, by creating a portrait of Stephen for this biography, had "written his precursor's characteristic work." In this reading, the "achievement" of Hardy's recollections of Stephen in Maitland is Hardy's appropriation of Stephen's "characteristic" role as biographer.

"The Schreckhorn," I would further argue, enacts not only Hardy's desire to appropriate Stephen's literary legacy, but to climb Stephen's mountain. As Hardy knew, Stephen had struggled mightily in his ascent of the Schreckhorn in 1861.[7] The poem, however, suggests that once Hardy himself drew near the mountain, he saw its limited power and was able to conquer it effortlessly with his words ("less it seems/A looming Alp-height"). Hardy's reduction of the awe of the Schreckhorn and of the literary world it represents in the poem thus allows him not only to diminish the greatness of Stephen's achievements, but also to stand above them, in judgment. In this reading, "The Schreckhorn" articulates Hardy's desire to empty out, reread, and rewrite Stephen's rightful legacy as a fearless climber and major literary figure, as Hardy conquers both the mountain and the literary world more effectively. The movement of the poem from Stephen's conquest to his eternal silence also illustrates Hardy's need to redefine Stephen's status. No longer a heroic mountaineer, or a literary figure to be reckoned with, by the end of the poem Stephen is conquered, silenced, and entrapped. Moreover, as the poem concludes, a new and more vital hero emerges, one unafraid of the awe of the mountain; the climber at dawn, tramping over the snowy and haunted voice of Stephen. Here we encounter the new conqueror of the mountain, of literature, and of Stephen himself: the poet, Thomas Hardy.

The Influence of Thomas Hardy's "The Schreckhorn"

While I have demonstrated here that Bloom's Revisionary Ratios can be utilized to explore a suspicion that Hardy desired literary prowess and wanted to "unseat" Stephen, I am also aware that "The Schreckhorn" is only *one* poem. Can the dynamics at work in this poem confirm that Hardy saw Stephen as a literary "precursor" whom he needed to "slay"? Or might I further argue that Hardy's publication of the poem in Maitland's biography was itself an act of revolt, as it insured that Hardy's reimagined portrait of his "precursor" would be circulated, and thus influence the way that Stephen would be remembered? If this is so, then Hardy's contributions to Maitland could account in part for both men's current canonical statures: Hardy usurped Stephen's place in the canon by successfully promoting Stephen as a weak and unimportant figure. But *did* Hardy's portrait of Stephen affect other, later images of him? How important was Hardy's depiction of Stephen to current perceptions of him?

One person upon whom Hardy's poem had a decided impact was Stephen's daughter, Virginia Woolf. Woolf's first letter to Hardy was prompted by the inclusion of "The Schreckhorn" in a collection of Hardy's poems entitled *Satires of Circumstance,* published in 1914. She wrote to Hardy on January 17, 1915:

> I have long wished to tell you how profoundly grateful I am to you for your poems and novels, but naturally it seemed an impertinence to do so. When however, your poem to my father, Leslie Stephen, appeared [. . .] I felt that I might perhaps be allowed to thank you for that at least. That poem, and the reminiscences you contributed to Professor Maitland's Life of him, remain in my mind as incomparably the truest and most imaginative portrait of him in existence (*LVW* 2:58).

Woolf's assessment of Hardy's "portrait" of her father as "incomparably the truest," I would argue, provides strong evidence that Hardy's contribution to Maitland does indeed influence the way in which Stephen is remembered: our current image of Leslie Stephen is primarily gleaned from Woolf's own depictions of him. Indeed, as I will demonstrate in chapter six, Woolf's renderings of her father echo those that Hardy provides in Maitland. Moreover, the images of Leslie Stephen that both Woolf *and* Hardy created are quite different from those offered by some of Stephen's other contemporaries. To most of his peers, Leslie Stephen was a man destined for some kind of greatness, a firm candidate for long-term canonical standing.[8] Stephen's historical importance, it seems, was only called into question after his death.

Certainly, at the time of his death Leslie Stephen was counted among the most respected members of what Noel Annan in his 1951 biography of Stephen calls the "aristocracy of intellect" (Annan, 1951 2), a man whose family ties all but assured him greatness. His father, Sir James Stephen, was for many years the Permanent Under-Secretary of State for the Colonies and was married to Jane Venn, the daughter of the Rev. John Venn, Rector of Clapham in 1814. Interestingly, the surname "Venn" surfaces in Hardy's novel *The Return of the Native,* as the name of the mysterious reddleman. Later in this chapter I will explore the possible connections between Leslie Stephen and that character, "Diggory Venn."

All biographies tend to take interest in family histories and genealogies, but I would argue that the available biographies of Stephen insist conspicuously upon the "greatness" of all the men in the Stephen line. Stephen's own accomplishments, that is, are figured in these studies as an inheritance: such works suggest that like all the "Stephen" men, he was born to "greatness." Thus, the manner in which Stephen's pedigree is offered to the reader can itself be read as a reinvention or re-reading of Stephen, and as his biographers' argument for his literary status. These works imply that his canonicity is all but assured, for Sir Leslie had literary primacy as his birthright. Once more in this chapter, then, the biographical genre has surfaced as a central means of producing literary history and canonical status. Indeed, I would align the posthumous portraits created by Stephen's biographers with the reimagined Stephen that Hardy's poem provided: all seem to insist upon Stephen's lack of influence upon his destiny.[9] If Hardy's contributions to Maitland hint that Stephen would be unable to secure literary immortality, the biographers in their own way portray Stephen's importance as out of his own hands. While Stephen's biographers make note of his literary accomplishments, their insistence on the power of his heritage implies that such achievements were not derived from personal merit, but from a familial legacy of "greatness." Being a "Stephen," they hint, was all Sir Leslie needed to achieve canonical status.

One example of this perception of Stephen is found in the opening of Noel Annan's 1951 biography. Here, Annan relates his own rather elitist theory about the nature of intelligence, which devolves into a treatise on the heritage of superiority of those children born into the aforementioned intellectual aristocracy. Annan then continues: "Stephen was born into this class and to understand him we must study his provenance" (1951 2). For Annan, then, Leslie Stephen is like a prized antique, whose provenance is of central importance: it is not Stephen himself but his heritage that Annan deems to be of value. This view of Stephen as a pedigreed specimen carrying greatness as his birthright appears in virtually all biographies of him.[10] The first biography of Stephen, Maitland's *The Life and Letters of Leslie Stephen,* is no exception. While the author begins by stating: "[o]f Leslie Stephen's ancestry little need be said" (Maitland 7), he nonetheless proceeds with an entire chapter on that very subject, fittingly entitled "Parentage."

In this chapter, Maitland offers the names and life-dates of the descendants of James Stephen (c.1733–1799), who came from Aberdeenshire to England (and whom Maitland calls "James Stephen I" [7]). Soon after, Maitland provides his sense of the character of a true Stephen, "[o]n many a page in the catalogue at the British Museum his progeny have left their mark, for whatever else a true Stephen might do he would at all events publish some book or at least some pamphlet for the instruction of his fellow men" (Maitland 7). Annan and Maitland, Stephen's earliest biographers, thus saw his life as tied to the accomplishments of his ancestors, and therefore informed by their status and their historical importance. As Gillian Fenwick argues in her authoritative bibliography, *Leslie Stephen's Life in Letters,* "the biographies and evaluations of [Stephen's] achievement have been written" but "[w]hat Leslie Stephen *wrote* is largely ignored" (Fenwick 2, my emphasis). Thus, Fenwick reminds us that it is not Stephen's works that his biographers deem to be of interest, but rather the idea of Leslie Stephen himself. Stephen as editor of *Cornhill;* Stephen as editor of the *Dictionary of National Biography;* Stephen as the son of Sir James; brother of the second Sir James; widower of Minnie Thackeray and Julia Duckworth; father of Virginia Woolf; Sir Leslie Stephen's tangential connections with great figures are what concern his biographers.

Most important from the point of view of my study, "what Leslie Stephen wrote" strengthens his association with the "greatness" of others. While Stephen's biographers insist upon his inheritance of the "Stephen status," Stephen himself was deeply involved in the process of cataloguing the achievements of other men, through his work on the *Dictionary of National Biography.* Such a personal and familial privileging of the importance of what Annan calls "leaving one's mark" (1951 2), must have affected Stephen's perception of his own life and work—his was an awesome heritage to live up to. One might further wonder at the impact that meeting a man from such a family must have had on Thomas Hardy; a struggling but ambitious architect-turned-writer from Dorset.

Censorship and Friendship:
Far From the Madding Crowd

One topic of debate between Hardy and Stephen was the elder man's distaste for what he viewed as "vulgarity" in the works of some writers of his time. For an insight into this stance of Stephen's, it is useful to look once again at his family history. While Stephen's biographers make much of his heritage of literary pursuits, Stephen's "moral fibre" has also been dwelled upon in these works, which portray his morality as similarly bequeathed to him by his ancestors. One example of a posthumous portrait of Stephen that discusses his ethics is the introduction to Phyllis Grosskurth's biography, *Leslie Stephen,* published in 1968, "[i]t is amusing to speculate whether Lytton Strachey considered including Leslie Stephen in his gallery of Eminent Victorians. [. . .] Stephen's concentration on the moral values of the artist, would undoubtedly have provoked Strachey's irritation, as exemplifying the absurd earnestness of the previous generation" (Grosskurth 1). Grosskurth's statement here echoes the image of Leslie Stephen provided by Hardy in Maitland's biography. Grosskurth's assertions of Stephen's "concentration on the moral values of the artist," for example, and its "absurd earnestness," closely resemble Hardy's anecdotes of Stephen's prudery as an editor. What were Hardy's reasons for leaving behind this obviously persuasive portrait of Stephen as a censorious and overbearing figure? Furthermore, what were Stephen's own motives for his often harsh editorial intrusions upon Hardy's work? As I offer below some examples of Stephen's comments upon Hardy's texts, I hope to suggest some plausible responses to these questions.

In his letters to Hardy, Stephen generally cited the stupidity and ignorance of the reading public as the reasons for his strict editorial decisions.[11] However, even a cursory inspection of Stephen's essays on "morality" leads one to believe that while he wanted to placate his magazine's subscribers, he was also acting upon his own prejudices. As Noel Annan notes: "from his detestation of the attitude of French novelists towards sex, it is clear that many rejections and excisions which [Stephen] excused on editorial grounds, were agreeable to him for personal reasons" (1951 67). Stephen certainly had a duty to his *Cornhill* readership to remove anything explicitly offensive from Hardy's manuscript of *Far From the Madding Crowd*. Stephen's censorship of Hardy's work may arguably have arisen not only from his personal moral stance, but also from a fear of offending his subscribers, and thereby jeopardizing his own career. Such motives, however, do not account fully for Stephen's often harsh excision of passages in Hardy's novels: one would expect that Stephen used equal vigor in his editing of the novels of other authors, but the record reflects only this single major conflict over censorship with Hardy.[12] Was Stephen more censorious of Hardy's texts than those of the other contributors to his magazine? Or was Hardy more sensitive to Stephen's editorial approach than other contributors? I take it that the answer falls somewhere in between.

While Stephen's censorship of *Madding Crowd* has been criticized as overbearing, it is important to consider that Hardy's later novels, in particular *Tess of the D'ubervilles* and *Jude the Obscure,* did excite the anger of many readers of his time.[13] The vehemence of the outrage against these novels suggests that Stephen was indeed justified in detecting danger in Hardy's prose. Stephen's major concern as an editor was to please his subscribers, and while modern-day readers may find it regrettable that he did not treat Hardy's texts with more leniency, as Annan tells us, "it was part of [Stephen's] trade to pander to the taste of the *Cornhill* public [. . .] granted that he regarded the post primarily as a safe job which gave him leisure to write" (1951 67). There were, however, other magazine editors in London at that time who were less afraid of notoriety. Perhaps most notable among these was Mary Elizabeth Braddon, whose husband owned the *Belgravia;* Braddon herself was largely responsible for publishing the French novels that Stephen found so distasteful. As Annan asserts, however, it was not in Stephen's professional or personal interest to fly in the face of public opinion. Stephen was not, perhaps, any more strict in his censorship than John Blackwood at *Blackwood's* magazine, or George Bentley at *Temple Bar:* both of these editors also turned down the opportunity to publish Hardy's *The Return of the Native,* which was finally serialized in Braddon's *Belgravia.*

If the actions of Bentley and Blackwood and the public outrage over the sensuality of Hardy's later novels justify Stephen's fervor in censoring *Madding Crowd,* there nevertheless seems to have been a very personal negotiation taking place in Stephen's editorship of the novel. The nature of this negotiation is suggested both by Hardy's premature memorial poem for Stephen, and by Stephen's zealous bowdlerization of *Madding Crowd.* The two men, I would argue, were engaged, however unconsciously, in a battle for literary status and canonical space. Unfortunately, it is difficult to locate an unbiased account of Hardy and Stephen's relationship, as Maitland's *Life* remains the foremost source of such information, and Hardy himself wrote the recollections contained there. As Maitland noted with regard to Hardy's contribution to the book: "I am anxious that Mr. Thomas Hardy should speak. An apology for speaking of himself as well as of Stephen I suppress as unnecessary, and it will be allowed that I was happy when I asked for notes and drew a poem" (cited in Maitland 270). As I have suggested, Hardy's generosity in contributing this poem may well have been informed by ulterior motives. Is there a similar agenda at work in Hardy's other anecdotal tales of Stephen in Maitland?

To answer this question, I will examine events surrounding the first encounter between these two men, as recounted by Hardy in the biography. This description is related by Hardy in poetic terms, as Hardy notes that Stephen's first letter to Hardy had been dropped by the postman in a muddy lane, and was serendipitously rescued by a laboring man and delivered to Hardy. Stephen's letter is reproduced in Maitland as follows:

Dear Sir,—

I hear from Mr. Moule that I may address you as the author of "Under the Greenwood Tree." I have lately read that story with very great pleasure indeed. I think the description of country life admirable, and, indeed, it is long since I have received more pleasure from a new writer.

It also occurred to me [. . .] that such writing would probably please the readers of the *Cornhill Magazine* as much as it has pleased me. "Under the Greenwood Tree" is, of course, not a magazine story. There is too little incident for such purpose; for, though I do not want a murder in every number, it is necessary to catch the attention of readers by some distinct and well-arranged plot.

If you are, as I hope, writing anything more, I should be very glad to have the offer of it for our pages.

Yours Truly, Leslie Stephen (cited in Maitland 270–271)

One would imagine that when a struggling young author is attempting to secure a future for himself, he would be very excited to receive such a letter from the editor of the most distinguished literary magazine of the day, as *Cornhill* was. *Cornhill* had, after all, a circulation of some 50,000, and since its founding by William Makepeace Thackeray in 1860, had published fiction by George Eliot, Trollope, Thackeray, Wilkie Collins, and Mrs. Gaskell, among others.

Hardy's reply to Stephen's letter, however, reflects none of the elation one would expect: "A reply that I could send [Stephen], when free—though that would not be for some time—a pastoral tale which I thought of calling 'Far from the Madding Crowd,' [. . .] brought another letter immediately. He said that the idea of the story attracted him, that he liked my proposed title for it, and that he hoped I would call and talk it over when next I came to town" (cited in Maitland 271). Hardy's apparently calm reaction and rather brusque response to Stephen's request seems strange. Indeed, in his recent biography of Hardy, Martin Seymour-Smith questions the possible reasons for the novelist's reluctance to work with Stephen, which this letter suggests. "[Hardy] did not," Seymour-Smith writes, "as almost all aspiring young authors would have done, rush to make Stephen's acquaintance. He bided his time, and did not call upon him until months later, on 8 December 1873, when arrangements for the serial had already been made" (Seymour-Smith 172). Why, I wonder, did Hardy react in this way, and furthermore, what occurred in the year between Hardy's receipt of Stephen's invitation to meet in December 1872, and their actual meeting in December 1873? As Seymour-Smith notes, Hardy was furiously attempting to finish his novel *A Pair of Blue Eyes* that was being serialized in *Tinsley's* magazine during this period, and this may explain in part his initial hesitance to commit anything to *Cornhill.* It does not, however, account for the blasé tone of Hardy's answer to Stephen's letter.

After receiving Hardy's reply, Stephen left him to finish *Blue Eyes,* and did not write to him again until April 1873, when he repeated his request for a contribution to *Cornhill:*

Since I wrote to you last circumstances have occurred which make it desirable for me to ask whether the novel of which you then spoke to me is in a sufficiently advanced state to allow of my seeing it with a view to its appearance in the *Cornhill,* and if so, at what time you would be able to let me publish the first number. It would not be necessary to have the whole story

before beginning. . . . You spoke of coming to town in the spring. If you
should be here I should be very glad to see you (cited in Maitland 271–2).

Hardy's reaction to this second request was again hesitant, as he once more
declined the opportunity to meet with Stephen. Such reluctance seems all
the more curious since, as Seymour-Smith notes, Hardy was in fact in London that spring: "Although [Hardy] then got down to some serious work on
the book [*Madding Crowd*], he still did not take advantage of the invitation.
[. . .] Instead, he sent a few chapters, which Stephen approved but did not
immediately accept" (Seymour-Smith 172). Is it thus possible to detect signs
of a power struggle between the two men, even in this early stage of their acquaintance? These letters, and the circumstances under which they were
written, clearly suggest to me that both men were "sizing up" the other, and
defining the terms of their future association.

Hardy in particular seems to have refused to insinuate himself into
Stephen's good graces. But why not? Was Hardy put off by Stephen's im-
politic suggestion that " 'Under the Greenwood Tree' [was] of course, not a
magazine story," or by his assessment of it as poorly arranged? "There is too
little incident for such purpose" (cited in Maitland 271), Stephen wrote.
Perhaps, then, Hardy's hesitance to meet Stephen was a reaction against such
unsolicited criticisms. If Hardy's delay in meeting with Stephen did stem
from wounded pride, he did not forgive quickly. In fact, he waited for
Stephen to request the story from him twice more before he finally decided
to submit *Madding Crowd* to *Cornhill*.

In the end, the hesitance that Hardy displayed toward Stephen's approaches had worked in his favor: upon Stephen's third request, they began
to negotiate generous terms of payment for the serialization of *Madding
Crowd*.[14] Hardy's reluctance may have brought about more than this monetary gain, however. There was now another beneficial change in his career:
Stephen began to approach Hardy with much greater diplomacy. Indeed,
there is a dramatic difference in tone between Stephen's first, condescending
letter to Hardy requesting a story, and his third, successful one written five
months later: "Since I wrote, arrangements have been nearly concluded
which will, I think obviate any necessity for hurrying you. . . . I should like
to see a specimen of your story before I go abroad, which will be in the middle either of June or July—most likely—the latter" (cited in Maitland 272).
Hardy finally agreed to submit his story to Stephen after receiving this deferential note.

Soon afterward, a bond began to evolve between the two men. Indeed,
despite any bad faith that can be read in Hardy's later reminiscences of
Stephen, it is clear that at least for a time, the two were friends. This friendship, it seems, may well have arisen from their mutual skepticism about or-

ganized religion. As an agnostic, Stephen looked at social evil scientifically, and endorsed morality not for the sake of a place in heaven, but for practical, charitable purposes. Hardy himself drifted between churchgoing and agnosticism and one could surmise from the ideas espoused in his prose and verse, that his was not a blind faith in a benevolent God. Stephen's beliefs were based on principles of humanitarianism, coupled with an intense hatred of hypocrisy. Intellectually, he could find no justification for the existence of God, and resented being forced to profess faith in something that he could not prove. In his essay "An Agnostic's Apology," for example, Stephen wrote: "[y]ou tell us to be ashamed of professing ignorance. Where is the shame of ignorance in matters still involved in endless and hopeless controversy? Is it not rather a duty?" ("Agnostic" 13). Like Stephen, Hardy professed ignorance on the subject of God, preferring to decry a careless fate in his works, than to bow to a provident being. Such similar, and unpopular, philosophies may thus have helped organize their friendship.

I would further suggest, however, that there was an additional motive that informed Hardy's befriending of Stephen. Notwithstanding their shared beliefs, in 1874, Stephen as editor of *Cornhill* was in a position of power, and Hardy wanted to be aligned with a powerful ally.[15] For a time Stephen was a strong supporter of the younger, struggling Hardy. Nonetheless, Hardy's later reminiscences in Maitland indicate the difficulty that these two ambitious and obstinate men encountered during the serialization of *Madding Crowd:* the editing process required compromise, and both Hardy and Stephen were often reluctant to "give in." As Hardy recounts in Maitland: "As soon, therefore, as I could, I forwarded a few chapters of the story, with some succeeding ones in outline, which, briefly, he was pleased to characterise in terms that, coming from such a quarter, were more eulogistic than I was aware of. He hoped I should hurry on 'the elopement of the heroine'" (cited in Maitland 272). As this recollection illustrates, even at the start of their work together on *Madding Crowd,* Hardy was finding Stephen's critiques difficult to decipher. Stephen's judgments were "characterise[d] in terms" that did not sound like praise to Hardy, but "coming from such a quarter" were in fact "eulogistic." While the "terms" of his editor's assessments were at first misunderstood by Hardy, the requests Stephen made at this time seem fairly innocuous: he wanted the writer to "hurry on" with his tale. In this early correspondence, therefore, there is no hint of the strict censorship for which Stephen's editorship of *Madding Crowd* was later remembered.[16]

Indeed, Hardy's first chapters must have appeared fairly tame to Stephen, as he undertook publishing the novel without having read its conclusion. Stephen's faith in Hardy seems in turn to have thawed the novelist's original reticence toward him: it was at this time that Hardy finally decided to visit

Stephen at home. Hardy in Maitland provides a version of their first visit as follows:

> [. . .] and on that day, owing to my remissness in not going sooner as he had wished, we met for the first time. [. . .] He welcomed me with one hand, holding back the barking "Troy" with the other. The dog's name I, of course, had never heard till then, and I said, "That is the name of my wicked soldier-hero." He answered caustically: "I don't think my Troy will feel hurt at the coincidence, if yours doesn't" (cited in Maitland 273).

The jovial banter Hardy recalls here belies the serious subtext of their meeting: each man, I would argue, was once again sizing up the other. As Hardy tells it, he was several hours late to their scheduled meeting, and Stephen's gruff demeanor could well have been a response to this breach of etiquette. Hardy nevertheless relates that in his view, this introduction to Stephen had a positive conclusion. As he writes in Maitland: "[p]erceiving, what I had not gathered from his letters, that I had a character to deal with [. . .] I felt then that I liked him, which at first I had doubted. The feeling never changed" (273).

Hardy's "feelings" toward Stephen do appear to have changed in the years after Stephen's death. Nevertheless, during the early part of 1874, their friendship underwent a "honeymoon" period, and at this time they shared a close, and enjoyable, working relationship. In January 1874, for example, Stephen wrote to Hardy following the first installment of *Madding Crowd* in *Cornhill:* "I am glad to congratulate you on the reception of your first number. Besides the gentle *Spectator* which thinks that you must be George Eliot because you know the names of the stars, several good judges have spoken to me warmly of the Madding Crowd. [. . .] The story comes out very well, I think, and I have no criticism to make" (cited in Seymour-Smith 179).[17] Stephen's wholehearted approbation for the first chapters of *Madding Crowd* in this letter thus confirms the friendly and supportive nature of their relationship at this time.

Hardy too seems to have changed his approach to Stephen during this period; perhaps his first taste of critical success had convinced him to place more trust in his editor. In February of 1874, Hardy wrote to Stephen with a tone of deference unprecedented in their correspondence. Admitting of his inexperience, Hardy wrote:

> The truth is that I am willing, and indeed anxious, to give up any points which may be desirable in a story when read as a whole, for the sake of others which shall please those who read it in numbers. Perhaps I may have higher aims some day, and be a great stickler for the proper artistic balance of the completed work, but for the present circumstances lead me to wish merely to be considered a good hand at a serial (*CLTH* 1:28).

This statement, I believe, serves as a telling commentary on the spirit of Hardy's ambitions at this time. Like Stephen, who was willing to dramatically alter any submission to *Cornhill* in order to avoid provoking his subscribers, Hardy himself was in his own words "willing, and indeed anxious, to give up any points" so that he could be "considered a good hand at a serial." While Hardy envisioned his future self as a "stickler for the proper artistic balance," at the start of his career he wanted, in a word, success.

If Hardy did have this agenda in mind, he must have been aware that a powerful editor like Stephen could help him to achieve his goal. Nevertheless, Stephen was a harsher judge of what was "proper" material for *Cornhill* readers than was Hardy, and this difference soon began to irritate them both. As Seymour-Smith remarks: "[Stephen] was genuinely offended by Hardy's persistent eroticism, but there was nothing he could say about it which would not implicate him in the Grundyism of which he pretended to be ashamed" (Seymour-Smith 187). Thus, while both Hardy and Stephen considered themselves as friends, by the midpoint of *Madding Crowd's* serialization their differing stances on "propriety" were becoming more and more difficult for them to resolve amicably.

Rosemarie Morgan's *Cancelled Words* provides compelling documentation of the extent of Stephen's "Grundyism" in his editing of *Madding Crowd*. Such evidence, moreover, strengthens the argument that Stephen's censorship of the novel had a profound effect on his relationship with Hardy. As Morgan notes, "[a]lthough Stephen maintains, in his correspondence with Hardy, a low profile on his role of censor, this does not reflect the regularity and rigor of his editorial intervention in actual practice" (Morgan, *Cancelled* 23). At the beginning, Stephen's requests appeared reasonable to Hardy, who was, as he admitted, a relative newcomer to serialized fiction. As his letter to Stephen clearly stated, he was at first willing to give in to his editor for the sake of the serial's success. But, in practice, as Morgan points out, Hardy did not always submit easily to Stephen's editorial "improvements."

While Hardy agreed to small changes to his text, such as Stephen's substitution of the word "backs" for "buttocks," some of Stephen's more intrusive suggestions for plot modifications met with Hardy's resistance. Hardy's reluctance to incorporate these larger changes to the tale, however, was countered with Stephen's dire predictions of public censure. In the end, Hardy usually resigned himself to following his editor's advice. Thus, as Morgan's research shows, Hardy was often complicit in Stephen's censorship of the novel. Nevertheless, Hardy's contribution to Maitland suggests that in later years, he came to regret the free reign that he had allowed to Stephen. Moreover, in his later accounts of the serialization of *Madding Crowd,* Hardy downplayed his own role in the censorship of his text. In Maitland, for example, Hardy does not mention his own stated willingness to "give up any points" to ensure his story's success, but he does offer several examples of Stephen's attempts to pander to his reading public. Recounting a letter he received from Stephen during the serialization, Hardy cites:

> "I have ventured to leave out a line or two in the last batch of proofs," [Stephen] wrote soon afterwards, "from an excessive prudery of which I am ashamed; but one is forced to be absurdly particular. May I suggest that Troy's seduction of the young woman will require to be treated in a gingerly fashion. [. . .] I mean that the thing must be stated, but that the words must be careful. Excuse this wretched shred of concession to popular stupidity; but I am a slave" (cited in Maitland 274–5).

I would argue that Hardy, by offering this example of Stephen's "slavery" to popular morality, provides Maitland's readers with a portrait of Stephen not as a judicious editor, but as a coward. Furthermore, this contribution ignores Hardy's own participation in these "concessions to popular stupidity": Hardy, in Maitland, projects the blame for the censorship of his novel solely onto Stephen.

As Hardy's recollections in Maitland continue, however, Hardy appears to momentarily vindicate Stephen's censorship. Hardy mentions that *Cornhill* had indeed received complaints about the impropriety of *Madding Crowd* from "[t]hree respectable ladies and subscribers" (cited in Maitland 275). Nevertheless, Hardy quickly qualifies this testimonial to Stephen's judgment. He recalls that: "I reminded him that though three objectors who disliked the passage, or pretended to, might write their disapproval, three hundred who possibly approved of it would not take the trouble to write, and hence he might have a false impression of the public as a body" (cited in Maitland 275). As he concludes this anecdote, Hardy leaves the reader in no doubt as to whom was the victor in this disagreement. Hardy recalls that the *Times,* after the novel's publication in volume form some years later, commended the very passage that had offended the ladies of *Cornhill.* As Hardy relates, he was anxious at that time to tell Stephen of this turn of events:

> As soon as I met him, I said, "You see what the *Times* says about that paragraph; and you cannot say that the *Times* is not respectable." [. . .] I then urged that if he had omitted the sentences [. . .] I should never have taken the trouble to restore them in the reprint, and the *Times* could not have quoted them with approbation. I suppose my manner was slightly triumphant; at any rate, he said, "I spoke as editor, not as a man. You have no more consciousness of these things than a child" (cited in Maitland 275).

As Hardy's contribution illustrates, he was glad of the opportunity to "triumph" over this example of Stephen's poor editorial judgment: the *Times* had praised the passage that Stephen had wanted removed. Hardy's anecdote thus makes clear to Maitland's readers that despite Stephen's accusations of Hardy's "childishness," it was *Hardy's* writing, and not Stephen's editing, of which the *Times* approved.

This recollection also contains another statement that calls for attention: Hardy's assertion that he would not have "taken the trouble" to restore sentences that Stephen struck is blatantly untrue. As Morgan points out, the original copy-text of *Madding Crowd* was lost after the serialization was complete. Hardy was therefore never able to revise from it for later editions. Morgan's research, however, confirms that Hardy used painstaking effort to restore his novel to its previous form for volume publication. As Morgan notes:

> [T]he reality of working under Stephen's censorious eye exacted enough unwilling compromises to warrant an effort, on Hardy's part, to collect and reinstate (for volume publication) numerous specific words and passages that had been cancelled for the *Cornhill*. This, despite the fact that his manuscript was never returned to him, which meant that such reinstatements had to be drawn entirely from memory (Morgan, *Cancelled* 50).

Such a concentrated attempt to replace the words "cancelled" by Stephen may confirm Hardy's eventual *lack* of trust in Stephen's judgment as an editor. Indeed, it may be that the critical approval of Hardy's work that the *Times* had offered had caused him to doubt Stephen's editorial perceptions.

This change in Hardy's view of Stephen, as indicated by these reminiscences in Maitland, seems to have occurred long after their work together on *Madding Crowd*. In fact, as Morgan demonstrates, during most of the serialization Hardy kept to his word and gave in to Stephen's modifications to the text. Not until April of 1874 did Hardy make any strong stand against Stephen's invasive editing. In that month, Stephen suggested to Hardy that Fanny Robins' baby might be removed entirely from the tale, for propriety's sake. Stephen wondered whether the baby was "necessary" and remarked, "I am rather necessarily anxious to be on the safe side, and should somehow be glad to omit the baby" (cited in Seymour-Smith 188). Not surprisingly, Hardy would not submit to this change, and in the end the two reached a compromise. Stephen settled for the removal of the description of the dead baby that Bathsheba sees when she opens Fanny's coffin.

As Morgan suggests, the scene as originally written by Hardy presented a much more dramatic crisis for Bathsheba as she looks down with sympathy upon the dead pair. According to Morgan, "Stephen had a peculiar sensitivity toward any mention of babies, particularly illegitimate babies" (Morgan, *Cancelled* 29), but it was not only babies to which Stephen objected. Despite Hardy's sensitive description of Fanny's seduction by Troy in his original manuscript, Stephen's bowdlerization also denied readers of *Cornhill* any knowledge of Fanny's "lost character." The result of this constriction was that in *Cornhill's* serialized version of the text, the baby that Fanny's coffin contains appears out of nowhere: due to Stephen's censorship, *Cornhill* readers had been kept ignorant of Fanny's sexual relationship with Troy.

Morgan argues that Stephen's revisions to *Madding Crowd* amounted to an overbearing and unjust censorship, exercised with no regard for overall loss of meaning in the text. Strangely, though, while Stephen's editorship took a toll on Hardy's novel, it did not seem to affect their personal relationship: the friendship between these men continued. In fact, despite Hardy's later hints of his distrust in Stephen's judgment, during the serialization of *Madding Crowd* he continued to like him personally and to value him as an editor. The eventual cost of this friendship to the integrity of Hardy's novel may have been high. As Seymour-Smith asserts, "Stephen, in spite of himself, began to slice out the candour from Hardy's writing" (Seymour-Smith 188), while Hardy, I would add, allowed Stephen to do so.

Such circumstances reveal that Hardy's account of his working relationship with Stephen, as contained in Maitland, is not entirely candid. Moreover, although Hardy's anecdotes describe Stephen as uncomfortable with the sensuality of *Madding Crowd,* other events undermine this idea: in December of 1874, Stephen wrote again to Hardy and, congratulating him on the completion of *Madding Crowd,* asked him for another story. Despite Hardy's later recollections, then, their work together on *Madding Crowd* must have been mutually beneficial: Hardy agreed to submit his next story, *The Hand of Ethelberta,* to Stephen for serialization in *Cornhill.*

Their joint decision to work on Hardy's next novel can be explained by the fact that despite their disagreements over *Madding Crowd,* Hardy and Stephen were now close friends. The strength of this friendship is illustrated by an episode that Hardy recounts in Maitland. On March 23, 1875, Hardy received a "mysterious note" from Stephen, asking him to come that evening, as late as he liked. As Hardy recalled, "he said he wanted me to witness his signature to [. . .] a deed renunciatory of holy orders, under the Act of 1870. He said grimly that he really was a reverend gentleman still, little as he might look it, and that he thought it as well to cut himself adrift of a calling for which, to say the least, he had always been utterly unfit" (cited in Maitland 263–4). Stephen, by now a confirmed agnostic, was renouncing the holy orders he had pledged to years earlier.[18] Stephen's choice of Hardy as a witness to his renunciation is perhaps a more convincing indicator of the closeness of their relationship, than are Hardy's later stories of their battles over censorship.

Hardy's contributions to Maitland thus demonstrate the power of the biographical genre in shaping perceptions of historical subjects. As I have suggested, Hardy's recollections promote a reading of his relationship to Stephen as a negotiation of power. Writing of Stephen *after* his death, Hardy privileges an image of him as an overbearing censor, while simultaneously downplaying the importance of their friendship. By doing so, I would argue, Hardy was attempting both to obstruct Stephen's entrance into literary history and to ensure his own: in Maitland, Hardy denies his lack of artistic integrity by laying the blame for any failure in his novel directly at Stephen's door. I have also noted that virtually all the later biographies of Stephen rely on Hardy's assessment of him in Maitland's *Life*. More to the point, these works tend to merely repeat Hardy's indictments, rather than question their objectivity. In these biographies, therefore, the relation between these two men is rendered as Hardy's recollections direct: with sympathy for "the censored" Hardy and indignation toward "the censoring" Stephen.

Hardy's contribution to Maitland thus illustrates that in later years he adopted an openly skeptical view of the editor he had once greatly admired. This reassessment of Stephen, however, also surfaces in fictional form, in texts that Hardy composed before Stephen's death. The first of these cryptic attacks on Stephen is contained in Hardy's *The Hand of Ethelberta,* which Stephen edited for *Cornhill.* Their collaboration on the serialization of this novel was fraught with difficulty, as the friendship born of their mutual beliefs became eclipsed by their growing sense of opposition. It appears to have become clear to both men that while Stephen, as he told Hardy, might "hope [to] shock the orthodox" (cited in Maitland 272) with his agnosticism, "free-thinking" and "plain-speaking," he himself was shocked by Hardy's brand of revolt. Stephen saw no place in novels for eroticism and open sexuality, considering these embellishments both unnecessary and immoral. Stephen's position on such matters is made quite plain in his essay entitled "Art and Morality":

> [. . .] when a man is accused of writing an immoral book, he has of course any number of excuses. One is that the book is perfectly moral; another is that it has nothing to do with morality; a third is that it is not written for children, but for men; a fourth that if it not express the morality of Philistines and prudes, it embodies a higher morality, which lies outside of the poor old Ten Commandments ("Art and Morality" 91).

What is perhaps most striking about Stephen's attack on immorality in novels in this essay, is that he ran it in the July 1875 issue of *Cornhill:* the same number in which the first four chapters of Hardy's *Ethelberta* appeared.

Was Stephen, I wonder, pointing a finger directly at Hardy when stating in this essay that "if a man really has the impudence to say that immorality is right because it is artistic, he is either talking nonsense or proposing a new law of morals that is too absurd to require confutation" ("Art and Morality" 91)? The sentiments that Stephen refers to here as "too absurd" are certainly similar to those that Hardy's works espoused. Indeed, the idea of a "higher morality," which Stephen belittles in this article, could be seen as the central argument of Hardy's major novels. Hardy's texts frequently interrogate accepted views of morality by portraying those views as inhumane, and therefore *immoral:* Henchard in *The Mayor of Casterbridge* is "a man of character," for example, and Tess d'Uberville is called "a pure woman." Stephen argues in "Art and Morality" that such a belief in a "higher morality" outside the "poor old Ten Commandments" is "nonsense," and this judgment may itself be a reiteration of his admonition that Hardy had "no more consciousness of these things than a child" (cited in Maitland 275).

In "Art and Morality," Stephen argues that the worst crime that an artist can commit is to use his talents to corrupt: "[n]ow if he is not only corrupt himself and anxious to corrupt others, but also uses his great talents to carry out his immoral purpose, the case [. . .] is a good deal worse" ("Art and Morality" 92). Was Thomas Hardy the talented but "corrupt" artist of whom Stephen wrote, or was the appearance of "Art and Morality" in this number of *Cornhill* a mere coincidence? If Stephen's essay *was* meant as a sermon of sorts to Hardy, its publication alongside Hardy's new serial could well be the first evidence of the dissolution of their friendship. Certainly, "Art and Morality" provides an indication of Stephen's central concerns at this time. His fear of the magazine's subscribers being somehow tainted by "new laws of morality" speaks volumes about the differing philosophies that were beginning to interfere in his relationship with Hardy. While Hardy attempted to throw light on matters of sexuality and morality, Stephen preferred to keep his readers in the dark, rather than risk their "corruption." An examination of Hardy's *The Hand of Ethelberta* will help to illustrate this growing rift between Hardy and Stephen, and how it came to inform this novel.

The Revenge of the Novelist:
Thomas Hardy's Fictional Portraits of Leslie Stephen

Unusually for a Hardy novel, much of the action of *Ethelberta* takes place in and around London. Rosemarie Morgan traces the origin of *Ethelberta*'s city setting to Hardy's reluctance to become labeled as a writer of country tales. As Morgan notes, by doing so Hardy was in clear defiance of Stephen's recommendations: in composing *Ethelberta,* Hardy had firmly turned his back on the Greenwood Tree–type tale that Stephen favored. Hardy's refusal to follow Stephen's advice is, for Morgan, evidence of his lapsing faith in his editor's judgment. Moreover, Hardy's inclusion of Stephen's petty criticisms of

Ethelberta in Maitland signals his later desire to voice these doubts publicly. Hardy cites some of Stephen's critiques there as follows:

> [May 1875.] "I doubt (to mention the only trifle which occurred to me) whether a lady ought to call herself or her writings 'amorous'. Would not some such word as 'sentimental' be strong enough? But I am hypercritical perhaps" [August.]—"I may be over particular, but I don't quite like the suggestion of the very close embrace in the London churchyard. Otherwise I have no criticisms to offer" [October.] "Remember the country parson's daughters. *I* have always to remember them!" (cited in Maitland 276)

By publicizing these examples of Stephen's "hypercritical" judgments, Hardy once again promotes an image of Stephen as a cowardly and prudish editor.

Was Stephen himself equally attempting to undermine *Hardy's* work, both through his zealous censorship, and by publishing "Art and Morality" in the same number of *Cornhill* as *Ethelberta?* If so, I could further suggest that Stephen, by mocking the higher morality in which Hardy believed, was simply retaliating for Hardy's attack on *him:* as I will illustrate, the foolish character of Alfred Neigh in Hardy's *The Hand of Ethelberta* can be read as an unflattering caricature of Stephen. As Martin Seymour-Smith notes: "One of Ethelberta's absurd suitors is Alfred Neigh, some of whose characteristics unquestionably resemble [. . .] Leslie Stephen's: the large red beard, his preoccupied measuring of it with his fingers, the egotism, and above all, what Gittings (who first noticed the resemblance) calls the 'false self-deprecation'" (Seymour-Smith 213).[19] The identification of Neigh (whose name suggests one task of an editor, that of saying "nay") with Leslie Stephen produces an interesting scenario: Hardy, insulted by Stephen's bowdlerization of his work, creates a demeaning caricature of his editor. At the same time Stephen himself sabotages Hardy's serial both by intrusive editing, and by publishing an essay on the lack of moral virtue in modern novels alongside Hardy's new tale. But does a reading of *Ethelberta* support this supposition?

Seymour-Smith notes that writer Robert Gittings first pointed out Stephen's likeness to Neigh. Describing Hardy's first acquaintance with Stephen's London literary circle, Gittings argues that "[I]n *Ethelberta* [Hardy] gives a minute and exact description of just such a coterie. [. . .] It is even possible that he drew certain aspects of his introducer, Leslie Stephen, in the person of the literary man Alfred Neigh" (Gittings 17–8). It is indeed "possible" to uncover similarities between Neigh and Stephen. In the novel's introduction to this character, for example, Neigh is portrayed as spouting the kind of learned literary jargon for which Stephen himself was known. Speaking of the meter of Ethelberta's poems, Neigh remarks: "[w]ritten I presume you mean in the Anacreontic measure of three feet and a half-spondees and iambics?"[20]

The description Hardy gives of Neigh, the would-be poet, is very like the man he would later describe in Maitland's biography: a gaunt and difficult specimen, a formidable, well-educated, and condescending man. Hardy describes Neigh as follows: "Neigh was a man who never disturbed the flesh on his face except when he was obliged to do so, and paused semicolons where other people only paused commas; and, as he moved his chin in speaking, motes of light [. . .] caught, lost, and caught again the outlying threads of his burnished beard" (*Ethelberta* 32:242). As Gittings suggests, the red beard Hardy gave to Neigh is a further indication of the character's connection to Stephen, while the pauses between words here ascribed to Neigh were also a characteristic of Stephen's: in a letter to Virginia Woolf years later, Hardy would recall her father's own "long silences."[21]

A strange, proleptic image of Stephen is also evoked by Neigh in the following passage. While Hardy's novel predates Stephen's editorship of the *Dictionary of National Biography* by some eight years, he seems here to anticipate Stephen's involvement in such an undertaking. Neigh tells his friend that "the only people I care to honour as deserving real distinction are those who remain in obscurity. I am myself hoping for a corner in some biographical dictionary when the time comes for those works only to contain lists of the exceptional individuals of whom nothing is known but that they lived and died" (*Ethelberta* 32:258). By placing these words in the mouth of this unsympathetic character, Hardy lends an air of hypocrisy to them. Neigh is shown to demean the "distinction" of being honored in "some biographical dictionary," but nonetheless hopes for a "corner" in one. His false humility is laughable, as he professes his idea of being noted as exceptional through the fact of his obscurity. Was this, perhaps, Hardy's view of Stephen's own self-deprecation? If Neigh is in part a depiction of Stephen, what influence might this caricature have had on later images of him? Interestingly, this mediocre, would-be writer, veiled in false humility, is similar in many ways to Virginia Woolf's fictional portrait of her father as Mr. Ramsay in *To the Lighthouse,* as I will illustrate in chapter six.

If Neigh *is* a sketch of aspects of Stephen, what reason would Hardy have for creating such an unflattering portrait of his editor at this time? Some possible answers can be inferred both from evidence of Hardy's insecurity over the quality of *Ethelberta,* and from Stephen's increasing criticism of it. Letters between the two demonstrate that from the start, Stephen did not consider *Ethelberta* to be as well written as *Madding Crowd.* Thus, Stephen's editorial critiques were now focused not only on the content and propriety of the story, but on Hardy's writing style as well. Hardy's sensitivity to such criticisms, and his resultant sense of vulnerability, are articulated in a humble letter that he wrote to Stephen at this time. Here, Hardy asks his editor for advice on what authors he might read in order to improve his writing. Stephen's response must have come as a painful surprise to Hardy:

> 16 May 1876
> I should advise [. . .] Shakespeare, Goethe, Scott, etc, etc, who give ideas and don't prescribe rules. [. . .] I think I should exhort you above all to read George Sand, whose country stories seem to me perfect, and have a certain affinity to yours (cited in Seymour-Smith 225).

As Martin Seymour-Smith argues, Stephen's condescending tone in this letter deeply embarrassed Hardy, and reinforced his paranoia of being considered an uneducated country bumpkin by the London literary community. Hardy, Seymour-Smith suggests, had opened himself up to Stephen by requesting his guidance, and felt humiliated by this response: Stephen's suggestions were no more than one might give a school boy. Hardy, an accomplished Latinist, and a widely read, if self-taught scholar, was mortified by this letter. Was Hardy's satirical portrait of Stephen as Alfred Neigh thus created in response to Stephen's slight? If so, what more can this character tell us about Hardy's sense of Stephen at this time?

Some possible answers to these questions can be posited via an examination of an unusual and macabre scene in *Ethelberta*. In this episode, Neigh is discovered to be not merely foolish or self-deceiving but dangerously corrupt. Hardy portrays Ethelberta secretly surveying Neigh's property in the countryside, when she comes across a group of starving and emaciated horses waiting to be sold to make dog food. There, "in the midst of the yard stood trunks of trees as if they were growing, with branches also extending, but these were sawn off at the points where they began to be flexible, no twigs or boughs remaining" (32:738). The trees themselves are hung with horses' heads and torsos, which are to be fed to the ravenous dogs who cry out nearby.

I suggest that as this gruesome episode is so unlike any other Hardy depicted in this novel, its singularity is evidence of his need to communicate a truly disturbing vision. If Neigh is indeed a caricature of Stephen, then this grotesque rendering of Neigh's estate may reflect Hardy's serious and deepening distrust of Stephen's priorities. Neigh here is shown to be a profiteer trading on the misery of others, willing to lop the arms off trees "at the points where they began to be flexible." This act of brutality may in fact be symbolic of Stephen's role as editor: to constrict the flexibility and the creativity of the writers who peopled his landscape, by cutting out the "twigs or boughs" of dangerous ideas. In this reading, the resulting mutilated "torsos" described by Hardy could be equated with the stories serialized by Stephen. Like the horses Neigh has hacked apart, the tales that Stephen "cuts" may once have been powerful, but now are hung "in parts," in order to cater to the needs of the howling crowds of *Cornhill* subscribers.

As my reading of this passage implies, Alfred Neigh characterized what was most abhorrent to Hardy: a pleasant exterior combined with a corrupt soul, an immoral man masked in conventional morality. If he did choose such a character to portray aspects of Leslie Stephen, it is clear that their once friendly relationship was coming to an end. Whomever or whatever Alfred Neigh symbolizes, it is certain that after the serialization of *Ethelberta* Stephen published no more of Hardy's work. Hardy's version of this breakdown of their association is recounted in Maitland as follows:

> [I]n 1877, on my starting another novel, "The Return of the Native," we had some correspondence about its suitability for the *Cornhill*. But [. . .] he feared that the relations between Eustacia, Wildeve, and Thomasin might develop into something "dangerous" for a family magazine, and he refused to have anything to do with it unless he could see the whole. This I never sent him; and the matter fell through. It was the last contribution that I ever offered him (cited in Maitland 276–7).

According to Seymour-Smith, after the poor reviews that *Ethelberta* had received, Hardy felt that "[b]oth his income and his integrity [. . .] might be at stake" (Seymour-Smith 224). Hardy's later view of the novel was that it had been "published thirty years too soon" (cited in Maitland 276). If here Hardy assigned the relative failure of this novel to the ignorance of the reading public, the dissolution of his friendship with Stephen at this time suggests that in fact Hardy laid the blame firmly upon his editor.

If the failure of *Ethelberta* was one unexpected blow to Hardy's ego, he soon received another: Stephen refused to publish *The Return of the Native* without first seeing the whole manuscript. This condition must surely have taken Hardy by surprise, as Stephen had serialized both *Madding Crowd* and *Ethelberta* without having read them in full. Hardy's unwillingness to submit to Stephen's terms may further illustrate the umbrage that he now bore toward his former friend. As I noted earlier, Hardy decided to approach John Blackwood, editor of *Blackwood's* magazine, with his story. Unfortunately for Hardy, Blackwood rejected the manuscript, and then a third editor, George Bentley of *Temple Bar,* also declined to publish the work. Leslie Stephen, it seems, was not the only editor to question the acceptability of Hardy's work.

Mary Elizabeth Braddon, herself no stranger to censorship, finally took on *The Return of the Native* for serialization in her husband's magazine, *Belgravia,* at a highly discounted rate.[22] The financial repercussions of this debacle were high for Hardy, and the embarrassment of being turned down by Stephen, the man with whom he had enjoyed his first commercial success, must have been especially galling. Thus, over the course of a few years,

Hardy's perceptions of Stephen had changed dramatically: Hardy now saw Stephen as a false friend. As Seymour-Smith suggests, Hardy believed that Stephen had betrayed his trust by refusing to publish *Native*. Hardy's sense of Stephen's betrayal, moreover, appears to surface in this novel, in the form of the character who bears Stephen's mother's name: Diggory Venn.

Hardy's inspiration for the character of Venn, the mysterious reddleman in *The Return of the Native,* is difficult to chart, as the novel itself underwent extensive revisions before, during, and after serialization. As Seymour-Smith notes, "[t]he early drafts differed considerably from the serial and book editions. The names of four characters were different. [. . .] The role of Diggory Venn in the original conception is again, unknown: but he was not a reddleman" (Seymour-Smith 226). The differing names in Hardy's original conception of the story, and the fact that Venn was not at first a reddleman, prompts me to query the cause of this character's transformation. Seymour-Smith points out that: "it is impossible to say how satisfied Hardy was with his early draft; nor to know exactly what he sent to Leslie Stephen" (Seymour-Smith 227). Did Stephen find a reddleman named Venn when reading the first chapters of Hardy's new novel? Or, instead, did Stephen's refusal to publish *Native* inspire Hardy to transform aspects of one of his characters into a portrait of Stephen, giving him the name of Venn as a clue to his origin?

The name Venn is, of course, the best indication of a link between this character and Leslie Stephen, but other features of the reddleman also bear similarities to him. Like Stephen, Diggory Venn is a self-deprecating and condescending figure, as well as being severe, earnest, moral, grim, and silent. Further details support this association as well: the red stain Venn carries with him may be Hardy's rendering of Stephen's impenetrable and difficult demeanor, or, more simply, an imaginative portrayal of Stephen's celebrated red beard. Other physical descriptions of Venn also provide him with features much like Stephen's own: like Stephen, Venn is a gaunt and agile figure, a speed walker, an outdoorsman, and a pipe-smoker.

While such likenesses may suggest a relation between the reddleman and Stephen, Seymour-Smith, by contrast, envisions Venn as a self-portrait of Hardy:

> [Venn] is, as he stands, an ambiguous figure. Perhaps his transition from red-dleman—grotesque certainly, but also, and more importantly, poetic in his mysteriousness—to respectable burgher, man of money and dairyman, is Hardy's ironic way of alluding to himself: would-be poet turned "respectable" purveyor of fiction safe enough for inclusion in Mudie's financially all-important list (Seymour-Smith 237).[23]

Seymour-Smith's reasoning here, however, also allows for a different reading of Venn: a would-be writer turned respectable purveyor of fiction could allude to

Stephen as well as to Hardy. Seymour-Smith argues that Hardy's shame at having sacrificed poetry on the altar of commerce resulted in his creation of the reddleman. If so, an interesting convergence of Hardy's character and Stephen's own is found in the fictional Venn. In *Native,* Hardy projects his flaws onto Stephen by endowing a character named "Venn" with Hardy's own opportunistic motives.

Hardy's characterization of Venn, moreover, has affinities with his other portraits of Stephen. In the first introduction to the reddleman, for example, the narrator describes his appearance as follows: "his face, if not exactly handsome, approached so near to handsome that nobody would have contradicted an assertion that it really was so in its natural colour."[24] Although the red stain of his calling pervades Venn's being, Hardy tells us that there remains a strange attractiveness about him. This description of the reddleman, I would argue, anticipates one of Hardy's later reflections on Stephen. As Hardy wrote to Virginia Woolf in 1915, her father "had a peculiar attractiveness for me" (*CLTH* 5:76). As Hardy's portrait of Venn continues, this "peculiar" attraction is further examined: "[a] certain well-to-do air about the man suggested that he was not poor for his degree. The natural query of an observer would have been, Why should such a promising being as this have hidden his prepossessing exterior by adopting that singular occupation?" (*Native* 34:262). As we have seen in the excerpts from Maitland, Hardy had similarly considered Stephen's work as an editor as a "singular occupation" that served to obscure Stephen's inherent likeability in a veil of "grim & severe" condescension.

If I am to pursue this reading of Venn as an image of Leslie Stephen, I should further consider the change in Hardy's presentation of this character over the course of the novel. While at first Hardy depicts Venn sympathetically as a misunderstood outcast, by the close of Book One the reader has begun to be shown a supercilious Venn, a man whose pride and self-pity has brought about a self-imposed exile. "The reddleman lived like a gipsy;" Hardy writes, "but gipsies he scorned. He was about as thriving as travelling basket and mat makers; but he had nothing to do with them" (*Native* 35:6). Helpful as the reddleman is to other characters in the text, Hardy reminds us that he is not a purely beneficent force: Venn's own agenda of endearing himself to Thomasin informs his every move. Hardy's novel thus depicts Venn ambivalently, as his generous acts are always also self-serving. Moreover, as the reddleman is characterized in terms that anticipate Hardy's later depictions of Stephen, I would argue that this ambivalence has its origin in Hardy's perception of Stephen: Venn's self-centered motives may, in Hardy's vision, have echoed Stephen's own.

Hardy, I believe, saw Stephen's editorial censorship to be like Venn's good actions: a function of his need to retain his position. In Hardy's depictions, the staunch moral codes of both Venn and Stephen are produced by their personal agendas, not by altruistic ideals. Venn is shown by Hardy to be a "decently born and brought up" (*Native* 35:6) man who is looked down upon by men of a lower station. Far from trying to make himself agreeable to these fellow workers, however, the reddleman routinely scorns them: "he considered them low company and remained aloof" (35:6). Here the single word "aloof" may be enough to associate Venn and Stephen, as it predicts the opening verse of "The Schreckhorn" ("Aloof, as if a thing of mood and whim") that Hardy wrote some twenty years later. The condescension exhibited by the reddleman thus relates to aspects of Alfred Neigh in *Ethelberta,* and to Stephen's own personality, as depicted by Hardy in Maitland's biography.

Throughout the text, Venn's character and history continue to exhibit similarities to Stephen's. In the original serialized version of *Native,* Venn was not at first a dairy farmer, but a haulier. In this capacity Venn had once lived and worked on the farms of Egdon Heath, but had traded this occupation for the lonely and roving career of a reddleman after Thomasin rejected his proposal of marriage. Hardy notes that by "adopting the reddle trade," Venn "had shifted his position even further to the worse in the eyes of the stationary dwellers upon Egdon" (35:7). Here, Venn's change in occupation may represent an event in Stephen's own past: Stephen, by abandoning his Cambridge fellowship, had also made an abrupt and shocking shift in career. As Diggory Venn moves from haulier to reddleman, he simultaneously trades his life as a member of the farming community for the lone existence of an itinerant worker. Thus Venn's location as an outcast on Egdon Heath could also be connected with Stephen's personal history. Stephen's renunciation of holy orders, to which Hardy was a witness, similarly forced him out of the religious and academic communities to which he had once belonged.[25] Stephen's new career, like that of the reddleman, left him as an outsider with an axe to grind. Although writers and other creative people surrounded Stephen, he himself was a critic, not an artist. Thus, like Venn, Stephen's chosen profession denied him an equal part in the sphere in which he lived. As Hardy wrote of the reddleman: "among all these squatters and folks of the road he continually found himself; yet he was not of them. His occupation tended to isolate him, and isolated he was mostly seen to be" (*Native* 35:6). It is tempting to consider whether this description also articulates Hardy's perception of Leslie Stephen.

If Diggory Venn is indeed a portrait of Stephen, it is a highly ambivalent one, and quite different from the caricature of Alfred Neigh in *Ethelberta.* While Neigh is fully corrupt and one-dimensional, Venn is a shadowy and complex figure, by turns helpful and opportunistic. Perhaps, then, the differences between Neigh and Venn suggest a change in Hardy's vision of

Stephen. It may be that as Hardy moved away from Stephen's daily criticisms, he lost his desire to depict Stephen's character as bitterly as he had done in *Ethelberta*. Nevertheless, Hardy's ambivalent rendering of Venn suggests that he had not completely forgotten Stephen's "betrayal": the reddleman, if a more sympathetic character than Neigh, is equally guided by a secret, selfish agenda.

Hardy's final recollection of working with Stephen, as quoted in Maitland, confirms his equivocal sense of his former friend. Hardy writes, "[o]ur correspondence as editor and edited was thus broken off, but when I had published 'The Trumpet Major,' he expressed, with some perversity I thought, his regret that I had not given him the opportunity of bringing it out. [. . .] 'Though,' he added, in a saturnine tone, 'the heroine married the wrong man.' I replied that they mostly did. 'Not in magazines,' he answered" (cited in Maitland 277). In this portrait of these two proud and sensitive men, there are hints of a subtext of mutual misunderstanding. Did Stephen, as Hardy here implies, so underestimate the impact that his refusal to publish *The Return of the Native* had made on Hardy, that he jokingly wondered at Hardy's sending *The Trumpet Major* elsewhere? Or was he genuinely unaware of Hardy's perception of this act as a betrayal? Certainly the "perversity" that Hardy mentions here suggests his incredulity over Stephen's lack of sensitivity.

Moreover, Stephen's unsolicited critique of *The Trumpet Major* ("the heroine married the wrong man") illustrates his continuing condescension toward Hardy: Stephen still believed he could offer Hardy advice on the "proper" formula for magazine serials. But Hardy no longer sought Stephen's approval. As he notes in Maitland, after this exchange over *The Trumpet Major*, "I saw him but very occasionally, until at length a ten years' chasm of silence came between us" (cited in Maitland 277). Thus it seems that Stephen's refusal to publish *Native* had cost both men a great deal. Hardy would never forgive Stephen, and Stephen, "perversely," would never understand why he was offered no more of Hardy's works. Their negotiations of power had undermined their friendship.

The End of the Line?
Epitaphs for Leslie Stephen and Thomas Hardy

As I have demonstrated, both of these men had a firmly entrenched desire for success. Leslie Stephen's career as editor of the *Dictionary of National Biography* would become a strange vehicle for his ambitions. This work assured Stephen of, as Neigh put it, a "small corner" in those volumes, and he in turn was largely responsible for choosing whom to include, and whom to exclude from them. Like Stephen, Hardy was keenly determined to succeed, and willing to sacrifice "any little points" in his stories for the greater good of popularity. Unlike Leslie Stephen, however, Hardy's name still enjoys that fame.

By the end of their respective lives, the priorities of both men shifted. Stephen, as I will illustrate in chapter six, began to belittle his achievements, and to look back upon his career as a waste of time: he was convinced that his name would ultimately be forgotten. Indeed, as F. W. Maitland recounts, Stephen had complained to him that: "[i]f ever a history of English Thought in the Nineteenth Century were written, his name would only appear in footnotes" (Maitland 491). Like the character of Alfred Neigh, then, Stephen was resigned to resting in some obscure "corner in some biographical dictionary." Indeed, were it not for the fame of Stephen's daughter, Virginia Woolf, and the current keen interest in biographical information relating to her, Stephen may well have disappeared from literary history.

By contrast, Hardy (who outlived his former friend by some twenty-five years) became obsessed with what would be written of him after his death. He was especially fearful that two of his harshest critics, G. K. Chesterton[26] and George Moore,[27] would survive him, and that their judgments of his works and his character would discredit his reputation in the future. In order to preempt any such reassessments of his life and work, Hardy began burning old diaries and unpublished poems, and made changes to the new editions of his novels, often with the subtle effect of sanitizing their more controversial ideas.[28] He flew into a rage at the publication of a book on his works, as it contained a chapter of unauthorized biography, and decided finally to write his own biography, dictating it to his second wife, and asking her to publish it under her name after his death.[29]

In Hardy's final hours, his anxiety over the security of his literary legacy had reached a fevered pitch. Leslie Stephen, now long dead, was no longer the focus of Hardy's venomous pen. Instead, he directed his ire at the two critics who would outlive him, Chesterton and Moore. In the last afternoon of Hardy's life, he composed and dictated two poems, the final lines he would ever write. These poems were not, as one might expect from a dying man, poems of regret or surrender, but rather, verses with a waspish sting: two epitaphs for Chesterton and Moore. Thus one can envision Thomas Hardy on his last day, spewing out the concluding verse of the poem entitled "Last lines dictated by T. H., referring to George Moore": "Heap dustbins on him:/ They'll not meet/ The apex of his self-conceit."[30]

The vehemence of Hardy's final outburst attracts my attention: is this an example of the "anxiety" of which Harold Bloom writes? Were these bitter epitaphs enactments of Hardy's desire to "clear imaginative space" (*Anxiety* 5)? Or are they more easily read as an illustration of Hardy's anxiety over his literary status, as an attempt to secure his future "canonical space"? Hardy's deathbed invective against his critics seems a clear attempt to discredit them.

Perhaps fearful that Chesterton and Moore might try to diminish his status (as Hardy himself had demeaned Stephen's accomplishments both before and after his death), Hardy sought to devalue his critics' opinions by depicting them as fools.

If Hardy's final words were an attempt to discredit his critics, thereby securing his posthumous reputation, this episode would confirm the importance Hardy placed on obtaining literary immortality. Indeed, this deathbed outburst may also be related to Hardy's negotiations of Leslie Stephen: Stephen, as I have shown, was less an aesthetic "precursor" for Hardy, than a rival for canonical status. Bloom argues that "poetic history" is indistinguishable from "poetic influence" since "strong poets make that history by misreading one another" (*Anxiety* 5). Is this, I wonder, the true dynamic enacted through Bloom's ratios? Does the appropriation of "aesthetic strength" lead a writer to obtain a place in the canon, or is poetic history the result of carefully articulated eulogies and character assassinations? Does the relation between Hardy and Stephen merely highlight such connections between the biographical genre and literary immortality? Is it coincidence that while Bloom's theory explicates a method for gaining aesthetic strength it mimics the structure of a more mundane struggle: that of the battle for popular success? These "which came first" conundrums will be explored in further detail in the chapters that follow.

For now, the strange case of Thomas Hardy and Leslie Stephen leaves me with these considerations: Hardy, who purposely protected his legacy by undermining the opinions of his critics and secretly penning his own "biography," still enjoys a strong reputation some seventy-five years after his death. Stephen, by contrast, convinced of his future "footnote" status, made no attempt to secure his future place in the canon. Unlike Hardy, however, Stephen appears to have rested in peace: having resigned himself to the idea of his eventual anonymity, he was, it seems, able to do so. He made no deathbed exhortations. Instead, on the final day of Stephen's life, just hours before he died, he requested that a poem be read to him: a poem by Thomas Hardy.

Chapter Three ❧

Three's a Crowd

Historicizing Influence among Thomas Hardy, John Middleton Murry, and Katherine Mansfield

In the previous chapter I argued that the language Harold Bloom employs in his theory of literary influence promotes a reading of texts as enactments of a struggle for power. While he maintains that it is "aesthetic power" that is fought for through his "Revisionary Ratios," a different kind of battle conforms to his paradigm as well: that of a writer's attempt to clear "canonical space" for himself. In the case of Thomas Hardy and Leslie Stephen, Hardy's struggle with his presumed precursor took place for the most part on public ground. Indeed, Hardy's strongest act of disempowerment was not his having *written* a premature epitaph for Stephen, but having *published* that poem in Maitland's biography. By doing so, Hardy ensured that his reimagined portrait of Stephen would be read and circulated: it would have influence. As Stephen's later biographers have tended to rely on Hardy's reminiscences, and even to cite "The Schreckhorn" in their works, Hardy's private desire to overthrow his precursor was successful: it became *public*. I would argue, therefore, that although Bloom's paradigm is meant to account for a personal, solipsistic negotiation of indebtedness, in fact Bloomian readings tend to locate those influences that are enacted upon publicly centered battlegrounds. Thus the usefulness of Bloom's theory as a critical tool may be limited; some literary influences are negotiated in private. In this chapter, I plan to explore the very different dynamics of artistic indebtedness as mediated through public and private means.

Bloom states in *The Western Canon* that there "can be no strong, canonical writing without the process of literary influence, a process vexing to undergo and difficult to understand" (*Canon* 8). Thus for him, the later poet's journey toward a public, canonical legitimacy begins with a personal, private agon: A later poet must slay his precursor on two distinct battlegrounds, one private and one public. Moreover, according to Bloom, both battles are related. A personal negotiation of indebtedness leads a "strong writer" to a public affirmation: canonical status. Within Bloom's theory, then, we find an overlapping of personal and public ambitions. The "major" poetic figures that he examines in *The Anxiety of Influence* are all also major canonical figures.[1] Thus, I would argue that Bloom's theory *privileges* a poet's public recognition over their private agon.

Other critics would argue that historically the very notions of "private" and "public" carry with them a gender-inflected distinction. As Jane Tompkins states in her essay "Me and My Shadow," the "public-private dichotomy, which is to say, the public/private *hierarchy,* is a founding condition of female oppression" (Tompkins 123). For Tompkins, "private" language is historically and culturally aligned with the voice of women; it is a language of feeling, of communication. "Public" language, on the other hand, is a tool of patriarchal authority, which, she claims, ignores "the human frailty of the speaker, his body, his emotions, his history" (Tompkins 129).

Tompkins' reading of the public and the private as a hierarchical structure may shed light on the exclusive character of literary influence and indebtedness, as theorized by Bloom. Because Bloom's theory relies on the works of major (and male) figures, it may in fact serve as an example of "female oppression." Bloom's reading of influence, that is, conflates public legitimization and literary value. Of course, detectable literary influence is necessarily that which has occurred publicly, by being enacted through the published text(s) of the later writer. But what of negotiations of influence that were never meant for publication, a writer's private interactions with literary indebtedness? Is there a paradigm that might measure or explain the nature of such a privately conducted influence? In this chapter, I will attempt to answer such questions, using Tompkins' idea of a gendered and hierarchical distinction between public and private discourse as a context for reading texts.

To begin, I will look at the works of two writers, John Middleton Murry and Katherine Mansfield, and their respective connections to one of the subjects of the previous chapter: Thomas Hardy. By historicizing these notions of gender, influence, public and private discourse, and relating them to events in the lives of these writers, I will suggest several different, and at times conflicting, readings of their texts. I will look first at the work of John Middleton Murry, the essayist and magazine editor, in whose works symptoms of what could be called "anxiety of influence" surface. His association with Thomas Hardy, moreover, was a highly public one, informed by Murry's own desire for a place in literary history.

John Middleton Murry's admiration for Thomas Hardy was often expressed in print. This being so, Murry's relationship to Hardy was not only informed by personal feelings, but also by the materialist mechanics of print production: Murry's published appreciations of Hardy were written with a certain audience in mind. Hardy's apparent influence on Murry, therefore, may have more to do with the tastes of Murray's readership than with any psychic "anxiety." An exploration of some of Murry's essays on Hardy will strengthen this argument. Examined together, these essays comprise a vast and verbose eulogy to Hardy, whom Murry described as the greatest living English writer of his time. As Murry wrote in 1926: "Indubitably the most singular phenomenon in the history of English literature during the last twelve or fifteen years was the rise of Thomas Hardy to a position of undisputed pre-eminence among contemporary writers" ("Supremacy" 207). This bold statement is echoed in several of Murry's published tributes to Hardy. At the same time, however, Murry's critiques and remembrances of Hardy bear similarities to Hardy's own belittling portraits of Leslie Stephen: Like Hardy, Murry negotiated his precursor through printed and published texts.

By contrast, the next writer I will consider here is Katherine Mansfield, whose relationship to Hardy's works was conducted privately. Unlike her husband, Murry, Mansfield never meant for her responses to Hardy's texts to be published. Her reflections upon Hardy and his works appear only in her letters and journals, which were brought to publication posthumously. Moreover, as Mansfield was a woman, a New Zealand "colonial," and an isolated invalid, her association with Hardy calls into question the relevance of Bloomian literary influence as a context for reading her works. Of what use are such theories for understanding a writer who is an "outsider" in literary tradition? Annette Kolodny argues in her essay "A Map for Rereading," that Bloom's influence theory does not account for influence that "takes place among readers and writers who in fact have been, or at least have experienced themselves as, cut off and alien from that dominant tradition" (Kolodny 48). My reading of the works of Murry and Mansfield, then, will offer a range of interpretations for their respective relations to Hardy, as informed by differences in gender, in cultural background, in the nature of public and private discourse, and by the material circumstances of their lives.

Perhaps unsurprisingly, Katherine Mansfield and John Middleton Murry first met through the medium of publishing, soon after she had begun writing professionally. Mansfield had been encouraged in this by her estranged first husband, George Bowden. In early 1910, Bowden suggested that Mansfield send the stories she had written while living in Bavaria to a magazine for which members of his circle also wrote, A. R. Orage's *New Age*.[2] Soon after her works began to appear in *New Age,* Mansfield's first book of short stories, *In a German Pension,* was published (1911). The volume was widely read and well received, and it seemed that the young writer was on her way to a bright career in literature.[3]

Mansfield's success with *In a German Pension* brought her to the attention of a young editor of a new literary magazine called *Rhythm*. That editor, John Middleton Murry, was to become Mansfield's second husband many years later.[4] After their first meeting in December 1911 Murry was suitably impressed and wrote to Mansfield immediately, requesting that she contribute reviews to his magazine. She had already sent Murry her story "The Woman at the Store" for consideration, and he now asked her to submit further works. Mansfield complied, and thus began their collaboration. Unfortunately, almost from the start, health and financial pressures plagued their lives. The *Rhythm* magazine collapsed in 1913, and in the ensuing year Murry contracted pleurisy. Shortly after nursing Murry back to health, Mansfield fell ill with what was later diagnosed as tuberculosis. She never fully regained her health, and for the subsequent nine years of her life Mansfield was on a perpetual journey, searching for a cure that never materialized.[5] After living together sporadically for several years, Mansfield and Murry married in May 1918. Soon after, as their journals and letters demonstrate, the two began to share an interest in the works of Thomas Hardy.

In early 1919, Murry was offered the editorship of the literary magazine *The Athenaeum,* at a salary of 800 pounds per year. This position was obviously advantageous to the newly married Murry; he and Mansfield were keenly aware that they would need both money and stability if they were ever to conquer Mansfield's tuberculosis. Running *The Athenaeum,* however, would not be easy. Once a leading literary magazine, it had floundered throughout 1917 and 1918, suffering a large loss in circulation. Murry would need to perform a miracle in order to forestall the magazine's closure. He hoped that such a miracle would occur in the form of contributions from Thomas Hardy, who was at this time nearly eighty years old. Thus, in early 1919, Murry wrote to Hardy, requesting a submission from him for the April 4 number of *The Athenaeum,* Murry's first as editor.

Why, one might ask, would Murry want to begin his tenure at *The Athenaeum* by publishing a poem of Thomas Hardy's? While Hardy was certainly considered a leading poet, his verse was hardly the fresh new blood of which *The Athenaeum* was in need. Why did Murry not seek out contributions from writers of his own generation instead? One answer is that Murry had recognized a resurgence of interest in Hardy's works among the young soldier-poets who were then coming into vogue.[6] Among these were Wilfred Owen, Siegfried Sassoon, and Walter De la Mare, who all befriended Hardy soon after their return from the war.

These young poets held Hardy in high regard, and formed among themselves a kind of "Hardy admiration society." They made visits to Hardy in

Dorchester, helped him with his correspondence, read aloud to him, and courted his advice on the writing of poetry. By approaching Hardy for a submission to *The Athenaeum,* then, Murry was calculating on the interest that he knew Hardy had once again begun to generate. Thus, Murry's first communication with Hardy had a self-serving, and public, agenda: commencing his reign as editor with a poem from Thomas Hardy would provide *The Athenaeum* with a stamp of legitimacy.

Hardy, however, turned down Murry's first request in the following letter, citing his age as an excuse:

> Dear Sir:
>   I have been searching everywhere for some poem that would meet your views, but so far have not been able to find anything at all up to date. [. . .] And I am not in trim for writing something special. So I fear I must forgo the honour [. . .] being in fact not so young as I was (Hardy, *CLTH* 5:297).

Hardy's response to Murry, in my view, echoes his first reply to an earlier editor: Leslie Stephen. In each case, Hardy was hesitant to submit his work. As I demonstrated in the previous chapter, however, Hardy did at last comply with Stephen's request for a contribution to *Cornhill* soon after he had received a deferential letter from Stephen. Similarly, Murry received a contribution from Hardy, after sending him these flattering lines: "It would be difficult to restrain my feeling while remaining 'this side of idolatry.' [. . .] We—I speak for a group of young writers who will be connected with the *Athenaeum,*—see in you and your work the embodiment of those qualities for which we are determined to fight in English literature. [. . .] In a real sense we desire to sail under your flag."[7] The poem that Hardy submitted to *The Athenaeum* was one he had written in 1917 entitled "According to the Mighty Working." Murry used the verses to head his first issue, printing Hardy's poem and name in large bold italics emblazoned across half of the first sheet.[8]

This first exchange between Murry and Hardy raises several questions about their earliest relations. Murry's admission of his near-idolatry of Hardy might, in a Bloomian reading, locate him as a "weaker talent." As Bloom argues: "Weaker talents idealize; figures of capable imagination appropriate for themselves" (*Anxiety* 5). Such a reading, however, ignores the circumstances surrounding Murry's "idealization" of Hardy. By paying such compliments to the elderly poet, Murry succeeded in "appropriating" Hardy's verses for the first issue of *The Athenaeum.* Indeed, Murry's communication with Hardy at this time seems to have coincided with a growing confidence in his own skills, as both an editor and a poet.[9] This self-assurance is evidenced by a bold gesture he made in July of 1919. Unsolicited,

Murry sent a copy of his recently published *Poems 1917–1918* to Hardy, inscribing it with the words "[t]o Thomas Hardy as a mark of devotion and gratitude from John Middleton Murry" (*CLTH* 5: 318*n*).

It seems curious that Murry, a fledgling poet, would send a book of his verse to the man he considered the leading writer of his day. What was Murry's reason for doing so? Was he seeking Hardy's praise, or was his gift, as he claimed, merely "a mark of devotion"? Hardy's own gracious, if noncommittal, reply to Murry's offering suggests that he was unsure of how to respond. In it, Hardy focuses on the printing quality of Murry's volume, rather than the verses themselves. "I have just received your beautifully printed sheaf of poems, & as I shall read them but slowly I write now. I am sure that they will be as good inside as they are out, from glimpses I have taken. The very kind inscription I have certainly not earned" (*CLTH* 5:318). One might presume that Hardy's cool response to Murry's "sheaf of poems" ("I shall read them but slowly") would have been a disappointment to the younger writer. But in fact, Murry's unshaken confidence in his poetic gifts during this period is illustrated by another event that occurred soon afterward. As F. B. Pinion notes in his biography of Hardy, in October of 1919 the poet Siegfried Sassoon presented Hardy with a belated seventy-ninth birthday gift. It was, Pinion notes: "[a] bound collection of the autograph poems he had collected from 43 younger poets" (Pinion 345). The volume was entitled *Poets' Tribute* and contained poems by Sassoon and G. K. Chesterton, among others, and a forward by Robert Bridges. Pinion also notes that "a curious late addition from J.M. Murry, written as if after Hardy's death" (Pinion 345), was part of the collection.

Murry's premature memorial poem, entitled "To T. H.," was enclosed in a letter to Hardy of October 26, 1919. In this letter, Murry asks forgiveness for writing "as though you were no longer among us": "For one thing I must ask forgiveness. You will find I have written as though you were no longer among us. For a moment, after I had decided to send my verses to you, I altered them. But on second thoughts, I felt I could not do otherwise than be honest. It is a virtue which you compel."[10] I find a startling similarity between this poetic exchange and that between Hardy and Leslie Stephen: both Murry and the young Hardy wrote premature poetic epitaphs for a man they claimed to admire. There is, however, an important difference between these two poetic events. Hardy stated that after writing "The Schreckhorn" he had a sudden realization that "there might be something in it" that Stephen would not like (cited in Maitland 277). Thus, Hardy never sent "The Schreckhorn" to Stephen. According to Murry's letter above, Murry had also reconsidered presenting his "posthumous" tribute to its subject. Unlike Hardy, however, Murry decided in the end to send the verses unaltered, for "honesty's sake." What can Murry's lack of diplomacy toward Hardy tell us about the nature of their relationship?

In my view, the poem, "To T. H.," holds an interest beyond its ostensible value as a work of "tribute"; it provides an insight into Murry's curious sense of Hardy. The length of the poem precludes my citing it here in full. I will, however, offer a sampling of the verses that will provide a general sense of the piece.

To T. H.
He is gone,
Of all we knew the mightiest, he whose voice
Fell like a doom of silence on the noise
Of lesser lips and meaner questionings,
So that we listened to forgotten things
Minded of him alone
And his great peers of whatsoever line
[. . .] set their lips against the comfortable lie.
Were his keen blasts then vainly blown
Like Roland's in the cold, estranging mountain-peak?
[. . .]

He shall not vainly seek
Young hearts responsive to his summons stern
So long as in the human mind shall burn
Though fitfully and weak
The grim flame of the will to know the truth
[. . .]

Verily he was our champion who foreknew
What steely scourge should pass
Among the wasted ranks of that too happy crew
Whom life once seemed to love, whose minstrelsy
Drowned his sad, monitory prophecy
Of what Life is and was.
[. . .]

So, till the speech of man is slowly stilled
His clarion voice shall sound
In aching souls, and wasted hearts be filled
With eager human courage to refrain
From meaner consolation than his brave disdain
Of comfort for his wound.
J. M. M. October 25, 1919[11]

In a cursory reading, Murry's poem endows Hardy with a dark and important vision, which has for some time been unheeded. These verses suggest that while earlier, light-hearted poets (that "too happy crew") were oblivious to the coming of war, Hardy had long foreseen "what steely scourge should pass." In these lines, Murry's poem renders Hardy as a prophet of doom, for which the postwar generation has a heightened appreciation and understanding. "To T. H." thus offers high praise both for Hardy's refusal to accept "the comfortable lie" of a lasting peace, and his brave, though sorrowful, adherence to his grim prophecies.

Nevertheless, the poem begins with the words "He is gone," and this dismissal of Hardy's existence prompts me to question "To T. H." as a simple tribute. Not only was Thomas Hardy *not* gone in the year 1919, he was to live another nine years, and publish three more volumes of poetry before his death.[12] How, then, does Murry's poetic epitaph compare with Hardy's own premature eulogy for Leslie Stephen in "The Schreckhorn"? Can Murry's poem similarly be interpreted as an enactment of his desire for literary status? Earlier, I argued that "The Schreckhorn" could be read as Hardy's attempt to undermine Leslie Stephen's place in poetic history. Does Murry's poem do the same?

Through its anticipation of Hardy's death, the opening of "To T. H." might suggest Murry's willingness to "slay" his precursor. The balance of the first stanza, however, belies this reading, as it honors Hardy's poetic strength. As Murry describes Hardy as "of all we knew, the mightiest," Murry's portrayal of Hardy's "voice" is very unlike the entrapped and silenced Leslie Stephen of "The Schreckhorn." For Murry, the power of Hardy's voice is unquestioned, as it "[f]ell like a doom of silence" on those "lesser lips and meaner questionings." Far from attempting to diminish Hardy's importance in this poem, then, Murry endeavors to enhance it. Hardy's poetic vision becomes in Murry's verses a "keen blast," a "trumpet's solemn note," a "clarion voice," and a "monitory prophecy."

Murry's rendering of Hardy's "immortal" power therefore seems to contradict any suspicion of his need to belittle Hardy. However, despite the tone of praise that Murry employs in "To T. H.," the fact that the poem begins with Hardy's death must undermine the ostensible worship of Hardy articulated by the rest of the poem. Examining "To T. H." in light of its opening lines, I find in it, no less than in Hardy's "The Schreckhorn," evidence of the poet's constrained relationship to his precursor. Nevertheless, if Hardy's desire for success had informed his portrait of Stephen as a "low voicing haunt," Murry's agenda when writing "To T. H." was slightly different.

Murry's praise of Hardy in this poem is not simply homage toward his hero; it is also a very public display of self-congratulation. This poem suggests that while others failed to appreciate Hardy's importance, Murry himself was wise enough to heed Hardy's grim prophecies. Such an interpretation is strengthened by a reading of the third and fourth lines of the poem, in which Hardy's voice "[f]ell like a doom of silence" on "lesser lips." Here, the "I" of the verses asserts the importance of Hardy's voice, but the very existence of Murry's poem indicates that he has not included himself among those muted "lesser lips." In these lines, the poet's own voice is aligned with the might of Hardy's: Murry's "questionings," unlike "lesser ones," have not been silenced by Hardy's power, for his vision and Hardy's are one and the same. In this reading, the opening words of the poem must imply that with "T. H." gone, Murry can replace him as an inheritor of Hardy's dark prophecies. In this sense, the poem may be read as a self-aggrandizing portrait of Murry, one that privileges him as an interpreter of Hardy's poetic vision.

Although Murry's poem declares that Hardy's "great peers" "as he are gone," it also asserts that his "keen blasts" were not "vainly blown"; there are "young hearts responsive to his summons stern." Through Murry's belated addition of this poem to the *Poets' Tribute,* these followers appear to be associated with the soldier-poets whose works were included in the collection. By thus equating his appreciation of Hardy's "summons stern" with the admiration for Hardy already demonstrated by these popular writers, Murry here aligns himself not only with *Hardy's* fame, but with the fame of the soldier-poets as well. "Verily he was *our* champion" Murry writes, and by doing so locates himself in the vanguard of literature.

This interpretation of Murry's poem as an exercise in self-promotion stands in interesting relation to my reading of Hardy's "The Schreckhorn." While Hardy's "tribute" to Stephen served to subtly undermine Stephen's historical prowess, Murry's poem does the opposite. I would argue then that if Hardy had wanted to "clear" a place for himself in poetic history, Murry, by contrast, was willing to *share* canonical space. By writing this poem, and contributing it to the *Poet's Tribute,* Murry was publicly associating himself with Hardy and with the soldier-poets who admired Hardy. If, therefore, "The Schreckhorn" is a misreading of Leslie Stephen, Murry's poem is a misreading of *himself,* and of his own importance in the world of literature. Murry, by portraying himself as a peer of the more successful poets of his era, positions his own, unknown poetry alongside theirs. The memorial tone of "To T. H." serves to confirm this view, as it implies that "the value" of Thomas Hardy is not found in his present or future poetic visions, but rather, in his influence on the "young hearts responsive to his summons stern." This memorial poem thus suggests that Hardy is *not* the future, indeed he is already "gone," but his "clarion voice shall sound" through his inspiration of younger poets, among whom Murry includes himself.

What was Hardy's reaction to this strange memorial? His reply to the poem and Murry's letter was as follows: "The verses are very striking I think, & they will keep. It will be for others to judge of their content. I must limit myself to admiring their form. [. . .] I am glad you did not alter them"

(*CLTH* 5:336). Hardy refrains here from any critique of Murry's poem, implying that its complimentary nature disallows him to "judge of their content." Later in the letter, Hardy tells Murry that the poem did serve to remind him of "matters connected" with his own death, and intriguingly, that he is "glad" that the poem was not altered. Why would Hardy have responded to Murry's letter and poem so graciously? Why would he have admired the "form" of a poem that portrayed him as already dead? Is it possible that Murry's premature eulogy recalled to Hardy his own memorial for Stephen, "The Schreckhorn?" It is often the fate of the curious reader to resign oneself to the fact that the most intriguing questions tend to remain unanswered: unlike the other subjects of this study, Hardy kept no proper journal in which he might record his private thoughts on Murry's poems.

The record does show, however, that Murry was aware of the singularity of sending a memorial poem to its (very much alive) subject. In a letter Murry wrote to Katherine Mansfield, he enclosed a copy of "To T. H.," and noted that "seized by characteristic passion I sent it off to T. H. hot from the oven: considering I treated him as dead it was a bit thick."[13] Murry seems to have been delighted with Hardy's reply, as he forwarded this to Mansfield as well, remarking: "I send you what he sent me. Preserve it. It's one of the most precious things I have. Send it back registered. I *love* the old man" (Murry, *LJMM* 199n). As Malcolm Woodfield notes in his introduction to a collection of Murry's essays, Hardy was not the first or the last idol that Murry was to worship. As Woodfield describes it, the "paradigm for Murry's 'story' is the conversion experience" (Woodfield 2).[14] Woodfield demonstrates that throughout Murry's career he was to vehemently defend, and eventually abandon, a number of "idols" and belief systems. In Murry's essays and journals, Woodfield argues, Murry propounds and later renounces, for example, the causes of socialism and pacificism, along with the works of several literary figures, D. H. Lawrence among them.

Such "conversions" suggest that Murry was an opportunist, eager to associate himself with current literary and ideological fads, and quick to abandon those movements when they fell out of favor. Is this what we find in his relation to Hardy? If Murry's "conversion" to "Hardyism" had been equally short-lived, it might hold little interest. But, in fact, Murry's "love" for Hardy, which began during his editorship of *The Athenaeum* (1919–20), continued throughout Murry's career. Woodfield offers one explanation for Murry's constancy to Hardy, when he remarks that "Murry looked constantly [. . .] for a return to a 'kind of seriousness' which he perceived as having 'been lost' by English culture and society" (Woodfield 2). The works of Thomas Hardy may thus have provided the "seriousness" that Murry was seeking. I would also point out another, more concrete reason for Murry's fervent admiration for Hardy: *The Athenaeum,* with its contributions from Hardy, was becoming a success.

As Woodfield notes:

[T]he journal was one of the four most important literary journals in post-war England. Two of them, the *London Mercury* and the *New Statesman* were associated with specific circles [. . .] the other two, *The Athenaeum,* and *The Egoist* associated with their editors, respectively Murry and T. S. Eliot. Murry and Eliot were by far the two most respected critical "voices" at this moment (Woodfield 14).

Murry's continued reliance on the Hardy name to enhance *The Athenaeum*'s popularity reinforces the very public nature of his indebtedness to Hardy. Contributions from Hardy and articles on Hardy's works allowed Murry to make repeated use of Hardy's prowess to increase *The Athenaeum*'s readership.

In a review of Hardy's newly collected poems, written in 1919, Murry once again paid tribute to Hardy, noting that "[h]e is the master of the fundamental theme; it enters into, echoes in, modulates and modifies all his particular emotions. [. . .] Each work of his is a fragment of a whole" (Murry, "Poetry of Mr. Hardy" 1147). This critique, I believe, raises questions about Murry's true sense of Hardy's worth. Here, that is, Murry emphasizes the importance of the collection's overall theme, rather than praising the beauty or power of any single Hardy poem. For Murry, as this essay makes clear, Hardy's poems are "fragments of a whole." Moreover, Murry's use here of the terms *echo, modulate,* and *modify* to describe Hardy's works reinforces his view of the verses themselves as somehow incomplete. Murry's language implies that Hardy's poems require an interpreter, a critic like Murry himself, who can perceive in these fragments a "fundamental" whole, and translate that vision to the reader.

As the article continues, Murry remarks: "Mr. Hardy stands high above all other modern poets by the deliberate purity of his responsiveness. The contagion of the world's slow stain has not touched him" ("Poetry of Mr. Hardy" 1149). This comment offers the reader an ambiguous vision of Hardy's work. While Murry places Hardy "high above" other poets, he also points out the oxymoronic "deliberate purity" of his poetic vision. Murry's observation begs the question: if the "contagion of the world's slow stain" had failed to taint Hardy, why must he be "deliberate" in his purity? Does Murry suggest here that Hardy's "purity" is an intrinsic part of his poetic vision, or perhaps that it is a "deliberate" stance? Furthermore, of what interest were the poems of one so removed from the "world's slow stain" to Murry's postwar readership?

While Murry defends Hardy's relevance throughout this article, the language he employs to do so simultaneously frames Hardy's poems as difficult and fragmented. I would argue that by making these equivocal judgments, Murry was not so much attempting to diminish the power of Hardy's poems, but rather was emphasizing *his own importance* as an interpreter of Hardy's vision. By locating himself as a translator, able to piece together Hardy's fragments into an understandable whole, Murry once again aligns his own work with Hardy's resurgent popularity. In this way, Murry could glean from Hardy's literary status some measure of his own. In the conclusion of this review Murry states that "no poet since poetry began has apprehended or told us more" (1149). This claim of Shakespearean eminence for Hardy again demonstrates Murry's desire to be publicly associated with, and to champion, a figure of importance: if Hardy were the greatest poet "since poetry began," Murry as his staunch proponent would stand in the reflected light of Hardy's glory.

On November 8, 1919, Hardy responded to Murry's review by sending him the following letter: "I have been struck with some of your casual remarks. One is: 'There is no necessary connection between poetic comprehension & poetic method.' You could throw a flood of light on the history & art of poetry by using that as text for a long article" (*CLTH* 5:341). Hardy's complimentary suggestion that Murry "could throw a flood of light" on the "art of poetry" seems to have gratified Murry. Indeed, not long after receiving this letter he sent Hardy a new collection of his essays on art and literature, the less than humbly titled *The Evolution of an Intellectual*. Hardy accepted this gift in silence, and there was no further correspondence between them until the following spring.

Questions of Authority:
Katherine Mansfield's Journals

While Murry was thus occupying himself with the demands of *The Athenaeum,* Hardy was not forgotten. Indeed, in a letter to Mansfield that December, Murry reiterated Hardy's importance to him. Trying to cheer his ailing and creatively frustrated wife, Murry writes:

> Don't fret [. . .] get well, keep up heart. We're going to win. By win I mean not be triumphant [. . .] but quiet & confident and humble like Hardy. One day people will turn to us as we turn to that old man. [. . .] We are fated to survive, you & I. We have something to give to England, and English literature, that no-one else can give. It shall be given. We belong to Hardy; and we shall have known more happiness than he has (*LJMM* 234).

Murry's assertion that he and Mansfield "belonged" to Hardy seems to have strengthened Mansfield's growing interest in Hardy's works during this period. As he remarked in the letter above, Murry felt that their connection to the "old man" had something to do with a common importance to "England and to English literature." Mansfield, on the other hand, did not appear to be concerned with Hardy for the same reasons. Moreover, unlike Murry, Mansfield did not compose her responses to Hardy with publication in mind: she transcribed poems and portions of poems from Hardy's volume *Satires of Circumstance* into her private journals. The first of these transcriptions appears in December of 1919. At this time, Mansfield was in the midst of several different projects. As she wrote reviews for *The Athenaeum,* and revised stories for her collection *Bliss,* Mansfield's productivity during this period belied the fact that she was slowly dying from tuberculosis. Although she continued to write, her illness was exacting a heavy toll on her marriage, as Mansfield was forced to be separated for months at a time from Murry, in order to avoid the London winters. Making matters worse, the financial implications of her invalidism meant that Murry must continue his work at *The Athenaeum* indefinitely, leaving little hope for them to share a life together.

It was during this difficult period that Mansfield copied Hardy's poem "Bereft, She Thinks She Dreams" into her diary. At this time she was once again without her husband, convalescing at the Casetta Deerholm near San Remo on the French-Italian border. This separation was meant to offer Mansfield a rest cure in the sun, but the villa itself was run-down and inadequately heated. Mansfield was thus acutely aware that despite her sacrifices, she was not, in fact, getting better. The Hardy poem that Mansfield chose to transcribe at this time seems to articulate some of the dark emotions she was then experiencing.

Mansfield cites from the beginning of Hardy's poem as follows:

> 'I dream that the dearest I ever knew
> Has died and been entombed.
> I am sure it's a dream that cannot be true'[15]

Hardy's poem continues:

> But I am so overgloomed
> By its persistence, that I would gladly
> Have quick death take me [. . .] (Hardy, *Complete Poems,* poem 314)

Mansfield, however, does not transcribe the poem's central stanzas, but notes the final verse:

> 'Yet stays this nightmare too appalling,
> And like a web shakes me

> And piteously I keeep on calling, [sic]
> And no one wakes me' (Mansfield, *JKM* 190)

Directly below the Hardy poem, Mansfield also wrote a phrase from Checkhov's story "Peasants" into her journal: "Whenever there is someone in a family who has been long ill, and hopelessly ill, there come painful moments when all, timidly, secretly, at the bottom of their hearts long for his death" (Checkhov, "Peasants" cited in *JKM* 190). A note of her own then follows this excerpt: "And even write poems" (*JKM* 190). Mansfield's transcriptions of these tragic passages from Hardy and Checkhov demonstrate that something in these works spoke to her. Perhaps more important, however, by citing only a portion of Hardy's poem, and then combining these verses with Checkhov's words as well as her own, Mansfield creates a kind of hybrid voice to articulate her thoughts. As Mansfield pieced together those fragments, the words she left out of her transcription tell as much about her state of mind as those she chose to cite.

The first stanza of Hardy's poem that Mansfield copied conveys that the "I" of the verses believes her lover's death to be only a dream. In the last stanza, also cited by Mansfield, the dreamer discovers that she is not asleep, and that the nightmare she experiences is real. Written from the point of view of the surviving lover, the central verses in which the "I" of the poem would "gladly/ Have quick death take me" and hopes each "minute and hour" for a reprieve, were not transcribed by Mansfield into her journal. Her deletion of these central verses, then, rewrites the sense of Hardy's poem: Mansfield's "version" denies the survivor the relief of a "quick death," and ignores her illusion that she will find her dead lover "as usual in the bower." Was Mansfield here alluding to her own relationship with Murry, envisioning him as the widowed lover? If so, her removal of these central verses could be read as an anxious denial of Murry's possible reaction to her death. Mansfield, that is, would not give space in her journal to the suicidal longing for death that Hardy's survivor voices. When the Hardy verses are combined with the passage from Checkhov and Mansfield's own words, however, a more bitter view of the surviving lover emerges. Perhaps Mansfield believed that Murry, as the Checkhov citation suggests, "timidly, secretly" longed for her death.

If this is so, her failure to transcribe the central stanzas of Hardy's poem could be an expression of Mansfield's anger toward Murry, the presumed survivor in their own marriage. Her copy of the poem allows the widowed lover no hope of a "quick" reprieve from "this nightmare too appalling." Mansfield's own remark at the end of this entry—"[a]nd even write poems"—further suggests that, in her view, the true victim is the lover who is dying—and not the one who is fortunate enough to survive, and to continue to write. If, as this journal entry implies, Mansfield was using the words of other writers to verbalize her own feelings, how might this act be interpreted? Why would a gifted writer like Mansfield rely on others to give voice to her emotions in her own private journal? As critic Jane Tompkins argues, the distinction historically drawn between public and private discourse is both gender-inflected and hierarchical. Mansfield's transcription of the words of two successful male authors in her diary, therefore, is intriguing on several levels. There, in her private world, Mansfield employed a public, culturally legitimized, and masculine language to articulate her deepest emotions. As I will demonstrate, Mansfield would do so throughout her short life.

As this journal entry illustrates, at this time Mansfield was suffering from a self-imposed exile. She longed to be with Murry, but would not beg him to visit, and so she remained alone. For his part, Murry seems to have been either unaware of the depth of his wife's loneliness, or else distracted by their very real need for financial stability; he remained hard at work on *The Athenaeum*. However, as Mansfield's diary indicates, she found little solace in the money that Murry's editorship was providing. In fact, in the same month that she transcribed the Hardy and Checkhov passages into her diary, Mansfield mailed Murry a malevolent poem she had composed, entitled "The New Husband." As Claire Tomalin notes in her biography of Mansfield, these verses were written when she "had a fever" and "accused [Murry] of abandoning her and predicted that his place would be taken by another husband: a husband called death" (Tomalin 194).

Mansfield's accusatory poem begins: "Someone came to me and said/ Forget, forget that you've been wed./ Who's your man to leave you be/ Ill and cold in a far country?"[16] The emotional affinity between "The New Husband" and the Hardy verses Mansfield had copied into her journal is clear: both verbalize her fear, her loneliness, and her anger at Murry. This connection between the Mansfield poem and her version of Hardy's verses provokes an interesting interpretation. Perhaps Mansfield was attempting to legitimize her feelings through transcribing portions of Hardy's poem into her diary, thus expressing herself with the words of a public figure. Having done so, moreover, Mansfield was then able to speak those emotions in her *own* voice, by writing her bitter poem, "The New Husband."

This reading of Mansfield's manipulation of Hardy's works as an attempt to legitimate her own experiences could also account for her later references to Hardy. Mansfield's private reliance on the words of such important literary figures, I would argue, illustrates her sense of being marginalized, as a woman, as an invalid, and as a foreigner. Unlike Murry, who seems to have used Hardy's work to enhance his own reputation, Mansfield's use of Hardy's voice in her diary suggests an uncomfortable relation to her *self*. Mansfield, that is, conscious of being an outsider, needed to have her feelings validated: she used Hardy's poems in her journals to do just that. The content of Hardy's poems, of course, no less than their cultural authority, must also have appealed to Mansfield. The Hardy poems that Mansfield transcribed often articulate a sense of moral outrage at the cruelty of fate and these concerns were also addressed in Mansfield's work. As Kate Fulbrook notes in her short study *Katherine Mansfield:* "Mansfield sees the failure of many human relationships as grounded in a collaboration of victim and victimizer who are caught in a cycle of self-falsification" (Fulbrook 9). Mansfield's stories, Fulbrook argues, concern the "terror at the clash between the self that exists in the world in its masked and inauthentic form, and the vulnerable, confused and unstructured self beneath the mask" (9). Perhaps then, for Mansfield, Hardy's poems recalled just such moments of unmasking: the sense of ethical terror that haunted her relationships, and came to inform her works.

Mansfield was aware that she did not have long to live, as her poem "The New Husband" illustrates, and this knowledge made her long for complete honesty in her relationships. As her illness isolated her from friends and colleagues, she seems to have engaged in "conversations" with Hardy's poems, employing them in her private papers both for validation and to work out her own ideas of honesty and mortality. One could argue that Mansfield's re-working of Hardy's poems in her journal thus constitutes evidence of a Bloomian "influence" scenario: Mansfield was attempting to "clear imaginative space" (*Anxiety* 5), or even canonical "space," for herself. Other evidence suggests, however, that Mansfield's concentration on Hardy's work was more closely connected to her marriage than to any battle for aesthetic prowess. The bed-ridden Mansfield often had at her side a book of Hardy's poems, which Murry had given her, and was aware of his idolatry of Hardy. It may be, then, that her transcriptions of Hardy were the result of her desire to share a common interest with her husband.

In December of 1919, Murry, disturbed by his wife's recent letters, joined her at the Casetta, and then returned to London in early January. On January 15, once again without her husband by her side, Mansfield copied over the fifth stanza of Hardy's six-stanza poem "The Spell of the Rose." Her journal entry for that date begins "[s]at in my room watching the day change to evening. [. . .] *Thinking of the past* always; dreaming it over. [. . .] P.O. strike. No, no letters" (*JKM* 193). I will give a portion of the Hardy poem below, noting the verses that Mansfield quotes in her journal. The poem begins:

"The Spell of the Rose"
'Yes; I will build a hall anon,
Plant roses love shall feed upon,
And apple-trees and pear' (Hardy, *Complete Poems* poem 295).

As the poem continues, the masculine "I" neglects his vow of planting roses "love shall feed upon," and so his love begins to starve. The woman of the poem then decides to grow the roses herself, rather than let their love die:

> 'This', said I,
> 'May end our divisions dire and wry,
> And long drawn days of blight.' (*Complete Poems* poem 295)

Mansfield quotes the next stanza as follows:

> 'But I was called from earth—yea, called
> Before my rose-bush grew;
> And would that now I knew
> What feels he of the tree I planted,
> And whether, after I was called
> To be a ghost, he, as of old,
> Gave me his heart anew' (*JKM* 193)

The poem ends:

> 'Ay there beside that queen of trees
> He sees me as I was, though sees
> Too late to tell me so!' (*Complete Poems* poem 295)

Once again, there is a personal pathos evoked by the verses that Mansfield chose to transcribe, one of tragic loss, of unfulfilled love, of a life cut short. Here, Mansfield disregards the earlier stanzas of Hardy's poem, which accuse the surviving lover of breaking promises, and also those that point to the dying lover's efforts to "end our divisions dire." Instead, she transcribes only the stanza in which the dead woman bemoans her ignorance of her lover's feelings.

Hardy's poem, when read in its entirety, projects a gloomy self-pity on the dead lover, but the one stanza that Mansfield copied has little such sentiment: it simply reinforces the sense of distance between the lovers. In these lines the dead lover fires no blame on the other, but instead wonders whether, even now, he could give her "his heart anew." Similarly, Mansfield did not quote the last, most damning verse in the poem, "He sees me as I was, though sees/ too late to tell me so!" This selective transcription from "The Spell of the Rose," then, illustrates another of Mansfield's very personal readings of Hardy's poems. These verses echo the movement of her own emotions; on a day when she was "thinking of the past," and received "[n]o, no letters," her bitterness toward Murry gave way to a consideration of her loneliness, and her own life after death. As Mansfield pieced together this journal entry, she articulated a painful reassessment of her feelings: at this time, it seems, Mansfield's anger at Murry's inability to support her either emotionally or financially was countered by her fear of being alone.

I would argue then that the material circumstances of Mansfield's life, its physical and emotional hardships, informed the nature of Hardy's influence on her private writing. Mansfield, that is, appropriated and rewrote Hardy's poetic visions in her journal, but not for the purpose of destroying him or his legacy, nor to create her own place in poetic history. Instead, she did so in order to clarify, legitimate, and voice her own, conflicting emotions. Hardy's verses gave Mansfield a language with which to explore her illness, her imminent death, and her relationship with Murry. During these last terrible years of her life, Mansfield's letters to Murry accuse him at times of being distant and unsympathetic, but also frequently acknowledge the demands her illness puts upon him. The portions of Hardy's poems that she cites in her journal give voice to these contradictory emotions. If some display anger, others, through Mansfield's selective transcriptions, seem to cover, and perhaps deny, the depth of that anger.

Katherine Mansfield's transcriptions of Hardy, therefore, do not seem to fit into a Bloomian influence paradigm. Although there is evidence of Mansfield having rewritten and displaced some of Hardy's words with her own in her journal, she, unlike Murry (or Hardy himself in relation to Stephen), made no attempt to publish such exercises: her negotiations of Hardy's poems were conducted in private. When I further consider Mansfield's awareness of her husband's "love" of Hardy, I find an alternative reason for her citations of Hardy's poems. Perhaps Mansfield cited and revised Hardy's verses, not to secure canonical status, but rather to explain her conflicting feelings in terms that her husband might understand: the words of Thomas Hardy.

Mansfield's need to locate a language through which to clarify her emotions and communicate them to Murry anticipates Jane Tompkins' argument of the gender-inflected and hierarchical distinction between public and private discourse. Mansfield may have recognized that in order for her feelings to be understood by her husband, they must be spoken in *his* terms, through the words of the (male) poet he most admired. But why would Mansfield need to "translate" her thoughts through this masculine, public language? As Annette Kolodny asserts: "for survival's sake, oppressed or subdominant groups always study the nuances of meaning and gesture in those who control them" (Kolodny 62*n*). While Kolodny's "master" and "slave" relation may not be analogous to the structure of Mansfield's marriage, her argument nevertheless offers an insight into Mansfield's transcriptions of Hardy's work. Mansfield, for "survival's sake," was willing to speak with Hardy's words, as these were a language that Murry could understand. Further examples of Mansfield's transcriptions of Hardy's poems also promote this reading. In some of these entries, Mansfield appears to cite Hardy's poems as illustrations not only of her anger and fear, as in the two examples above, but also of her anxiety over being forgotten after her death.

An example of this anxiety can be found in a journal entry of 1920. On January 21 of that year, Mansfield left the Casetta for L'Hermitage, a nursing home in Menton. As her diary indicates, she was extremely disappointed with her doctors there, and with her own inability to "work."[17] During her first week there, she transcribed the second half of Hardy's poem "The Year's Awakening" into her journal. The transcription begins as follows:

> 'How do you know, deep underground,
> Hid in your bed from sight and sound,
> [. . .]
> That light has won a fraction's strength,
> And day put on some moment's length
> [. . .]
> O crocus root, how do you know,
> How do you know?' (*JKM* 196–7)

Hardy's poem depicts a sense of winter desolation through the relation of the speaker to the crocus root he looks upon. Here, Hardy does not dwell on the flower's promise of spring, but on his own difficulty with perceiving an end to winter.

Mansfield's reaction to these verses is suggested by her own poem, "Winter Bird," written just beneath "The Year's Awakening" in the same journal entry:

> My darling, my darling,
> Calling through the cold of afternoon
> Those round, bright notes,
> Each one so perfect,
> Shaken from the other and yet
> Hanging together in flashing clusters!
> [. . .] (*JKM* 197)

The first stanza of Hardy's poem (not transcribed here by Mansfield) also refers to a bird in winter:

> And never as yet a tint
> of spring
> Has shown in the Earth's appareling;
> O vespering bird, how do you know,
> How do you know? (*Complete Poems* poem 275)

As Mansfield joins her verses and Hardy's together in this journal entry, her "Winter Bird," in a sense, displaces Hardy's. There is, moreover, an interesting difference between the two "species."

Hardy's bird is granted an almost mystical knowledge through its connection to natural cycles; he endows this "vespering creature" with an instinctual faith in the coming of spring. Mansfield's bird, on the other hand, lives in opposition to the pattern provided by nature, thriving and singing "round bright notes" even in the "cold of afternoon." Here, as in the previous examples, Mansfield's version of Hardy's poem gives rise to an intriguing reading. As the title implies, "The Year's Awakening" points to a hopeful conversion from winter desolation to springtime joy brought about by a meditation on the mysterious workings of nature. Mansfield's "Winter Bird," by contrast, depicts a creature able to find joy *outside* of, or *despite* the gloom that nature provides. If, as one might argue, Hardy's age had inspired in him a vision of a world that continues despite the sorrows or joys of the individual, Mansfield's own struggle with illness may have equally informed her poem. Hardy's bird sings in anticipation of spring, but Mansfield's lives for today, defying the decrees of nature by extracting happiness in spite of the winter's cold. Mansfield's revision of Hardy's poem, then, suggests that each individual must follow his or her own path, and struggle against the current. The title of her poem is a clue to this vision, for while Hardy's bird was only one participant in "The Year's Awakening," Mansfield's poem concentrates on the singular "Winter Bird."

If, at times, Mansfield used Hardy's poems as a means of working out and communicating her feelings toward Murry, in this example she appears to do something very different. Here, Mansfield employed Hardy's words as a starting point for a different kind of discourse: for speaking to *herself*. Harold Bloom argues in *The Western Canon* that the reading of canonical works "enables us to learn to talk to ourselves," and provides us with a "proper use" of our "solitude whose final form is one's confrontation with one's own mortality" (*Canon* 30). Is this, then, what Mansfield's transcriptions of Hardy's poems enact? Did his verses teach her to talk to herself, and to contemplate her "mortality"? Or is it possible that Mansfield's creative deletions and substitutions of Hardy's poems are in fact evidence of the *distance* between her vision and Hardy's own? Critic Julia Kristeva argues in her essay "Women's Time" that "sexual difference" "is translated by and translates" a difference in one's "relationship to power, language and meaning" (200). Did the gender difference between Hardy and Mansfield thus inscribe a difference in their relationships to power, language, and meaning? If so, Hardy's verses were not perhaps tools that enabled Mansfield to talk to herself, but were instead a foreign and patriarchal discourse that required translation. As Mansfield cut and pasted Hardy's words into her journal, that is, she knitted a composite language to communicate her meaning: revising these poems, Mansfield bridged the gap between Hardy's words and her own.

Thus, Mansfield's diary entries provide a poignant example of one writer's difficult relation to poetic history, power, language, and meaning. While the ever-confident Murry publicly aligned himself with Hardy and the popular solider-poets of his time, the far more talented Mansfield was secretly piecing together a hesitant, cautious language, using the words of the past to validate her own perceptions. Moreover, as Mansfield may have perceived a gendered and hierarchical distance between Hardy's verses and her own private voice, this "distance" may itself have informed her transcriptions of his poems: by employing a "foreign language" in her journals, Mansfield was able to maintain some degree of remove from the difficult emotions she explored in her journals.

One possible example of this distancing tactic can be found in Mansfield's diary on the second anniversary of her mother's death. Here, Mansfield cites the whole of Hardy's poem "Lament" (*Complete Poems* poem 283). She notes at the beginning of the entry: "A. B. B. [Anne Burrell Beauchamp] died August 8 1918" and then quotes "Lament" as follows:

> 'How she would have loved
> A party to-day!—
> [. . .] But
> She is shut, she is shut
> From friendship's spell
> In the jailing shell,
> Of her tiny cell.' (*JKM* 206)

By transcribing Hardy's poem on the anniversary of her mother's death, Mansfield again exhibits her constrained relation to her own emotions. In this journal entry, she allows Hardy's words to give voice to her loss, thus privileging his verses as messengers of her private feelings. In doing so, moreover, Mansfield removes herself from the tragedy these lines depict. Here, as elsewhere, Mansfield's sorrows are legitimized, translated, and distanced through Hardy's masculine, public, and foreign voice.

Courting Fame:
J. M. Murry's Public Negotiations of Thomas Hardy

While Mansfield was conducting this private negotiation of Hardy's work, Murry continued to pursue a public relationship with him. After a brief period of silence between them in early 1920, Murry once again requested a contribution from Hardy for *The Athenaeum* in April. Hardy's response was as follows: "I have found some verses which at first I thought would only suit publication in a *daily* paper dated April 30th. But I find that by accident there will be an Athenaeum on April 30th. next, [sic] and therefore I shall have pleasure in sending you the verses" (*CLTH* 6: 12).[18] Murry's obvious delight in Hardy's contribution can be seen in his letter to Mansfield dated April 8, 1920: "I had a letter from Hardy to-day asking if I would like a poem for the *Athenaeum* of April 30. Wouldn't I ! [. . .] It's very mysterious, because he says it's quite essential that it should appear on *April 30* & no other day [. . .] I'm very excited" (*LJMM* 310). Murry's "excited" state seems to have led him to "rewrite" the content of Hardy's note in his letter to Mansfield. Hardy had said that he had "found by accident" that *The Athenaeum* would be published on April 30, but Murry recounts to Mansfield that "[h]e was going to send it to the *Times* when he suddenly realised that the *Athenaeum* comes out on the 30th." The subtle difference in the two letters is one of many examples of Murry's misreading of his relationship to Hardy. Although Hardy offered Murry the poem in order to ensure its appearance on April 30, Murry appears to have understood Hardy's contribution as a compliment to himself. Murry's misinterpretation of Hardy's words, moreover, seems to have exacerbated his already-inflated sense of his own importance. As Murry's letters to Mansfield demonstrate, Hardy's unsolicited contributions to *The Athenaeum* were, for Murry, evidence of his success as an editor.[19]

Murry's growing sense of self-importance at this time can be surmised from a conflict he had with Mansfield in December of 1920. A flirtation had arisen between Murry and Princess Elizabeth Bibesco as Mansfield was convalescing at the Isola Bella in Menton.[20] Mansfield, alone and ill, was disgusted by Murry's confession of the affair. The situation worsened when, in a series of letters, Murry told Katherine of his feelings for Bibesco, and begged her forgiveness. Soon after, the publication of an edition of Murry's collected essays, *Aspects of Literature,* drew biting criticism from his wife. Mansfield regarded Murry's preface as pompous, and she scolded him in the following letter: "How could a person say such a thing. It's so naive as to be silly, or so arrogant as to be *fantastique.* Suppose I wrote: 'I have dated my stories as I venture to hope my readers may enjoy tracing my development—the ripening of my power . . . ' What *would* you think! You'd faint! It is indecent, no less, to say such things. And one doesn't think them!"[21] In addition to this critique Mansfield went on to attack Murry's essay on Hardy in the collection. "Your Hardy doesn't quite come off to my thinking" she wrote. "You seem to be hinting at a special understanding between yourself and the author. That's not fair: it puts me off" (*LKM* 618). Mansfield's derision of Murry's "arrogance" here confirms her sense of his self-important attitude, but it also offers an insight into Mansfield's view of their respective relationships to Hardy.

If Mansfield's critique of Murry's essays is informed by her anger over Murry's affair, she seems equally annoyed by his "hints" at intimacy with Hardy. She tells Murry, for instance, that in his "tremendously just desire to prove [Hardy] a major poet, you mustn't make yourself Counsel for the Prisoner!" (*LKM* 618). "That's not fair," Mansfield exclaims, and in the context of her argument these words articulate the difference between Murry's relation to Hardy's work and her own. As this letter suggests, in Mansfield's view Murry's essay "arrogantly" publicizes his "special understanding" of Hardy, and plots it as a point in the "ripening" of Murry's own powers. While Mansfield had employed Hardy's words in private, she seems to have found Murry's public parading of his "special" status with Hardy distasteful and shocking. Mansfield's harsh critique of her husband's work in this letter had a profound effect on him. In a move that Murry later believed had pushed him to the sidelines of literature for the rest of his life, he left *The Athenaeum,* and joined his ailing wife in Menton.[22] Thomas Hardy had recently contributed a New Year poem to *The Athenaeum,* and this appeared in Murry's final edition of the magazine. Hardy's poems thus "framed" Murry's editorship of *The Athenaeum,* by appearing on the front pages of Murry's first and last issues of the paper.

Murry's relationship with Hardy, however, was far from over. Having spent most of the winter with his wife, Murry returned to London in the spring of 1921, and was able to fulfill a great ambition: the Hardys invited him to their home at Maxgate in Dorchester. Just as Mansfield might have predicted, Murry later turned his visit into a publishing opportunity. Murry recorded his memories of the trip immediately afterward, but he waited until 1934—six years after Hardy's death—to print them. What follows is an excerpt from that published account: "I first met Thomas Hardy at Dorchester in May, 1921. I had long desired to see him; but when the volume of his collected Poems appeared in the winter of 1919 the desire became almost a monomania. Certainly I had never longed to see a living person so much" ("Hardy," *Defending Romanticism* 297). In the opening of this essay, as elsewhere, Murry is profuse in his adulation of Hardy. Nevertheless, the "monomania" for meeting Hardy that Murry relates here is in fact undermined by the account that follows it. Throughout the article, despite Mansfield's earlier cautions, Murry exploits and exaggerates the "special understanding" between himself and Hardy.

Murry's retelling of the origins of their acquaintance, for example, differs significantly from the events detailed in their biographical records. Indeed, in Murry's version, it seems as if Hardy were a devotee of Murry's, rather than the reverse. Murry writes, "Hardy had sent me some very kindly letters, and in particular one concerning a review of the 'Collected Poems' which I had written for *The Athenaeum.* In that letter he was generous enough to say that the history of English poetry ought to be re-written in accordance with the principles I had tried to establish in regard to his own" ("Hardy" 297). When mentioning Hardy's letters, Murry neglects to inform the reader of his own repeated approaches toward Hardy, his virtual bombardment of Hardy with notes, poems, and requests for magazine contributions. In my view, Murry's interpretation of Hardy's response to his review is little short of ego-maniacal: surely Hardy's suggestion that Murry might write a long article to shed light on his "casual remarks," was not an assertion that Murry rewrite the history of English poetry in accordance with those principles.

As the essay continues, Murry attempts to justify his Hardy "monomania" to the reader, qualifying his feelings in terms of the historical moment in which they met. He writes "[i]t was at the end of the year of complete despair and disillusion which followed the Armistice of 1918" (297). England was gone, Murry felt; "the England of Hardy alone was left to us; not the country or the characters of his novels, but the great and achieved simplicity, the all but terrifying candour, of the mind which had conceived them" (298). Here again, then, Murry's commentary privileges not Hardy's achievements, but rather Murry's own interpretation of them as the "England of Thomas Hardy." Murry next takes to task the insights of earlier admirers of Hardy's work, arguing that it is not "the country or characters of his novels" that are important, but rather the poet's "achieved simplicity." Because this phrase echoes the "deliberate purity" that Murry had earlier cited as Hardy's greatest legacy, it emphasizes Murry's ambiguous perception of Hardy's importance. Once again in this critique, that is, Murry raises more questions about Hardy's poetry than he answers. What, for instance, is the nature of a purity that is "deliberate," a simplicity "achieved," and does not such determined innocence belie the idea of Hardy's "candour"?

Adding further ambiguity to his reading of Hardy's legacy, in this essay Murry repeatedly promotes his own importance, as he explains his "right" to pay a visit to Hardy: "I had been told that he believed that editors were important people, and that newspapers existed primarily in order to communicate what they believed to be the truth; I had also been told that it would be the easiest thing in the world for me, who was then an editor, to see him, if I would only ask" (298). Bearing in mind Hardy's publishing history, it is difficult to imagine that such a statement could be written about him. Hardy's career as a novelist was continually threatened and finally ruined by his battles with the censorship of magazine editors. Is it possible then that Hardy believed "editors were important people" and that "newspapers existed" to communicate the truth? Would not Hardy have been more likely to consider editors as destructive, and newspapers as pandering to a hypocritical reading public? Again, while Murry states that he did not want to invite himself to Maxgate, this hesitance contradicts his earlier assertion that he was "monomaniacally" hoping for an invitation. "Still, I knew I should see him" Murry writes, "it was impossible that it should be otherwise" (298). Such confused perceptions of Hardy, and of Murry's relation to him, continue throughout the essay.

Interestingly, the circumstances surrounding Murry's visit to Maxgate seem to reproduce the events of Hardy's own first meeting with Leslie Stephen years earlier; Murry, like Hardy, repeatedly deferred his visit, and arrived late on the day of their eventual meeting. As Murry notes, he had to "send a telegram canceling one day and fixing another, then another telegram to cancel that" (298). Surely this is an unexpected response to an invitation from the object of Murry's "monomania." Why would Murry have postponed his meeting with Hardy, and furthermore, why would he have mentioned this fact in his published recollection of their first visit? Perhaps Murry's inclusion of these cancellations in this essay is another example of his (public) negotiation of Hardy. Murry, that is, informs his readers of his own importance here, by publicizing his nonchalance at changing plans on the great Thomas Hardy. Hardy, in any case, was willing to reschedule the visit from his admirer, and Murry was welcomed at Maxgate in May of 1921. Murry's first reaction to Hardy is recounted in this essay as follows: "It is true. I scarcely noticed Hardy [. . .] [he] seemed very small. As he sat there sideways turned away from the light of the window, he seemed not so much old as shrunken" ("Hardy" 299). As here Murry portrays his supposed *idol* as "small" and "shrunken," I wonder at his reasons for offering the reader these particular observations.

In recording such sad details as Hardy's "old brown suit, so well worn, [that] must have fitted him well once; it hung loosely on him now" (299), was Murry merely depicting the pathos of Hardy the fragile genius? Or is there another project at work here? As the essay continues, Murry notes that eventually their conversation turned to literature: "[Hardy] said how he had enjoyed Katherine Mansfield's story, 'The Daughters of the late Colonel,' how he had laughed when his wife had read it to him. [. . .] What a lot of verse was being written now! He felt he must be getting out of touch; there was very little of it that he could appreciate" (304). In this passage, Murry informs the reader of Hardy's feeling "out of touch," though this idea is belied by Hardy's familiarity with Mansfield's story, which had only just been published.[23] Moreover, in recounting this exchange, Murry once again suggests his "special status" with Hardy. Though Hardy remarked on his lack of appreciation for most works being written "now," he *did* show interest in the writing of Murry's wife.

Murry's recollection thus combines two differing visions of Hardy. Murry portrays Hardy as shrunken and feeble, but also relishes his attentions, and endows his words with great meaning. His tone toward Hardy shifts throughout from disappointment to reverence, and at the end of the essay, to irritation. He notes:

> I heard continually the faint *plack-plack* of Hardy's teeth as he chewed. It drowned every other sound to my ear; it reasserted itself at every moment. [. . .] *Plack, plack, plack, plack.* Yes he was very old. [. . .] I was glad when dinner was over. For a moment I was alone with Mrs. Hardy in the drawing-room. "I hope I'm not tiring him." And I felt a sudden sense of acute shame that I should be talking of Hardy behind his back, as though he were a child (305).

Murry's ambivalence toward his subject is demonstrated clearly in this passage. For although Murry admits to his "acute shame" at talking behind Hardy's back, and viewing him as a "child," this "shame" did not prevent him from publishing these observations. Indeed, this emasculated, childlike portrait of Hardy is emphasized throughout Murry's essay. Later on, for instance, Murry depicts Hardy as being "mothered" by his wife, and as wanting in business skills. As he tells it, Hardy asked for Murry's advice on a simple business matter: "There's one thing I would like your advice upon. A man who works for the Clarendon Press was here the other day; and he urged me to have a thin India-paper edition of my poems printed [. . .]What do you think?" (cited in "Hardy" 306). Once again, I pause to question the candor of Murry's observations. Was Hardy, with his team of helpers and admirers flocking to Maxgate, really in need of Murry's publishing advice?

In Murry's version of the visit, he gave Hardy the help he needed, and prepared to take his leave. According to Murry, Hardy then requested that he return soon: "He said I must come back with a bicycle and ride over the Dorset country; it was worth the knowing. A bicycle made traveling delightful. Now for him it was only a weariness of the flesh—the packing, the getting to the station, the hotels. But in the old days [. . .]" (cited in "Hardy" 308). Thus the final image of Hardy that Murry provides in this essay contrasts Murry's youth and strength with Hardy's age and impotence. Like Hardy's own reminiscences of Stephen in Maitland's biography, Murry's recollection of his visit to Maxgate creates a belittled image of Hardy, as an idol now fallen. There are, in fact, several similarities between Hardy's contribution to Maitland and Murry's article above.

As I suggested in the previous chapter, Hardy endowed his portrait of Stephen with some of his own flaws. In particular, his accusations of Stephen's editorial cowardice seem to be an attempt to cover Hardy's own complicity in the censorship of his tales. His reinvented image of Stephen, therefore, was in some respects a portrait of Hardy's own dark side, as he endowed Stephen with those failings that he sought to deny in himself. I would argue that in this essay Murry renders a similar projected persona in his recollection of Hardy. Hardy's weakness and childishness as portrayed by Murry are astonishingly similar to Murry's *own* character flaws. Likewise, Murry's insinuations about Hardy's lack of business knowledge could well be read as a projection of Murry's own inability to control his finances.

Despite these similarities between Hardy's rendering of Stephen and Murry's recollections of his visit to Hardy, there are also several differences between each man's negotiation of their literary "precursor." If Hardy had attempted to diminish Stephen's importance by recounting his failings in Maitland, this "overpowering" of Stephen's legacy was nevertheless conducted secretly, in a coded language requiring a good deal of curiosity to decipher. Even Leslie Stephen's daughter Virginia, as her letter to Hardy suggested, saw no threat in Hardy's portrait of her father. Murry's essay, by contrast, provides a clearly drawn image of Hardy as a fallen legend, a shrunken idol. In this recollection, Murry publicly announces the failure of Hardy to live up to Murry's "monomaniacal" fantasies of his "greatness."

Sexual Difference and the Public/Private Debate

Thus I can draw a distinction between Murry's public negotiation of Hardy, and Hardy's more covert mediation of Leslie Stephen's influence. But what framework can explain Katherine Mansfield's very different approach to Hardy? A Kristevan reading might suggest that Mansfield's sense of "sexual difference" "translates" her relation to "power, language and meaning." If so, how does such a translation surface in Mansfield's responses to Hardy's verse? One answer would be that while Murry saw Hardy iconically, as an important public figure with whom to be aligned, Mansfield concentrated her attentions on Hardy's *texts:* it was Hardy's language that was of value to her. Therefore, while Murry misread and reinvented Hardy's legend, his public image, Mansfield was at work on her own private revisions of Hardy's words. This different approach to Hardy's work can be seen in Mansfield's last quotation of one of his poems, which appears in her unposted letter to Murry of July 25, 1921. Here, Mansfield writes that she is desperately worried about money owed to her doctor, and later, quotes from a bitter poem of Hardy's entitled "Ah, Are You Digging on My Grave?" (*Complete Poems* 269)

The poem recounts the thoughts of the deceased "I," who hears someone digging on her grave. She imagines that it may be a member of her family, a friend, her lover, or even an enemy, but discovers instead that it is only her dog that digs for a bone buried there. Mansfield cites the last stanza of the poem as follows:

> 'Mistress, I dug upon your grave
> To bury a bone, in case

> I should be hungry near this spot
> When passing on my daily trot.
> I am sorry, but I quite forgot
> It was your resting place.' (*JKM* 258)

Below this, Mansfield wryly notes that her cat, Wing, "would do this." As this example once again illustrates, Hardy's poetry provided Mansfield with images that she could fashion into a kind of mosaic of her own fear, anger, and loneliness. By fusing Hardy's verses with her own words, Mansfield was able to give voice to the complex set of emotions that had been brought about by her long-term illness. Her difficult feelings were thus articulated and legitimized by an equally difficult discourse: Mansfield, the outsider, attempted to translate Hardy's foreign, masculine vision, into a language of her own.

In the final months of her life, Mansfield invoked Hardy's name once more in a letter to Murry. In a moment of anger, Mansfield had told Murry not to come to her for Christmas, but now regretted her words and hoped that he would visit nevertheless. Writing to him from the Gurdjieff Institute in Fontainebleau, she said: "I *love* Christmas; I shall always feel it is a holy time. I wonder if dear old Hardy will write a poem this year" (*LKM* 696). Here, Mansfield seems to recall the New Year poem that Hardy had contributed to *The Athenaeum* in December of 1920, and her reminiscence evokes a poignant reading. As this letter indicates, for Mansfield the very word "Hardy" brought back memories of *The Athenaeum,* and the literary world from which she was now permanently removed. Moreover, thoughts of Hardy seem also to have led Mansfield to recall the "holy time" of her shared life with Murry, the past Christmases they had spent together, and their mutual excitement over Hardy's contributions to *The Athenaeum.* Here, as elsewhere, Mansfield's sense of Hardy was emotive, nostalgic, and personal. Perhaps Murry did not share that nostalgia: He did not come to his wife for Christmas, but arrived at her bedside in Fontainebleau on the afternoon of January 9, 1923. Katherine Mansfield died that evening, at the age of thirty-four.

If Mansfield's relationship to the works of Thomas Hardy was indeed one of literary influence, it was an influence that oscillated between her private desires and her need to communicate them through a legitimized, public discourse. Mansfield's negotiation of Hardy's work, therefore, was an uncomfortable compromise. While she admired his poems, her transcriptions of them also demonstrate the constraints she found in his language, and the distance she saw between her vision and his. This distance itself, moreover, reproduces Mansfield's relation to Murry: a failure to communicate, an impenetrable language barrier, and the personification of the gap between male/female, public/private. As Kristeva's argument explicates, a gendered difference was inscribed in the respective relations of all three figures to power, language, and meaning. The evidence for this is found in Mansfield's private, and Murry and Hardy's published, texts.

Murry's own association with Hardy continued after his wife's death. If he had once exaggerated his "special status" with Hardy, after Mansfield's death Hardy himself sought out Murry's company. Soon, a real bond began to grow between them as the once-widowed Hardy offered sympathy for Murry's loss.[24] In January 1923, for example, a few weeks after hearing of Mansfield's death, Hardy sent Murry a letter of condolence: "I thought that I should like to tell you of my deep sympathy, & my wife's, with you in your loss. I have passed through the same experience as that you are now undergoing, & I know how very useless letters are at such times. But we go on writing them just the same. [. . .] Believe me, Always yours" (*CLTH* 6:184). Murry replied to Hardy's kind note, and soon afterward the two began to spend a good deal of time together. Their friendship was further cemented when Murry defended Hardy in the *Adelphi* magazine, after George Moore had attacked Hardy's work in *Conversations on Ebury Street*.[25] In fact, when Murry's second wife, Violet Le Maistre, gave birth to their first child, Murry asked the Hardys to be the little girl's godparents. They accepted.[26]

Shortly afterward, Virginia Woolf sarcastically recounted Murry's relationship with Hardy, through a bit of gossip she heard from E. M. Forster. In a letter to Vita Sackville-West, Woolf noted:

> Then [Mrs. Hardy] says "Who do you think should write my husbands [sic] life?" In order to feel the ground, Morgan says, "Well, Middleton Murry's a great admirer"—Whereupon Mrs. Hardy flames out (to all our joy) "No, no, Mr Forster, We should not like that at all"—in spite of the devotion of that worm, who took his wife to be delivered of a son, to be called Thomas, in Dorchester, but she was delivered, of a daughter, 50 miles away (Woolf, *LVW* 3:238).

While Woolf's dismissal of Murry as a "worm," and Florence Hardy's veto of him as Hardy's biographer, suggest that the Hardys disliked Murry, other evidence belies this. Hardy, by all accounts, enjoyed and encouraged the visits of Murry, his wife, and his child. Indeed, F. B. Pinion notes that Hardy, who had not long to live himself, was quite moved when learning in October of 1927 that Murry was desperately short of money.

According to Pinion, Hardy intervened to facilitate a grant for Murry: "Hardy asked Gosse [Sir Edmund] to inquire whether assistance could be provided from the Royal Literary Fund. This would have taken so long that Gosse appealed to Stanley Baldwin, the Prime Minister, emphasizing Hardy's support, with the result that a grant of £250 was made to Murry shortly afterwards"

(Pinion 386). It seems then that Murry's "Hardy monomania" had evolved over time (and through Mansfield's death) into a friendship, to which his many visits with Hardy in the mid-1920s attest. Despite this closeness, however, Hardy was reluctant to allow Murry, or indeed anyone, to write his biography. As I mentioned in the previous chapter, Hardy eventually wrote his life story himself, and requested that it be published posthumously, under his wife's name. Thus, Hardy's appreciation of the influential power of the printed word was demonstrated once again: Perhaps aware of the effect his own portrait of Leslie Stephen had on later assessments of Stephen, Hardy refused to allow Murry a similar power over *his* legacy. On December 11, 1927, Murry went to Maxgate once more, but on doctor's advice was not allowed to speak with Hardy. He never saw him again. On January 11, 1928, Thomas Hardy died.

(Auto)biography, Hagiography, and the Canon

With the deaths of both Mansfield and Hardy recounted here, this chapter now draws to an end. Before I conclude, however, I would like to pause for one further consideration. If, as I have argued throughout this chapter, Murry and Mansfield's relations to Hardy and his work were informed by differences in the public and private nature of their negotiations, what do such differences suggest about their respective places in literary history? With hindsight, was Hardy justified in protecting the future of his own public image so cautiously? Furthermore, did Mansfield's private relationship to Hardy's verses, and Murry's public association with the man and his work, have an impact upon how these writers are viewed today? As Jane Tompkins argues, private writing, such as is found in Mansfield's journals, is historically constructed as "feminine," and is therefore marginalized in a patriarchal culture. By contrast, public discourse, which could include Murry's reminiscences of Hardy and his critiques of Hardy's poems, is culturally located as the language of authority and power. Why then is Mansfield read and remembered today, while, for the most part, Murry is not?

As a result of my reading of the works of Stephen, Hardy, Mansfield, and Murry, I will hazard a possible answer. Writers, I posit, can achieve a place in literary history in at least one important way: like Mansfield and Hardy, they must gain popularity with respected critical contemporaries, and in some way retain that success posthumously. I maintained in the previous chapter that Hardy's canonical status was secured not only by his poetic power, but also through his diligent censorship of biographical images of him. By assuring that he had ghost-written his own biography, and refusing to authorize others written during his lifetime, Hardy took control of his biographical legacy.

In contrast, Katherine Mansfield's private journals and letters were left to her husband to publish after her death. Critic Gillian Boddy notes in her essay "Leaving 'All Fair'," that Mansfield had written the following note to Murry in 1922, requesting that he receive it only upon her death: "All my manuscripts I leave entirely to you to do what you like with. Go through them one day, dear love, and destroy all you do not use. Please destroy all letters you do not use. Please destroy all letters you do not wish to keep & all papers [. . .] leave all fair—will you?"[27] As Boddy points out, Mansfield's repeated use here of the words "destroy all you do not use" is confusing. Had she meant Murry to "use," that is to publish, some of her papers, and destroy the rest? Sometime later in 1922, Mansfield wrote a will, and included in it more specific instructions for Murry: "I should like him to publish as little as possible and to tear up and burn as much as possible."[28]

Murry obviously ignored this later plea, as he compiled from her various diaries and notebooks the *Journal of Katherine Mansfield,* which first appeared in 1927. Perhaps more important for this study, by publishing these excerpts Murry had made Mansfield's private words *public.* Murry's selective "opening" of Mansfield's secret world had a specific, traceable effect: as Boddy acknowledges, Murry's selections and omissions in editing the journal served to create the "Mansfield myth" (Boddy 12). Murry, that is, scrupulously removed evidence of Katherine's petty jealousies, her promiscuity, and her mood swings from her private papers before publishing them. Thus, the "Katherine Mansfield" of the journal of 1927 is a much saintlier and more secure figure than is found in the later "unMurryfied" edition of her journals.[29] Murry offered the world a censored view of the private Mansfield. Moreover, in this influential publication Mansfield's thoughts were once again voiced, as it were, in translation, through the editorial choices of her husband.

The Mansfield myth, informed by Murry's constraints, continued as he published further editions of her previously unseen works. In 1939 *The Scrapbook of Katherine Mansfield* was released, and the "Definitive Edition" of the *Journal,* also edited by Murry, came out in 1954. As Boddy remarks on this last: "although the 1954 edition described itself as 'Definitive' it was still highly selective" (Boddy, 16). Murry's carefully arranged and partially "sanitized" version of Mansfield's journals had cemented the reading public's interest in, and awareness of, a publicly acceptable Katherine Mansfield. Boddy posits that Mansfield herself would have found ironic "a cult which idolized her as a courageous, tragic figure, while ignoring many other aspects of her character" (Boddy 12). Nevertheless, such mythologizing has undoubtedly aided her posthumous popularity among readers.

As I illustrated in the previous chapter, Leslie Stephen did not exert control over the images of him that would be circulated after his death.[30] Instead

Hardy, and later Virginia Woolf, offered a wide range of readers their own "reinvented" portraits of Stephen. John Middleton Murry's reputation may also have suffered from a lack of say over his posthumous image: like Stephen before him, Murry received little attention after his death. Sharon Greer Cassavant notes that when Murry died in 1957, "the old rancors had abated" and "the last reviewers added judicious praise to largely patronizing accounts of Murry's feuds and ideological oscillations" (Cassavant 4). Still, those "oscillations" had won Murry more enemies than supporters. His publication of Mansfield's journals, for instance, was viewed by many of her friends as a profiteering exploitation, and, as Cassavant demonstrates, Murry's unpopular pacifist stance during World War II had estranged him from many in his old literary circle.[31] Hardy, as I have shown, carefully preempted attempts to sully his posthumous image, and Mansfield's own likeness after death was polished, refined, and "translated" by her husband. Murry's legacy, however, had no champion, and his frequent ideological "oscillations" allowed no definitive portrait of him to emerge. Murry's serial idolatry of other writers, Lawrence, Hardy, and Mansfield among them, seems, ironically, to have denied him the place in literary tradition that each of them have secured.

These examples of Hardy, Stephen, Murry, and Mansfield thus illustrate some of the dynamics at work in influential relationships among writers. If what I have described is not quite the battle to the death that Bloom's theory of influence articulates, I *have* found that subterfuge and anxiety, powerful desires and overwhelming ambitions informed these literary connections. Moreover, while examining these relationships, each writer's *public image* emerges as a location of struggle for themselves, and for those who followed them. As Bloom might predict, these negotiations of private desire and public reputation follow a patriarchal paradigm of battle, with winners and losers, victor and vanquished.

Is this, I wonder, what one would find when examining indebtedness between two women writers? How might literary influence operate if these two women were contemporaries, friends, and came from different cultural backgrounds? In *The Anxiety of Influence* Bloom demeans the idea of a cooperative relationship between writers as indicative of their being "minor or weaker" (*Anxiety* 30), and in *The Western Canon* he attempts to marginalize such shared generosity even further, by calling it peculiarly "feminine." In the future, he bemoans, true aesthetic strength will be lost to "the proper humility of shared sisterhood" (*Canon* 31). In order to explore these themes of cultural difference and shared-sisterhood among writers, in the next chapter I will examine the relationship and the texts of the two women in this study: Virginia Woolf and Katherine Mansfield.

Chapter Four ❦

Mother/Muse, Psychic Sister?

The Personal and Intertextual Connections between Virginia Woolf and Katherine Mansfield

In their 1979 text *The Madwoman in the Attic,* Sandra Gilbert and Susan Gubar describe what they see as the specific difficulty of Harold Bloom's theory of influence for the woman writer: "[h]er battle, however, is not against her (male) precursor's reading of the world but against his reading of *her,*" they claim (49). For these two critics, then, Bloom's theory accurately "analyses and explains" (49) the patriarchal nature of Western literary history, and in doing so simultaneously offers a reason for women's exclusion from that tradition: the woman writer is too preoccupied with deciphering misreadings of herself to engage in battle with her precursor(s). In order to remedy this difficulty, they suggest an alternate path for the woman writer, a "swerve" from Bloom's influence paradigm: "she can begin such a struggle only by actively seeking a *female* precursor who, far from representing a threatening force to be denied or killed, proves by example that a revolt against patriarchal literary authority is possible" (49). Is this what "successful" women writers have done?

One of the subjects of this chapter, Virginia Woolf, was certainly greatly interested in the idea of a female literary tradition. In *A Room of One's Own,* for example, Woolf describes the effect of a "change which came about towards the end of the eighteenth century," when "[t]he middle class woman began to write" (*Room* 98). As Woolf argues: "[w]ithout those forerunners, Jane Austen and the Brontes and George Eliot could no more have written than Shakespeare could have written without Marlowe" (98). Woolf's reasoning here anticipates Gilbert and Gubar's formulation of female literary precursors who provide "nurturing," rather than inducing "anxiety." "For," Woolf continues, "masterpieces are not single and solitary births; they are the outcome of many years of thinking in common [. . .] so that the experience of the mass is behind the single voice" (98).

Woolf's vision in *A Room of One's Own* of a collective voice, of literary influence among women writers as a strengthening force, has been explored in the works of some later feminist critics. In Jane Marcus' essay "Thinking Back Through Our Mothers," for instance, Marcus emphasizes Woolf's own reliance on the work of other women: "Woolf knew by experience how women influence each other. Far from Harold Bloom's concept of the 'anxiety of influence,' it is rather the opposite, affording the woman writer relief from anxiety, acting as a hideout in history where she can lick her wounds between attacks on the patriarchy" ("Thinking Back" 8). Like Jane Marcus, critic Ellen Hawkes similarly endorses the idea that Woolf saw the collective influence of women writers upon each other as a kind of "safe haven." In her essay "Woolf's Magical Garden of Women," Hawkes corroborates Marcus' assertion that Woolf's view of literary influence would not fit within Bloom's paradigm. Hawkes notes that Woolf's "is not the story of the 'anxiety of influence', but of its reassurance" (Hawkes 32). In Hawkes' view, Woolf's utopian image of a "magical garden of women" was that of "a safe surrounding in which women preserve and sanction their shared values derived from their special experiences as 'outsiders'" (32).

Like Gilbert and Gubar, then, both Marcus and Hawkes read Woolf's sense of literary influence among women writers as not only "nurturing," but also as a specific defense against the "wounds" inflicted by a patriarchal order. However, despite their indignation against the overwhelmingly male Western canon of literature, each of these feminist critics privileges a patriarchal paradigm of influence as, in some way, definitive. As these critics accept this traditional formulation as a norm, for them the woman writer becomes a deviation: wounded, revolutionary, an "outsider" in literary history. Gilbert and Gubar suggest that "actively seeking a *female* precursor" may provide the woman writer with a role model. Nevertheless, they argue that such a precursor must represent a reaction against patriarchy in order to be of help, proving "by example that a revolt" is possible (Gilbert and Gubar 49). Thus the "nurturing" influence that these critics envision among women writers is itself defined by, because in *revolt against,* "patriarchal literary authority."

Thus, the tropes these critics employ—"swerve," "denial," and "revolt"—reflect their negative reading of women's place in literary history, brought about by seeing women writers against a traditional norm. In her own attempt to locate a "positive" starting point for the woman writer, Virginia Woolf looked back to those "middle class women" of the late eighteenth century and envisioned not a deviant, but a parallel literary tradition for women: Austen, the Brontes, and Eliot alongside Chaucer, Marlowe, and Shakespeare. For Gilbert, Gubar, Marcus, and Hawkes, on the other hand, a mutually benevolent exchange among women writers necessarily enacts a "swerve" from patriarchal literary authority, as exemplified by, and enacted via, Bloom's paradigm of influence.

As these critics have employed Bloom's framework to represent the "norm" from which women writers must deviate, they might further consider how his theory perceives the sharing they endorse: for Bloom, generosity between writers is evidence of artistic weakness. As he asserts: "It does happen that [. . .] one poet's poems influence the poems of the other, through a generosity of spirit, even a shared generosity. But our easy idealism is out of place here. Where generosity is involved, the poets influenced are minor or weaker; the more generosity and the more mutual it is, the poorer the poets involved" (*Anxiety* 30). This passage, I would argue, demonstrates the difficulty that feminist critics encounter if they accept the Bloomian paradigm as definitive in any sense. If Gilbert, Gubar, Marcus, and Hawkes argue that the influence of women writers upon each other is reassuring, this need for comfort may itself mark those writers as "weak." Indeed, Marcus' argument describes the woman writer as unable to stand on her own two feet in literary history; she needs a "hideout" from that tradition, "where she can lick her wounds." Is there, then, no way out for the woman writer? Must she either collude with the patriarchal order or agree to be its wounded victim, searching for a nurturing muse, in order to achieve a place in literary history? Moreover, at the textual level, does either of these paradigms constitute a useful tool for understanding the creative process? Or do women writers deliberately "swerve" from such strategies in their texts, as an act of revolution?

That writers influence each other in a host of ways is indisputable. But if this does not occur through an orderly process such as Bloom's Revisionary Ratios, how does it happen? As ever, I would suggest that the dynamics of literary influence are far more complicated than our current theoretical models assume. In their essays, for example, Marcus and Hawkes focus on those of Woolf's texts that display her feminist/socialist belief in a "shared sisterhood" among women artists. Their high hopes about the positive nature of such a "sisterhood," however, may be belied by another concern that appears frequently in Woolf's private papers: her jealousy of the works of Katherine Mansfield. Woolf's journals often voiced her envy of the popular and/or critical success of other writers, but in 1923 she confessed that Mansfield's was "the only *writing* I have ever been jealous of" (Woolf, *DVW* 2:227, my emphasis). Such a declaration, I would argue, must complicate a benign view of Woolf's relation to other women writers. Jealousy of the works of Katherine Mansfield, that is, may be the snake in Woolf's "magical garden of women." In order to confront this intruder in the feminists' paradise, in this chapter I will examine the circumstances surrounding Woolf and Mansfield's association, and the impact of that relationship on their respective works.

First Impressions Count:
Virginia Woolf meets Katherine Mansfield

In my view, literary influence is best explored through a reading of the events that led to a given writer's interest in the works of another. In the case of Woolf, such an interest was clearly sparked by her desire to be introduced to the woman she saw as her literary rival. Woolf had been hearing a great deal about Mansfield through mutual friends and colleagues for several years when she finally decided that the time was right to meet her in person, and the two were formally introduced at the end of 1916. Earlier that year, however, in a letter to Lytton Strachey, Woolf wrote of an imaginary, fantasy meeting with Mansfield in which she described her sense of discomfort over the very idea of "Katherine Mansfield." Strachey had just written to Woolf to say that he had recently met Mansfield, and that she had praised Woolf's novel *The Voyage Out*.[1] In response, Woolf asked him to arrange an introduction between them, and remarked: "Katherine Mansfield has dogged my steps for three years—I'm always on the point of meeting her, or of reading her stories, and I have never managed to do either. [. . .] Do arrange a meeting—We go to Cornwall in September, and if I see anyone answering to your account on a rock or in the sea, I shall accost her" (Woolf, *LVW* 2:107).

That Woolf was already finding it difficult to negotiate her sense of Mansfield is evident in the language she employs in constructing this fantasy: "Mansfield has dogged my steps," "I have never managed" to read "her stories," "I shall accost her." This discourse of anxiety, and indeed hostility, demands our attention, particularly when we consider that Woolf composed this letter before she and Mansfield had ever met. What, I wonder, gave rise to such heated, emotional language? This "fantasy meeting" thus serves as an intriguing starting point for an examination of the later textual exchanges in their relationship. Furthermore, as I shall discuss later in this chapter, the place in which Woolf located this first "imagined" meeting with Mansfield may itself be significant: Cornwall became the setting for Woolf's first experimental novel, *Jacob's Room,* written several years later. Before I examine that work, however, I will look at the early encounters that formed the groundwork of Woolf and Mansfield's relationship.

Lytton Strachey did indeed arrange for the two writers to meet at the end of 1916.[2] At that time Woolf was thirty-four years old, and, although an accomplished critic, had published just one novel, *The Voyage Out* (1915). While this volume had received some critical appreciation, it was certainly not a financial success. Indeed, in Peter Alexander's book *Leonard and Virginia Woolf: A Literary Partnership,* he discusses Virginia's monetary gains from *The Voyage Out,* and notes that although "2,000 copies of the book were printed," less than 500 were sold in the years 1919 to 1929. In fifteen years, Alexander points out "Virginia earned less than £120 from it" (Alexander 98). Leonard Woolf later noted that if Virginia "had had to earn her living during those years, it is highly improbable that she would ever have written a novel" (Leonard Woolf, *Downhill* 17). As I noted in the previous chapter, Katherine Mansfield, Woolf's junior by six years, had by this time already established a career as a writer of fiction.

One could argue, then, that the "jealousy" of Mansfield to which Woolf admitted years later was informed by her awareness of Mansfield's popular success. If so, this envy could also account for the ambivalence of Woolf's early impressions of the younger writer. At times, as in Woolf's imaginary meeting with Mansfield, Woolf employs a clear tone of hostility toward Mansfield. In a letter to her sister Vanessa written only a few months after she had met Mansfield, Woolf referred to her as "an unpleasant but forcible and utterly unscrupulous character" (*LVW* 2:144). In another note to Vanessa in June of 1917, Woolf praises Mansfield for having "a much better idea of writing than most," but also exhibits her disdain of Mansfield's bohemian lifestyle. Here, Woolf tells Vanessa that Mansfield "seems to have gone every sort of hog since she was 17" (*LVW* 2:159). Such ambivalent and strongly worded judgments hint at Woolf's fascination with, and struggles over, her sense of Katherine Mansfield.

Mansfield's own response to her new acquaintance was similarly mixed. She remarked in a letter to Woolf in this same June, that she was a "bit 'haunted'" by her, and went on to state "[m]y God, I love to think of you Virginia, as my friend" (Mansfield, *CLKM* 1:313). Nevertheless, as this letter to Woolf continues, Mansfield appears strangely anxious to avoid the condescension of her "friend": "Dont cry me an ardent creature or say, with your head a little on one side, smiling as though you knew some enchanting secret: 'Well Katherine, we shall see' . . . But pray consider how rare is it to find some one with the same passion for writing that you have . . ." (*CLKM* 1:313). Throughout their relationship, Mansfield made private references that demonstrated her dislike of Woolf's snobbery. In Sydney Janet Kaplan's recent study of Mansfield, she argues that Woolf was frequently patronizing toward Mansfield, and claims that the reasons for this were culturally based: "Although Mansfield and Woolf were drawn together by their mutual interest in writing and in women, their feminism had developed along separate lines because of significant differences in experience, education and class"

(Kaplan 12). While Kaplan's work explores the ways in which Woolf and Mansfield's class differences informed their respective feminist visions, other evidence suggests that these differences affected their relationship on a personal, as well as political, level. Thus Woolf would refer to Mansfield's colonial "commonness" repeatedly in her journals, and Mansfield herself, as the early letter above implies, was frequently annoyed by Woolf's sense of superiority. Although their mutual love of writing would continue to draw these women together, such misunderstanding and distrust contaminated, and eventually undermined, their friendship. More interesting in terms of this study, this mutual ambivalence surfaces frequently in the texts each composed during the period of their relationship.

"To Hell with other people's presses!":
Katherine Mansfield's "Prelude" and the Hogarth Press

The first evidence of the material effect that their difficult association would have upon their respective works can be found by examining the circumstances that surrounded a joint project they undertook early in 1917. In April of that year, Woolf asked Mansfield for a story that she might publish, using the printing press she and Leonard had recently purchased.[3] Thus began their collaboration on "Prelude," which was later to become one of Mansfield's best-known tales. The printing of "Prelude" brought the two into close and frequent contact, and thus became an important framework for their relations, as well as a cause for mutual disappointment. The journals and letters of both women record their changing responses to the work and to one another. In October of 1917, for example, Woolf's diary records that she was setting type for "Prelude," and asked Mansfield to Hogarth House to see proofs of the first page. The following day, Woolf noted her and Leonard's sense of Mansfield: "We could both wish that ones first impression of K. M. was not that she stinks like a—well like a civet cat that had taken to street walking. In truth, I'm a little shocked by her commonness at first sight; lines so hard & cheap" (*DVW* 1:58). Here, Woolf's caricature of Mansfield as a "civet cat" demonstrates that despite her admiration for Mansfield as a writer, Woolf was nevertheless repelled by her "commonness." While, as Kaplan suggests, cultural and educational differences between these women may have been partially responsible for such an outburst of venom, a more tangible reason can also be proposed: by the end of 1917 the printing of "Prelude" had become an immense burden on Leonard and Virginia. Aware that their single press was not capable of printing Mansfield's story, the Woolfs were forced to purchase a second, larger one, and Virginia had begun to resent the enormity of the typesetting work involved.

This frustration over "Prelude"'s progress was not one-sided; Mansfield's own letters articulate her anger at the unprofessional functioning of the Hogarth Press. While Woolf privately scorned Mansfield as a "civet cat," Mansfield was complaining about Leonard and Virginia in her notes to her husband Murry. In a letter of February 17, for instance, Mansfield remarks: "I am sorry you have to go to the Woolves. I don't like them either. They are *smelly*" (*CLKM* 2:77). The childishness of Mansfield's insult and of Woolf's own comment on Katherine's "stink" is rather extraordinary, and may in fact be read as each woman's denial of the more "adult" reasons for their frustrations. For Woolf, who was admittedly jealous of Mansfield's literary success, such name-calling would serve to devalue both Mansfield and her work, thus making her a less threatening rival. Mansfield's own rude comment on the Woolfs could imply that she sensed Virginia's envy and condescension, and was reacting against it. Certainly, Mansfield's frustrations over the ongoing delays were growing. In a letter to Murry that February, Mansfield wrote: "I think the Woolfs must have eaten the Aloe root and branch or made a jam of it" (*CLKM* 2:87).

Mansfield's distress over the slow progress of "Prelude" added to the numerous pressures that she faced at this time. In this same February she had suffered from her first hemorrhage of the lungs, her ill health exacerbated by her wartime journey to Bandol the previous month. While she was thus undergoing a difficult period of sickness and upheaval, Woolf herself had embarked on a new project: her second novel, *Night and Day*. Mansfield returned to London in April, and met again with Woolf soon after her marriage to Murry in May. As Woolf noted in her diary, Katherine's illness had taken its toll on her appearance, and Woolf was shocked by her rapid decline. This same journal entry also suggests that in spite of their recent separation, Woolf now felt a shared sympathy with Mansfield: "Katherine [. . .] looks ghastly ill. As usual we came to an oddly complete understanding. My theory is that I get down to what is true rock in her, through the numerous vapours & pores which sicken or bewilder most of our friends. It's her love of writing I think" (*DVW* 1: 150). Mansfield recorded her own reaction to this "reconciliation" with Woolf in the following letter to Dorothy Brett: "I saw Virginia on Thursday. She was very nice [. . .] she *does* take the writing business seriously and she *is* honest about it and thrilled by it. One cant ask more. My poor dear Prelude is still piping away in their little cage and not out yet" (*CLKM* 2:169). Both Woolf's diary entry and Mansfield's letter thus suggest that although each of them sensed the rarity and value of the other, they were also aware that their shared "love of writing" was tempered by many personal differences. Though Woolf stresses her "understanding" of Mansfield in this diary entry, for example, she is equally aware that Mansfield could "sicken and bewilder" most others. Similarly, Mansfield counters

Woolf's ability to "take the writing business seriously" with her disappointment over Woolf's handling of her "poor dear Prelude."

Mansfield's frustration over the Woolfs' work on her story was further expressed in a letter to Murry that same May. Having just seen a mock-up of the binding the Woolfs were planning to use for her story, Mansfield fumed: "[j]ust a plain blue cover with Prelude on it. To Hell with other people's presses!" (*CLKM* 2: 203). According to Anthony Alpers, this reaction was justified. As he argues, the initial failure of "Prelude" was a direct result of the incompetence of the Hogarth Press, which finally published the story in July 1918: "For the little blue book called *Prelude* there was no general enthusiasm, no body of allies ready to promote it, and no demand in the bookshops. Few review copies were sent out and the papers hardly noticed it, for its appearance was unprofessional" (Alpers 284). As Alpers also asserts, for Mansfield this result was particularly frustrating as she saw "Prelude" as her first truly personal story. This view is corroborated by Mary Burgan in her 1994 study of Mansfield, entitled *Illness, Gender and Writing: the Case of Katherine Mansfield*. Burgan argues that by composing "Prelude," Mansfield was able to work through the death of her brother Leslie, and thus "seems to have broken through the writing block that had unsettled her sense of her vocation after the publication of *In a German Pension* in 1911. The publication of 'Prelude' [. . .] seems to have put her doubts securely behind her" (Burgan 143). Both Alpers and Burgan thus emphasize the personal and professional importance of "Prelude" to Katherine Mansfield: the lackluster presentation of the text coupled with the critical dismissal in which its "unprofessional" appearance resulted, were thus almost impossible for Mansfield to bear.

Leslie Beauchamp: "Prelude"'s Lost Brother

Apart from the circumstantial difficulties that Woolf and Mansfield experienced in the production of "Prelude," the tale itself would come to have a far-reaching effect on both writers. Mansfield's inspiration for the story, as well as the unusual narrative structure she employed in the text, seems to have triggered a whole new approach to fiction writing, one that was later explored repeatedly by both Woolf and Mansfield. According to Mansfield's journals, her inspiration for "Prelude" was the visit of her brother Leslie Beauchamp to London in the summer of 1915, only months before he was to die in military training.[4] Mansfield noted that her brother had implored her to write something "nostalgic" about their childhood in New Zealand. One month after Leslie's death, Mansfield promised herself to fulfill his request: "I feel I have a duty to perform to the lovely time when we were both alive. I want to write about it, and he wanted me to. We talked it over in my little top room in London. I said: I will just put on the front page: To My brother, Leslie

Heron Beauchamp" (*JKM* 90). Mansfield, however, had first begun the story that was to become "Prelude" in early 1915, that is, before Leslie's death. In its first incarnation, the tale was to be a novel, entitled *The Aloe.*

As Sydney Janet Kaplan remarks in her comparison of the unfinished novel, *The Aloe,* to the later "Prelude," "[t]he evolution of 'Prelude' from its initial conception as a novel *The Aloe* to its publication by the Woolfs in 1918 demonstrates [. . .] the true beginning of her *conscious* sense of a new shape for prose fiction. What began as a 'novel' eventually became something new: a mixed genre, a multileveled spatially ordered narrative" (Kaplan 103).[5] This "new shape for prose fiction" was ultimately realized as the sixty-eight-page "Prelude," written by Mansfield, published by the Hogarth Press, and largely typeset by Woolf herself. As I noted above, both the material circumstances surrounding "Prelude"'s publication, and the highly original creative strategies Mansfield employed in the text, came to have far-reaching effects upon the later works of Woolf and Mansfield.

Mansfield's "Prelude" is predominantly a tale of four women in a New Zealand family, and their move from the center of Wellington to a house in a less accessible, rural area. Mrs. Fairfield, the grandmother, her daughters Linda Burnell, a self-absorbed mother, her younger unmarried sister, Beryl, and Linda's daughter Kezia, are these main characters. Unusually for its time, the story is told from multiple viewpoints, and relates the inner lives of the various characters during this period of upheaval. Mansfield's depiction of the thoughts and dreams of Linda Burnell, for example, shows her struggles with her responsibilities as a mother and wife. These difficulties are manifested in Linda's private reveries, in which objects swell and grow before her eyes with frightening consequences. In one of these dreams, Linda picks up a small bird, "a tiny ball of fluff," which begins to "ruffle" and "grow bigger." It becomes "a baby with a big naked head and a gaping bird mouth, opening and shutting."[6] In Linda's dream, these swelling objects appear to symbolize both her fear of her growing children, and of sexual contact with her husband, Stanley.

In contrast to Linda, the character of Mrs. Fairfield is shown to revel in her nurturing and maternal impulses. As Linda rests and dreams alone in her room, her mother, Mrs. Fairfield, sets the new house to order. Soon after, Mrs. Fairfield gazes out the kitchen window and recalls the time when her own daughters were young: "And she remembered how Beryl when she was a baby [. . .] had been stung on the leg by a huge red ant. [. . .] Mrs. Fairfield caught her breath remembering. 'Poor child, how terrifying it was'" ("Prelude" 28–9). If Mrs. Fairfield's daydream illustrates her sympathetic character, her younger daughter Beryl is depicted through her fantasies as shallow and self-involved. Unlike her mother, who looks through the window into a metaphoric "outer world," Beryl gazes into mirrors, admiring her own beauty. Beryl also indulges in escapist fantasies while thus staring at her reflection: a "young man, immensely rich, has just arrived from England. He meets her quite by chance," she imagines ("Prelude" 22).

As Mansfield explores the imaginations of the figures in "Prelude," a clear connection seems to be implied among the female characters. Kaplan remarks "[t]he spatial organization suggests simultaneity, but the typical linear pattern of individual development is rather spread out among the female characters, who tend to represent the central consciousness at various stages of her life: early childhood, late adolescence, young motherhood, old age. The child, aunt, mother, and grandmother embody the female life cycle" (Kaplan 117). The symbolic associations that link the women in "Prelude" confirm Kaplan's reading of their interconnected roles in the text. The "simultaneity" of experience among these female characters is perhaps best exemplified by the young Kezia's own fantasy world, in which the windows, mirrors, and swelling and rushing animals found in the elder women's inner lives, all coexist. Alone in her old and empty home, Kezia looks out the window: "Kezia liked to stand so before the window. She liked the feeling of the cold shining glass against her hot palms" ("Prelude" 15). Later, in the buggy ride to her new home, Kezia tells the storeman who drives her: "I often dream that animals rush at me—even camels—and while they are rushing, their heads swell e-enormous" ("Prelude" 17). These images of windows and swollen heads thus align Kezia's thoughts with those of her grandmother and mother. Later, however, we see the child inhabit the inner world of her aunt as well, as the text concludes with Kezia and her cat gazing momentarily into Beryl's mirror: "she sat the cat up on the dressing-table and stuck the top of the cream jar over its ear. 'Now look at yourself,' she said sternly" ("Prelude" 59–60).

Thus, as Kaplan suggests, in "Prelude" Mansfield portrays episodes in the typical "female life cycle," and the struggles inherent in that cycle are themselves played out in Kezia's own imagination. In Mansfield's text, therefore, Kezia functions as a repository for a specifically feminine brand of fear, nurturing, and self-absorption, as she appears to "channel" the thoughts of the elder women. Kaplan further remarks that the "spatial rendering" in "Prelude" prefigures a similar technique employed by Woolf in *her* novel *Mrs. Dalloway*, written some ten years later. As Kaplan observes, both explore "a few days in the inner lives of [their] characters" (Kaplan 118). "Prelude"'s influence on Woolf's writing, I would argue, was actually in evidence well before this. Woolf's *Mrs. Dalloway* does indeed employ a multivoiced arrangement and a study of her characters' inner lives, as Kaplan argues, but this same technique was first attempted in Woolf's earlier novel, *Jacob's Room*. In order to provide a context for reading this stylistic connection between Mansfield's "Prelude" and Woolf's novel, I will take a moment to examine the changing nature of the relationship between these writers during the period that preceded the composition of *Jacob's Room.*

As Woolf's journal indicates, her reaction to Mansfield's "Prelude" was somewhat equivocal. An entry in the diary on July 10, 1918, shows that having spent the afternoon gluing and covering the newly printed work, Woolf realized that now she "must read the book through" (*DVW* 1:165). Two days later Woolf notes that when reading the story for the first time, she finds it "freely watered with some of [Mansfield's] cheap realities; but it has the living power, the detached existence of a work of art" (*DVW* 1:167). Woolf's diary entry thus implies that she had only just read "Prelude" "through" for the first time on the day of its final production. Can this be true? How, I wonder, could Woolf have been typesetting and proofing Mansfield's story for ten months without ever having read it? I am even more deeply intrigued by the ambivalent tone and terminology of Woolf's assessment. How was it possible for Woolf to have sensed "Prelude"'s "living power" when she scorned it as "watered" with "cheap realities?"

Perhaps Woolf's critique of "Prelude" can be read as a defensive response to the work of a rival. Such an interpretation would also be suggested by Woolf's other journal entries during this period, which indicate that she was having difficulties with her own writing, as she struggled with the first draft of *Night and Day.* On the other hand, Woolf's confusing assessment of "Prelude" could be further evidence of difficulties arising from cultural and class differences between herself and Mansfield. Just as her complaints about Mansfield's "cheap scent and cheap sentimentality," that is, had allowed her to dismiss Mansfield herself as "common," Woolf's reading of "Prelude" belittles the power of that text by naming Mansfield's realities as "cheap."[7]

Woolf repeated this view of Mansfield's personal and artistic cheapness soon after the publication of "Prelude" when Mansfield's short story "Bliss" appeared in *English Review.* Woolf's reaction to "Bliss," as recorded in her diary, confirms her growing dismissal of Mansfield's artistic powers:

> I threw down Bliss with the exclamation, "She's done for!" Indeed I dont see how much faith in her as woman or writer can survive that sort of story. I shall have to accept the fact, I'm afraid, that her mind is a very thin soil, laid an inch or two deep upon very barren rock [. . .] she is content with superficial smartness; & the whole conception is poor, cheap, not the vision, however imperfect, of an interesting mind. She writes badly too (*DVW* 1:179).

Here, once again, the terms Woolf employs to deride Mansfield's artistic strength belong to a discourse of class difference ("cheap" and "poor"), as if one judgment informed the other. Indeed it seems that although Woolf acknowledges Mansfield's vision as "smart," her works have no cultural value for Woolf; they have only a "superficial smartness," and are "badly" written, too.

As the diary entry continues, however, Woolf's focus changes from a critique of Mansfield's writing toward a more personal attack: "And the effect was as I say, to give me an impression of her callousness & hardness as a human being. [. . .] Or is it absurd to read all this criticism of her personally into a story?" (*DVW* 1:179). Here, Woolf notes wryly that her reading of "Bliss" rendered an "absurd" impression of Mansfield as "personally" hard and callous. Perhaps more absurd, however, is the fact that notwithstanding such comments, Woolf continued to meet with this "cheap" and "hard" "human being" almost weekly during the autumn and early winter of that year.[8]

Mansfield herself appears to have been overwhelmed by Woolf's kindness at this time. In a series of "thank you" notes that November, Mansfield was profuse in her gratitude, stating: "I wonder why I feel an intense joy that you are a writer—that you live for writing—I do. You are immensely important in my world, Virginia" (*CLKM* 2:288). Later in the same week, Mansfield declared "[y]ou do not know, Virginia, how I treasure the thought of you. Thats quite sober & true" (*CLKM* 2:289). Thus, like Woolf's frequent visits to Mansfield that winter, Mansfield's letters also suggest that alongside their privately voiced misgivings was an equally strong sense of shared affection and fascination.

An understanding of their relationship is further complicated by the "progress reports" that Woolf kept on her "patient," the ailing Mansfield. After one visit on November 9, for example, Woolf wrote in her diary, "Katherine was up, but husky & feeble, crawling about the room like an old woman. How far she is ill, one cant say. She impresses one a little unfavourably at first—then more favourably. I think she has a kind of childlikeness somewhere which has been much disfigured, but still exists. Illness, she said, breaks down one's privacy so that one can't write" (*DVW* 1:216). As here Woolf considers the debilitating effects of "illness" on the writer, I am reminded that her own struggles with mental illness had periodically robbed her of the ability to write, delaying the publication of *The Voyage Out* for several years.[9] This notion of illness, and feminine illness in particular, as a context in which to read Mansfield's works is suggested and examined by Mary Burgan's study, noted above. In the introduction to this work, Burgan argues that Mansfield's "sense of the body" was as "the instrument of a perception mediated by the culturally determined metaphors of sickness, especially feminine sickness" (Burgan xvii). While Burgan does not claim that Mansfield's struggles with tuberculosis were the only strong influence upon her writing, her study nevertheless provides an intriguing account of the way that Mansfield negotiated her illness through her art. Moreover, Burgan quite rightly draws a comparison between Mansfield's sickness and Woolf's own: both writers saw themselves *as* ill. In Burgan's view, this awareness surfaces in their texts: "for Katherine Mansfield, as for Virginia Woolf, the creativity of women was inflected by illness. As madness haunts the writing of Virginia Woolf, physical disease haunts Mansfield's fiction" (Burgan 172).

This similarity of experience might be supposed to have forged a further connection between Woolf and Mansfield. In Woolf's journal entry above, however, she seems strangely objective, if not entirely unsympathetic, toward Mansfield's difficulties. Rather than containing a concerned account of her friend's ill health, here Woolf's diary portrays Mansfield as a pathetic, almost fictional, character. In these passages Woolf sees Mansfield as both "like an old woman" and "childlike," and, moreover, "one cant say" the extent of her illness. As the entry concludes, Woolf narrates the speech of this "character": "Illness, she said, breaks down one's privacy." Woolf's reporting of Mansfield's words as an indirect quotation serves to enhance the fictional quality of the scene she records. While Woolf often employed this indirect narrative style in her diary, her use of this form to detail her visit to Mansfield inscribes a palpable distance between them.

Here, that is, Woolf does not articulate her empathy for a fellow sufferer, but instead monitors Mansfield, defining her as a "patient." Woolf's rendering of this visit thus implies a more removed stance toward Mansfield than her weekly visits might otherwise suggest. Woolf's "progress note" is thus evidence of her desire for emotional remove from Mansfield, and their biographical records strengthen this view: soon after the visit that Woolf recalled in November 1918, a temporary estrangement arose between them. Woolf and Mansfield did not meet again until March of the following year.

Emotional Distance and Biting Critiques:
Woolf and Mansfield in 1919

While Woolf may have attempted to distance herself emotionally from Mansfield at this time, her diary nevertheless contains evidence of her painful reaction to their separation:

> It is at this moment extremely doubtful whether I have the right to class her among my friends. Quite possibly I shall never see her again. Upstairs I have letters in which she speaks of finding the thought of me a joy, dwelling upon my writing with excitement. [. . .] But the last is dated December, & now it is February. The question interests, amuses, & also slightly, no, very, decidedly pains me (*DVW* 1:242).

In this journal entry, Woolf's response to the loss of Mansfield's friendship moves from interest, to amusement, to pain, and thus reconfirms Woolf's conflicting and ambivalent feelings toward her "friend." These lines thus evince Woolf's ostensible ease in her dismissal of their friendship, but also demonstrate her reluctance to admit sorrow at their estrangement.

The pain of this loss, however, was soon to end: a few days after Woolf wrote the lines above, she received a letter from Mansfield. Woolf recorded her reaction to this note as follows: "But all this is made to appear rather fine drawn & exaggerated by the simple fact that I have a letter this morning from K. M. herself asking me to tea on Monday. [. . .] Also, I am asked to write for the Athenaeum, so that little scratch in my vanity is healed" (*DVW* 1:243).[10] Woolf's collaboration with Murry and Mansfield on *The Athenaeum*, which began with this request, continued throughout 1919. By April, Murry had become editor of the magazine and Woolf was regularly contributing essays and reviews to it.[11] Brought together once more by a shared literary project, Woolf and Mansfield's friendship was revived. After a meeting with Mansfield in March, Woolf noted her renewed respect and admiration for her: "And again, as usual, I find with Katherine what I don't find with the other clever women a sense of ease & interest, which is, I suppose, due to her caring so genuinely if so differently from the way I care, about our precious art" (*DVW* 1:258). As Woolf records here, the "precious art" of writing was the bond that continued to draw these women together. Nevertheless, their doubts about each other's talents and the dissimilarities in their respective lifestyles still created obstacles in their friendship. Woolf privately noted, for instance, that Murry and Mansfield had the "shadow of the underworld" about them (*DVW* 1:159), and that she was envious of her friend's critical success. Mansfield, on the other hand, was less envious of Woolf's *writing* than of her seemingly stable home and marriage.

In a letter to Woolf of April 1919, for example, Mansfield wrote: "A husband, a home, a great many books & a passion for writing—are very nice things to possess all at once—It is pleasant to think of you & Leonard together—I often do" (*CLKM* 2:314). While Mansfield thus records her observations on Woolf's lifestyle, her own desire to possess such "nice things" "all at once" is also clearly implied here. Thus it appears that as Mansfield's illness deprived her of husband and home, her thoughts had turned to the seemingly enviable world of Virginia "and Leonard together." Mansfield's response to Woolf's home life indicates her feelings of self-pity, but her sense of Woolf's writing during this period is equally complicated. Mansfield, for instance, commented as follows on Woolf's essay "Modern Novels" in this letter to Woolf written that same April: "You write so *damned* well, so *devilish* well. There are these little others, you know, dodging & stumbling along, taking a sniff here and a start there—& there is your mind so accustomed to take the air in the 'grand manner'—To tell you the truth—I am *proud* of your writing" (*CLKM* 2:311).[12] Despite such explicit praise, Mansfield's use of the term "grand manner" to describe Woolf's style once again hints at her perception of a flaw in Woolf's work. As this critique suggests, in Mansfield's opinion, Woolf's writing had a tendency toward coldness and condescension. Thus, couched within Mansfield's declaration of "pride" in her friend, was a seed of doubt that would soon grow into an angry and mistrustful view of Woolf's work as sterile and aloof.

Evidence of this change in Mansfield's response to Woolf's writing can be found in her review of Woolf's short story "Kew Gardens," published in Murry's *The Athenaeum* in May of 1919.[13] In this article Mansfield argues that Woolf's story "belongs to another age. It is so far removed from the note-book literature of our day, so exquisite an example of love at second sight" ("A Short Story" 459). Here, as in her letter to Woolf above, Mansfield cautiously praises Woolf's "exquisite" vision and qualifies it as "removed" and "belonging to another age." Mansfield also implies that this distanced stance has a tangible impact on the reader: the story elicits no immediate response, but rather exemplifies "love at second sight." In this ambivalent review, then, Mansfield's suspicion that "Kew Gardens" "belong[s] to another age" is voiced in the midst of admiration for the experimental nature of the work. Interestingly, Mansfield reiterated this same critique in less flattering tones several months later in her review of Woolf's second novel, *Night and Day.*

Night and Day was published in October of 1919 and was fairly well received, having been praised by *The Times Literary Supplement,* for example, as a work of "wisdom" and "brilliance."[14] Katherine Mansfield, however, saw Woolf's novel in quite a different light, as her review, entitled "A Ship Comes into the Harbour," denotes. Mansfield begins this critique with a discussion of the viability of the modern novel, noting that "[w]e are told on excellent authority that it is dying; and on equally good authority that only now it begins to live" ("Ship" 1227). Mansfield then asserts that there is only one resolution to this dichotomy: "If the novel dies, it will be to give way to some new form of expression; if it lives it must accept the fact of a new world" ("Ship" 1227). As the review continues, Mansfield's sense of *Night and Day* in relation to this modern imperative becomes clear: in her view, Woolf's novel *does not* "accept the fact of a new world."

In this essay, as its title suggests, Mansfield employs the metaphor of the novel as a "ship," and locates herself "down at the harbour" gazing upon "the strange sight of *Night and Day* sailing into port serene and resolute" ("Ship" 1227). Soon after, she offers an explanation for this serenity in Woolf's novel. *Night and Day,* Mansfield hints, ignores the war, shies away from "the age of experiment," and unfolds in a safe and "privileged" world. Next, Mansfield emphasizes her suspicions that Woolf's own emotional remove has deadened the novel she has composed: "The strangeness lies in her aloofness, her air of quiet perfection, her lack of any sign that she has made a perilous voyage—the absence of any scars" ("Ship" 1227). Throughout this critique, Mansfield continues to allude to Woolf's novel as a "ship," and this troping allows her to refer to *Night and Day* in the feminine. Thus, Mansfield's judgments on "her aloofness" "her air," etc., are easily read as a critique of the text, *and* of Woolf personally. This elision is reproduced as Mansfield goes on, and her desire to distinguish between the novel and the novelist becomes more and more questionable.

Mansfield suggests that the "perilous voyage" and the "scars" it has left are the imperative issues in the postwar "new world." Through Mansfield's metaphoric associations, however, both Woolf's novel and Woolf herself are shown to disregard those important topics. She argues that so far from representing a modern vision, *Night and Day* should be compared "with the novels of Miss Austen" for it shares with those works "a tribute to civilisation." By thus linking Woolf's work with Austen's, here Mansfield not only questions the modern relevance of *Night and Day,* but also scrutinizes its political status. Like Mansfield's comment on Woolf's "grand manner" in her review of "Kew Gardens," this parallel with Jane Austen similarly locates Woolf's work as aloof, serene, and, of course, privileged. As I recall Mansfield's envy of Woolf's lifestyle, of her possessing so "many nice things" at once, I must question whether Mansfield's comparison of Woolf and Austen was informed by jealous motives. Mansfield's review, I suggest, throws a suspicious eye on the very kind of stable and civilized life that illness denied her. If this is so, her equation of novel and novelist in this article indicates that Mansfield's critique was influenced by her private sense of Woolf. As the piece continues, Mansfield elides Woolf with her text even further, remarking "[t]here is not a chapter where one is unconscious of the writer, of her personality, her point of view, and her control of the situation" ("Ship" 1227). Here, as Mansfield points to her continual consciousness of Woolf when reading *Night and Day,* it seems that she had no wish to separate the two.

Perhaps Mansfield's hostile perspective in this review was fuelled by the circumstances of her life at this time: Mansfield wrote the article while alone and convalescing at the Casetta Deerholm in Menton. During this period in late 1919, Mansfield had begun to confront the severity of her illness, and Virginia Woolf's life could well have seemed unfairly settled and privileged in comparison to her own. This notion that personal jealousy had contaminated the language Mansfield used in her review is strengthened by the passage that follows. After admitting to being "conscious" of the writer's personality, Mansfield adds: "We feel that nothing is imposed on her: she has chosen her world, selected her principal characters with the nicest care, and having traced a circle round them [. . .] she has proceeded, with rare appreciativeness, to register her observations" ("Ship" 1227). Mansfield's view of Woolf's ability to "choose her world," to have "nothing imposed" upon her, and to "trace a circle" around that world, can again be read as describing the very freedoms of which Mansfield's illness had robbed her. This seemingly envious censure of the privileged world of Woolf's characters, however, is here placed alongside Mansfield's praise of Woolf's skill as a writer. Mansfield asserts that within the "confines" of the "circle" that Woolf's characters inhabit, "she has proceeded, with rare appreciativeness, to register her observations" ("Ship" 1227). The ambivalence of Mansfield's critique, then, and its elision of novel and novelist, give voice to her frustrations with Woolf as a friend and a writer. Mansfield, it seems, felt that Woolf's rare gifts were squandered in portraying *Night and Day's* confined and exclusive world.

As the review concludes, Mansfield reiterates what she sees as the tragic flaw of the novel *and* its author. She argues that by ignoring the war and its effects, both *Night and Day* and, by implication, Woolf herself, display cowardice:

> We had thought that this world was vanished forever, that it was impossible to find on the great ocean of literature a ship that was unaware of what has been happening. Yet here is *Night and Day* fresh, new, and exquisite, a novel in the tradition of the English novel. In the midst of our admiration it makes us feel old and chill: we had never thought to look upon its like again! ("Ship" 1227).

In this passage, then, Mansfield accuses *Night and Day* of being "unaware of what has been happening." Privately, she confirmed in a letter to Murry that her dislike of the novel was based both on its refusal to confront the postwar world, and the cowardice that such a stance implied. She wrote: "My private opinion is that it is a lie in the soul. The war has never been, that is what its message is [. . .] the novel cant just leave the war out" (*CLKM* 3:82).

In this letter, as in the conclusion of her review, Mansfield asserts that her censure of *Night and Day* arises from its failure to address "the war." However, the other, personal critiques of Woolf's "privileged" world that "A Ship Comes into the Harbour" contains must complicate this explanation. Woolf's "control," her "privilege," and her ability to "choose her world" in which "nothing is imposed on her," seem equally to be under attack in Mansfield's review. Thus, although Mansfield justifies her dislike of *Night and Day* in political terms, her underlying personal jealousy of Woolf's privileged world seems also to have informed this opinion. This idea is further corroborated as Mansfield's letter to Murry regarding *Night and Day* continues: "Inwardly I despise them all for a set of *cowards*. We have to face our war—they won't" (*CLKM* 3:82). Here, "the war" that Mansfield believed Woolf would not face seems to encompass much more than the military actions in Europe.

For Mansfield, it stood for "our war," the death of Mansfield's brother, her financial and marital struggles, and perhaps most acutely, her tuberculosis and its attendant upheavals. These were the battles that Mansfield had fought on her own "perilous voyage," and perhaps, alone and ill, she begrudged Woolf's ability to float "serenely into port," her "absence of any scars."

That Mansfield's criticism of Woolf and her novel appeared in *The Athenaeum* is further evidence of her need to censure Woolf on both a personal and professional level. For while Murry was editor and Mansfield one of the main reviewers of that magazine, Woolf herself was also contributing to it on a regular basis.[15] The fact that Woolf's novel was criticized in a magazine with which she was so closely associated must have added to the impact of that critique upon her. Indeed, Woolf's shocked reaction to "A Ship Comes into the Harbour" was recorded in her diary on November 28, 1919, as follows: "K. M. wrote a review which irritated me—I thought I saw spite in it. A decorous elderly dullard she describes me; Jane Austen up to date. Leonard supposes that she let her wish for my failure have its way with her pen. [. . .] I need not now spread my charity so wide, since Murry tells me she is practically cured" (*DVW* 1:314–5). Mansfield was not, of course, "practically cured," despite what Murry may have told Woolf. Nevertheless, Woolf's "charity" visits to Mansfield did cease after the appearance of Mansfield's critical review. Thus, it appears that though Woolf claimed that Mansfield's words had merely "irritated" her, they had in fact hurt her deeply.

Mansfield's review, moreover, appears to have haunted Woolf in the months that followed. As Woolf once again pored over Mansfield's words in her diary that December, she resolved to continue to "write in her own way":

> Night & Day flutters about me still, & causes great loss of time. George Eliot would never read reviews, since talk of her books hampered her writing. I begin to see what she meant. I don't take praise or blame excessively to heart, but they interrupt, cast one's eyes backwards, make one wish to explain or investigate. [. . .] But I had rather write in my own way [. . .] than be, as K. M. maintains, Jane Austen over again (*DVW* 1:315–6).

If, as this journal entry implies, Mansfield's review had interrupted Woolf and forced her to "cast" her "eyes backwards," what did she see when she did so? One obvious answer is she saw the logic of Mansfield's critique: Mansfield's article had called for experimentation in modern novels, and shortly after reading this imperative Woolf herself began to search for "a new form for a novel" (*DVW* 2:13). As I shall demonstrate, Mansfield's critiques in "A Ship Comes into the Harbour" would have a great impact on Woolf's next project.

Ships, Bones, and Battlegrounds:
"Prelude" to *Jacob's Room*

By January of 1920, Woolf had visualized an experimental format for creating her next work, writing: "the approach will be entirely different this time: no scaffolding; scarcely a brick to be seen" (*DVW* 2:13). Woolf cast her "eyes backwards," and spent the next few months reading over both *The Voyage Out* and *Night and Day*. Soon after this rereading, she began to outline her next novel, *Jacob's Room*. Interestingly, Woolf's first mention of *Jacob's Room* appears in the same journal entry as the following observation about Mansfield: "Moreover, I can wince outrageously to read K. M.'s praises in the Athenaeum. Four poets are chosen; she's one of them. Of course Murry makes the choice, & its Sullivan who rates her story a work of genius. Still, you see how well I remember all this—how eagerly I discount it" (*DVW* 2:28).[16] Shortly below this, Woolf notes: "I'm planning to begin Jacob's Room next week" (*DVW* 2:28). The fact that these two thoughts coincide in Woolf's journal is intriguing. Might this suggest that Woolf's "wincing" jealousy upon reading "K. M.'s praises" on this day had somehow compelled her to begin *Jacob's Room*? Certainly, as this journal entry highlights, Woolf was making connections between Mansfield and *Jacob's Room* at this time.

By mid-1920, Woolf decided to confront Mansfield about her censure of *Night and Day*. Now in the midst of composing *Jacob's Room*, Woolf seems to have needed Mansfield to explain her critique of the earlier novel. In her diary, Woolf noted a discussion she and Mansfield had when they met that June for the first time in many months:

> A queer effect she produces of someone apart, entirely self-centred; altogether concentrated upon her "art": almost fierce to me about it, I pretending I couldn't write. [. . .] Then asked me to write stories for the A[thenaeum]. "But I don't know that I can write stories" I said, honestly enough, thinking that in her view, after her review of me, anyhow, those were her secret sentiments. Whereupon she turned on me, & said no one else could write stories except me. [. . .] Well but Night & Day? I said, though I hadn't meant to speak of it. 'An amazing achievement' she said. Why, we've not had such a thing since I don't know when—, But I thought you didn't like it? [. . .] Anyhow, once more as keenly as ever I feel a common certain understanding between us—a queer sense of being 'like'—not only about literature—& I think it's independent of gratified vanity. I can talk straight out to her (*DVW* 2:44).

Woolf's recollection of their meeting hints at several layers of mutual delusion in their relationship. She describes Mansfield as "self-centred" and "fierce," and such language clearly conveys Woolf's sense of constraint and circumspection during this conversation. Further uncomfortable feelings about Mansfield are demonstrated as Woolf recalls "pretending" deference, telling Mansfield "I don't know that I can write stories," and recounts her suspicions of Mansfield's "secret sentiments." If, then, Woolf's decision to talk to Mansfield about *Night and Day* ("though [she] hadn't meant to speak of it") suggests a certain frankness between them, Mansfield's praise of the novel as "an amazing achievement" belies this notion of candor: Mansfield had told Murry that the novel "positively frightens me" (*CLKM* 3:82). Despite this subtext of deceit, as Woolf concludes this entry she states that there is a "common certain understanding" between them. Finally, it appears, Woolf chose to ignore the elaborate negotiations that brought about this "understanding," as she claims without irony, "I can talk straight out to her."

Woolf noted that in a further meeting a few days later, Mansfield continued to praise *Night and Day:* "I lunched with K. M. & had 2 hours priceless talk [. . .] to no one else can I talk in the same disembodied way about writing; without altering my thought more than I alter it in writing here. [. . .] We talked about books, writing of course: my own. N. & D. a first rate novel, she said. The suppression in it puzzling, but accounted for by circumstances" (*DVW* 2:45–6). As in the earlier journal entry, here Woolf stresses the honesty of her "priceless talk" with Mansfield, but this claim of shared openness is once again questionable. Woolf states here that in speaking with Katherine she need not alter her thoughts. Nevertheless, as she noted previously, Woolf purposely "pretended" to Katherine that she "couldn't write," and was suspicious of Mansfield's "secret sentiments." Similarly, Mansfield herself was less than honest with Woolf in their discussion of *Night and Day.* As Woolf recalls, Mansfield told her that *Night and Day* was a "first rate novel," although privately she had told Murry that it was "a lie in the soul" (*CLKM* 3:82).

My purpose in examining "A Ship Comes into the Harbour" (and the textual responses to which it gave rise) is a simple one: in these texts we encounter both personal indebtedness and literary influence at work. As Woolf and Mansfield struggled over their literary perspectives of *Night and Day,* their private relationship was being negotiated as well. Mansfield had told Woolf that "the suppression" in *Night and Day* was "puzzling," but "accounted for by circumstances." Similarly the "puzzling" "suppression" of their own honest opinions of each other can itself be "accounted for by circumstances": both women were constrained by their mutual mistrust. Mansfield had "irritated" Woolf by her cutting review of *Night and Day.* Equally, Woolf's privileged world, and her portrayal of this world in *Night and Day,* was felt by Mansfield as a betrayal. Thus, Woolf's *Night and Day* and Mansfield's review festered in the back of both their minds, and poisoned later attempts to overcome their differences; their lives now began to drift apart in earnest.

In September of 1920, Woolf made a conscious attempt to separate herself from Katherine and Murry. After turning down an opportunity to do another review for *The Athenaeum,* Woolf noted in her journal, "[t]hank God, I've stepped clear of that Athenaeum world, with its reviews, editions, lunches, & tittle tattle—I should like never to meet a writer again" (*DVW* 2:66). Woolf made no further mention of Mansfield in the journal until December, when she remarked on the publication of *Bliss and Other Stories:* "everyone's book is out—Katherine's, Murry's, Eliot's. None have I read so far. I was happy to hear K. abused the other night. Now Why? Partly from some obscure feeling that she advertises herself; or Murry does it for her [. . .] yet in my heart I must think her good, since I'm glad to hear her abused" (*DVW* 2: 78–9). Woolf acknowledges her ambivalence toward Mansfield here, realizing that she "must think her good," since she "likes to hear her abused." Despite Woolf's claims of their mutual candor, however, she was clearly unable to confide these mixed feelings to Mansfield.

Woolf admits above, for instance, that she liked to "hear [Mansfield] abused," but she nevertheless wrote a congratulatory letter to Mansfield on this same day. In this note, Woolf declares: "I wish you were here to enjoy your triumph—still more that we might talk about your book—For what's the use of telling you how glad and indeed proud I am?" (*LVW* 2:449). This letter, which Woolf described in her journal as "insincere/sincere," is a further example of a failure in their friendship.[17] Although both Woolf and Mansfield claimed to be "proud" of one another, each secretly harbored doubts about the sincerity and talents of the other. Instead of expressing their conflicting feelings with the openness they claimed to share, however, the two seem rather to have avoided any such confrontation. As Woolf herself put it, she felt "[w]hat's the use of telling you" (*LVW* 2:449)? The physical distance between the two women had also played a part in the dissolution of their friendship; at this time Mansfield was convalescing in Menton. Woolf wrote to Mansfield there in February of 1921, but it was to be the last letter between them: Mansfield never replied.[18]

In the face of her advancing illness and constant relocations, Mansfield composed some of her most noted stories, including "The Garden Party," "At The Bay," "The Doll's House," and others in a burst of productivity in 1921. By contrast, 1921 was a frustrating year for Woolf in creative terms.[19] In January, for example, Woolf noted in her diary that she was at a crisis with *Jacob's Room,* which she had hoped to complete by the previous Christmas.[20] This "crisis" was prolonged, and Woolf was eventually forced to put aside any serious work on the novel for many months. By April, she had all but given up on *Jacob's Room,* remarking in her diary: "I'm a failure as a writer. I'm out of fashion; old; shan't do any better" (*DVW* 2:106). Woolf's self-criticism here may merely be the result of her creative crisis, but it is interesting to note that the words she employs to denigrate her efforts echo those Mansfield used in her critique of *Night and Day.* By describing her own work as "out of fashion" and "old," that is, Woolf "names" her failure in the terms that Mansfield's review had provided. In this moment of self-doubt, then, as Woolf's attempt to create "a new form for a novel" seemed doomed, Mansfield's critique may have taken on an added potency. Mansfield, as Woolf knew, had called for an "age of experiment," and on this day Woolf believed her own experimental novel to be a "failure." Once again, Woolf put *Jacob's Room* aside.

In February of the following year, Woolf bemoaned the state of *Jacob's Room* in light of Mansfield's own productivity, and wrote in her diary that Mansfield "bursts upon the world in glory next week" (with *The Garden Party and Other Stories).* She then complained that by the time *Jacob's Room* appears it will seem "sterile acrobatics" (*DVW* 2:161). Perhaps in response to Mansfield's recent accomplishments, Woolf began to work on *Jacob's Room* again in March. As she noted in her journal at this time: "So what does it matter if K. M. soars in the newspapers, & runs up sales skyhigh? Ah, I have found a way of putting her in her place. The more she is praised, the more I am convinced she is bad" (*DVW* 2:170–1). Having thus put Mansfield "in her place," Woolf proceeded with *Jacob's Room,* completing it at last in July 1922.

That month, Woolf noted Leonard's impression of the work as "unlike any other novel." While his assessment may be true, this new "form" can also be read as a response both to Mansfield's "Prelude" and her review of *Night and Day.* But what is the nature of this response? Did Woolf's personal jealousy of Mansfield's "skyhigh sales" and "soaring" popularity, for instance, lead her to attempt to "overwrite" Mansfield? Or is it possible that Woolf saw Katherine Mansfield as an inspirational muse, a female precursor pushing her toward greater achievements, in the way that Gilbert and Gubar might envision? The examination that follows indicates that neither of these paradigms can adequately account for the variety of textual connections between these Mansfield texts and Woolf's *Jacob's Room.*

From the opening page of *Jacob's Room,* the novel's association with Mansfield's work is, I believe, quite clear. Each moment in these early pages can be read as a negotiation of one of Mansfield's critical imperatives or fictional images. The first sign of the text's indebtedness to Mansfield is its setting. As I noted earlier, in her review of *Night and Day* Mansfield claimed that the reason she disliked the novel was that it denied the changes wrought by the war. There, Mansfield disparaged the world of Woolf's characters, noting: "It is so far away, so shut and sealed from us to-day. What could be more remote than the house at Cheyne Walk [. . .] and the knowledge that within a young creature is playing Mozart" ("Ship" 1227). In this appraisal, Mansfield does not question Woolf's brilliance, but her relevance, as she asks: "What could be more remote"? Woolf's novel *Jacob's Room,* as if written in response to this critique, begins on a beach in Cornwall, perhaps as far removed from Cheyne Walk in scenery and temperament as Woolf could imagine. It was here, in Cornwall, that Woolf had fantasized she would first meet Mansfield, and thus it is possible that Woolf had Mansfield in mind when choosing this location. This image of a confrontation with Mansfield "on a rock or in the sea" (*LVW* 2:107), which Woolf described to Lytton Strachey, informs my reading of the early scenes of *Jacob's Room,* which she located there.

By placing her novel in so remote a setting, Woolf appears to have been reacting to Mansfield's criticism of *Night and Day* on more than one count. Indeed, the entire opening chapter of the novel can be read as Woolf's attempt to "accost" Mansfield on the beach at Cornwall. In Woolf's struggle to create a "new form for a novel," that is, the first chapter of *Jacob's Room* serves as a battleground, as it answers Mansfield's criticism of "the aloofness" of Woolf's writings, and actively refigures moments from Mansfield's own "Prelude." A further indication of Woolf's intention to address Mansfield's "fact of a new world" is found in the name of the first character the reader encounters: Betty Flanders. As the action of the first chapter takes place around the turn of the century, the proleptic quality of Betty's surname implies that like the landscape of Flanders at this time, Betty is unaware of her future role as a victim of a war as yet unimagined. Thus on this opening page, Woolf appears to overturn Mansfield's critique of her artistic vision as "remote" and unaware of the concerns of the postwar world. Through Woolf's naming of Jacob's mother, Woolf immediately foreshadows the movements of Jacob's life, locating him as a victim. If Betty Flanders, as a mother, represents Jacob's "original place," her name simultaneously connotes his final, figurative resting-place in the historical imagination, the site of several of the most devastating World War I battles: Flanders fields. Betty Flanders' name thus betokens the whole of her son's life: Jacob's Womb, Jacob's Room, Jacob's Tomb.

In her review, Mansfield had also attacked Woolf's work for its coldness ("it makes us feel old and chill"). In defiance of any such critique, however, Woolf's Betty Flanders is shown as overcome by emotion from the start. Betty is at first seen writing, but is soon interrupted by her uncontrollable tears: "Slowly welling from the point of her gold nib, pale blue ink dissolved the full stop; for there her pen stuck; her eyes fixed, and tears slowly filled them. The entire bay quivered; the lighthouse wobbled" (*Jacob* 7). As the text's very first images dissolve in tears, like Betty Flanders' letter, this open display of sentiment suggests Woolf's intention to move away from her earlier "aloofness." Betty Flanders' weeping washes away the distanced stance that Mansfield had sensed in *Night and Day.* It is also possible, however, to read this first sequence in a different way: the emotion that Betty displays may also be interpreted as Woolf's critique of Mansfield's "cheap sentimentality."

As Leonard Woolf remarked in his autobiography, both he and Virginia felt that the "sticky sentimentality" that Mansfield's works evoked was the result of a corruption. In the Woolfs' view, Murry had imposed this overblown sentimentality upon his wife's work, thus obscuring her natural gifts for cynicism, realism, and humor (*Beginning Again* 203–5). This notion of emotional "corruption" informs Woolf's opening scene; Betty Flanders' tears blur her view of the world around her, making the lighthouse "wobble" and the bay "quiver." These tears, moreover, distort the meaning of the words Betty writes, "dissolving the full stop." As Woolf's novel begins, then, does she suggest that too much emotion, too many tears, serve only to corrupt one's image of the world? Perhaps this passage should be read as a defense against Mansfield's critique of Woolf's "aloofness." Here, that is, Woolf demonstrates that emotional control is necessary to the clarity of a writer's vision, and to the quality of a writer's text.

Recalling Woolf's intention years earlier to "accost" Mansfield on the rocks in Cornwall, I further question whether Betty Flanders, sitting on these same rocks, is in some way Woolf's portrait of Mansfield. Betty Flanders is, after all, a writer whose emotions distort the intelligibility of her texts. Like Mansfield herself, she has been forced by tragedy to move house. "[N]othing for it but to leave" (*Jacob* 7), Betty Flanders repeats, and the opening scene illustrates the aftermath of that upheaval, of being packed "like herring in a barrel" (7). That Woolf's novel begins with an uprooted family also indicates the indebtedness of *Jacob's Room* to another of Mansfield's works: "Prelude" similarly begins with the scene of a family on moving day.

As their respective stories open, both Woolf and Mansfield explore the emotional strain that the mothers of these families undergo as a result of their relocations. While Betty Flanders composes tear-stained letters, in the first scene of "Prelude" Linda Burnell speaks with a "voice trembling with fatigue and excitement" ("Prelude" 11). If these fictional mothers are thus emotionally linked, their children seem also to be connected. In both texts, for example, the children are introduced in the negative, and described as being without a space. At the start of Mansfield's "Prelude," the reader finds that "[t]here was not an inch of room for Lottie and Kezia in the buggy" ("Prelude" 11). Woolf introduces the Flanders children as follows: "'Well, if Jacob doesn't want to play' (the shadow of Archer, her eldest son, fell across the notepaper)" (*Jacob* 7). Both Woolf and Mansfield, then, mark the children in their stories as an afterthought, an absence. Jacob "doesn't want to play," Archer is a shadow, and Lottie and Kezia are left behind by their own mother. Linda Burnell sets out instead with her holdalls and boxes, the "absolute necessities that [she] will not let out of [her] sight for one instant" ("Prelude" 11).

If, unlike Linda Burnell, Betty Flanders is depicted as concerned for her children, Betty's thoughts are nevertheless, like Linda's, far away. Linda contemplates "casting" her children off ("Prelude" 11), while Betty Flanders thinks of Scarborough and Captain Barfoot: "[i]t was her native town" (*Jacob* 8). Mansfield's critique may also have informed Woolf's choice of Scarborough as the home of Betty Flanders. As I noted earlier, Mansfield had written in her review of *Night and Day* that the "strangeness" of that novel lies "in her lack of any sign that she has made a perilous voyage—the absence of any scars" ("Ship" 1227). I read the opening scene of *Jacob's Room* as, in part, a response to each one of these critiques. As Betty Flanders' tears defy any accusation of "aloofness," the "accident" and consequent uprooting of the Flanders family fulfills Mansfield's call for evidence of a "perilous voyage." Betty Flanders herself, whose name calls to mind wartime loss, answers Mansfield's last critique of the "absence of any scars" in Woolf's work. Not only does Woolf locate Betty Flanders as a future victim of the war, but also through her troping Betty is already scarred, being in fact from *Scar*-borough.

As I propose, Woolf was responding to Mansfield's critique "A Ship Comes into the Harbour" in this first scene of *Jacob's Room,* and that idea is strengthened by Woolf's use of nautical tropes in these passages; the bay that Woolf describes here could be a reinvention of the "harbour" that Mansfield envisioned in her article. There, Mansfield saw "the strange sight of *Night and Day* sailing into port serene and resolute." In *Jacob's Room,* however, the "quiet perfection" of that "ship" that Mansfield decried becomes an illusion for Betty Flanders as "the mast of Mr. Connor's little yacht was bending like a wax candle in the sun" (*Jacob* 7). In this scene, then, Woolf reimagines Mansfield's metaphor as a mirage, and in doing so may be further commenting on the sentimentality that she felt corrupted Mansfield's own work. For Betty Flanders, the quivering bay, the wobbling lighthouse, and melting yacht-mast are not only a temporary illusion, they are in essence *brought about by* her show of emotion. A quick "wink" restores these visions to their former perfection ("[t]he mast was straight; the waves were regular; the lighthouse was upright"), but it cannot redeem Betty's blurred letters: "the blot had spread" (*Jacob* 7). As this passage suggests, in Woolf's view even a momentary lapse into sentimentality permanently spoils one's text.

In her depiction of Betty's emotional illusion, Woolf appears to point to a connection between Betty and Mansfield by employing a trope that is found in the opening of "Prelude." At the beginning of Mansfield's story, there is "not an inch of room" for the children, and as Pat the handyman "swung them on top of the luggage they wobbled" ("Prelude" 11). While Mansfield here uses the term "wobble" to hint at the insecurity of the neglected Burnell children, the word takes on a different meaning in Woolf's opening paragraph. In *Jacob's Room,* it is not Betty's children who "wobble," but rather Betty's view of the bay: "The entire bay quivered; the lighthouse wobbled" (*Jacob* 7). The presence of this unusual word in the openings of both texts demands my attention, as does the difference in emphasis between Woolf's "wobble" and Mansfield's. Mansfield employs the word metaphorically, to symbolize the insecurity of Lottie and Kezia, while Woolf uses the term to suggest a temporary illusory change in Betty's vision. Thus, Woolf's reinterpretation of Mansfield's trope can again be read as a critique of Mansfield's "cheap realities." Unlike the Burnell children's very real dilemma, that is, the wobbling lighthouse that Betty sees is merely a mirage, which is brought about by her overtly displayed emotions.

As *Jacob's Room* continues, nautical metaphors, which recall Mansfield's review, continue to be echoed in the names of the men and the places of which Betty thinks. Woolf's use of language thus voices further indebtedness to Mansfield: "Scarborough is seven hundred miles from Cornwall: Captain Barfoot is in Scarborough: Seabrook is dead" (*Jacob* 7). By referring to the seaside locations of Cornwall and Scarborough, and naming "Sea-brook" and the "Captain," Woolf alludes to Mansfield's "A Ship Comes into the Harbour" on a linguistic level. Mansfield had envisioned lingering "down at the harbour, as it were, watching the new ships being builded [sic]" ("Ship" 1227). In my reading, Woolf provides Mansfield with her own view of that harbor, of the illusory quality of overt "scars" and of the most intriguing of those "new ships"—her own novel *Jacob's Room*.

In this reading, therefore, Woolf was negotiating Mansfield's review of *Night and Day* in the opening of *Jacob's Room*. Nevertheless, any definitive understanding of Woolf's response to that text is complicated by the introduction of another character to the novel. As if anticipating further critiques of her own art, Woolf offers the reader a panacea through the thoughts of a fictional artist: a painter on the beach named Charles Steele. Like Woolf herself, Steele is concerned with the critical reception of his work. Musing over his latest painting, for example, he concludes "[t]he critics would say it was too pale, for he was an unknown man exhibiting obscurely" (*Jacob* 8). Just as Mansfield had perceived *Night and Day* to be flawed by its serenity and cultivation, Steele imagines that his own critics will decry his work as "too pale." As I argued above, in the earlier passages from *Jacob's Room*, Woolf appears to confront Mansfield's censures of her writing. Soon after, Woolf portrays Steele himself as preempting the critique of "paleness" that he fears; upon hearing Archer's cry of "Ja-cob! Ja-cob!," Steele "struck the canvas a hasty violet-black dab" (*Jacob* 8).

Thus, Steele's location in Woolf's novel, combined with his preemptive strike of black paint in defiance of his imagined critics, identifies him at some level with Woolf herself. This view is further confirmed by his self-congratulatory remark, "Ah, one may learn to paint at fifty!" (*Jacob* 9). Woolf would later repeat this phrase in her diary: upon the completion of *Jacob's Room,* Woolf noted "there's no doubt in my mind that I have found out how to begin (at 40) to say something in my own voice" (*DVW* 2:186). This linguistic connection between Woolf and Steele hints at other similarities. Like Charles Steele, Woolf is self-congratulatory about her work: in this diary entry she too feels that she has finally found her voice. But Steele may also represent a darker aspect of Woolf's art. Importantly, neither Woolf's novel nor Steele's painting are solely the products of their creators' artistic visions, as both works are indebted to outside forces. In the case of the painting, Archer's cry of "Ja-cob!" (foreshadowing Bonamy's lament after Jacob's death) calls forth Steele's successful use of black paint: "it was just *that* note which brought the rest together" (*Jacob* 9). Through Woolf's later repetition of this cry, Jacob's eventual death seems to proleptically provide the darkness that Steele's "too pale" painting requires. Similarly, Mansfield's call for an awareness of the postwar world colored Woolf's *Jacob's Room.* Just as Archer's cry changed the tone of Steele's painting, Woolf's text is itself darkened by the shadow of the war.

The character of Steele may thus function as a kind of alter ego for Woolf within the text, an artist who is childless, "yet loving children" (*Jacob* 8). He is also, however, an artist of limited ability, unable to sketch fully the emotional Betty Flanders. If I read Betty Flanders as a re-creation of Mansfield (as is suggested by her location on the rocks in Cornwall, and the blurring impact of emotion on her writing) and Steele as a projection of Woolf, an interesting interpretation of the novel is produced. Here, Woolf draws a distinction between Mansfield's artistic vision and her own. As the opening scene of *Jacob's Room* recalls, Mansfield had once depicted insecurity through the physical "wobbling" of the Burnell children, and dismissed Woolf's writing for its "absence of scars." Woolf's own text responds by relying on a disembodied stance, critiquing that "wobbling" vision as an illusion. Thus, the sadness and loss of *Jacob's Room* are not depicted by the scars that Mansfield called for, but by a voice "[p]ure from all body. Pure from all passion" (*Jacob* 8–9). The "fact of a new world" that Mansfield further required is also seen here as Woolf suggests the impact that the war will have on both Betty and Steele. The opening passage hints, for example, that Betty's words and visions are distorted by her emotional response to the coming war: Betty cries because Jacob will die. By contrast, Steele, whose very name articulates his cold and unimpressionable nature, is presumably able to maintain his vision. Indeed, rather than allowing the war and the loss of Jacob to blur his work, Steele employs that sadness to deepen it.

If Woolf had envisioned Steele as a steadfast representative of her own artistic sensibilities, the power of Steele's distanced stance is nevertheless undermined by his inability to sketch Betty Flanders completely. At the moment he congratulates himself on employing the black paint, he sees: "a cloud over the bay. Mrs. Flanders rose, slapped her coat this side and that to get the sand off, and picked up her black parasol" (*Jacob* 9). Steele's brief revelation is gone forever, and the painting must remain unfinished. I would argue that this moment in the text is a dangerous one for Woolf, in which the pride and aloofness of the artist she created result in his failure to realize his vision fully: for Steele, no less than for the emotional Betty Flanders, that vision has become blurred. The "danger" that I see for Woolf in this passage is in its challenge to the objective "Steel-ey" stance that the text propounds in its initial pages. There, through Betty Flanders' tears, Woolf depicts overt sentimentality as the foil of artistic clarity. Charles Steele's incomplete painting, however, defies that argument: the failure of his painting is the result of Steele's hyperobjectivity, his cold unbending nature. Thus, if Woolf had attempted to demean a corrupted "sentimental" Mansfieldian stance in the opening of *Jacob's Room,* Steele's unfinished painting interrupts that critique. Instead, Steele's own weakness points to the inadequacy of the opposing position. His inability to complete the painting suggests that "aloofness," like sentimentality, can "corrupt" the clarity of an artist's vision.

That Woolf herself sensed a difficulty in the passage is indicated by the abrupt shift in the text that follows it. Once Steele's revelation is portrayed as unrealized there is no further mention of him. Instead, Woolf turns quickly to Jacob's point of view: "[t]he rock was one of those tremendously solid brown, or rather black, rocks" (9). In this swift movement I sense not only the "danger" of this moment for Woolf, but also her indebtedness to Mansfield. Here, the rocks upon which Woolf once imagined meeting Mansfield are transformed into "something primitive" (9), and Jacob's consciousness is entered via a scene that echoes "Prelude." Climbing to the top of the rock, Jacob grabs a "huge crab," and placing it is his bucket is about to jump down when he sees: "stretched entirely rigid, side by side, their faces very red, an enormous man and woman" (9). After seeing the couple and their "large red faces" (9), Jacob runs "deliberately " but "very non-chalantly" (10) away from them.

The origin of Jacob's fright, I would argue, can be found in the similar unnamed anxiety that plagues Mansfield's Kezia in "Prelude." As I noted previously, while riding in the buggy away from her old home, Kezia tells the storeman that: " I often dream that animals rush at me—even camels—and while they are rushing, their heads swell, e-enormous" ("Prelude" 17). Both Woolf and Mansfield thus employ these "enormous heads" to provoke fear in the children of their respective stories. These similar images nevertheless function very differently in each text. Kezia sees these swelling and rushing heads in her dreams, thus reproducing her mother's own anxieties, and establishing her fear as fated and inherited. Jacob's encounter with the "large red faces," by contrast, is merely a momentary distraction, an interruption in his adventures.

Indeed, Jacob's position in this scene is itself echoic of the conclusion of "Prelude." As Jacob runs "deliberately" but "very non-chalantly" (10) away, he seems to walk in the shadow of Kezia, who "tiptoed away, far too quickly and airily" (60). Both children thus take on a deliberate and disingenuous stance of calm in the face of fear: Their nonchalance and airiness is a mask for their primal fears of maternal loss. A similar refiguring of an image from "Prelude" that voices the children's shared fear of abandonment occurs soon after Jacob's frightening encounter by the rocks. As Jacob runs along the beach seeking comfort from this sudden shock, he heads toward an image he believes to be his "Nanny": "'Nanny! Nanny!' he cried, sobbing the words out on the crest of each gasping breath. The waves came round her. She was a rock" (*Jacob* 10). Like the large-headed figures, Jacob's vision of his nanny also recalls an image in the opening of "Prelude." There, Kezia rushes after her grandmother's buggy: "At the last moment Kezia let go Lottie's hand and darted towards the buggy. 'I want to kiss my granma good-bye again.' But she was too late" ("Prelude" 12). Both children are left temporarily distraught by the loss of their source of comfort, and struggle to control their tears, as "Kezia bit her lip" ("Prelude" 12), and Jacob's "face composed itself. He was about to roar" (*Jacob* 10).

Although these sequences in "Prelude" and *Jacob's Room* are, therefore, similar, the actual loss that they articulate is not. In "Prelude," Kezia's grandmother represents maternal love, and the moment in which her buggy drives away confirms her as "orphaned" and abandoned. As Kezia grows more accustomed to the insecurity of her mother's affections, she learns to submerge her tears in a false airiness that we see in the tale's close. The "Nanny" Jacob loses, however, is, like Betty Flanders' wobbling lighthouse, a mirage, an illusion caused by an outburst of tears, and thus not a measurable loss of any kind. There is, in this sense, no *con*textual explanation within Woolf's novel for Jacob's forced bravery and nonchalance: unlike Kezia, Jacob has lost nothing. Instead, I suggest, Jacob has inherited this response *inter*textually—from the hard-earned mask worn by Mansfield's Kezia, the child who is, in so many ways, Jacob's "prelude."

Just as the "primitive rock" that harbors Jacob's frightening vision may be a refiguring of the rocks upon which Woolf planned to "accost" Mansfield, the words and images of Mansfield's "Prelude" are themselves reimagined in *Jacob's Room*. Moreover, as Woolf overwrites Mansfield's text here, she frequently evacuates Mansfield's tropes of their sentimentality. Kezia's dreams, for example, are shown by Mansfield to invade her day to day life, but Jacob is not confronted with dream animals; two real people on the beach frighten him. Furthermore, Jacob's "real" encounter does not haunt him as Kezia's dreams do. Again, in "Prelude," Kezia's disappointment at being unable to kiss her grandmother goodbye causes her to bite her lip and fumble for a handkerchief. In *Jacob's Room,* on the other hand, Woolf sculpts Jacob's Nanny in stone, thus removing all sentiment from her tableaux of a child crying out for comfort. Unlike Mansfield's grandmother/child scene, Woolf constructs Jacob's abandonment as less than tragic. Indeed, like the "large red faces," Jacob forgets his loss when he is suddenly distracted:

> He was lost.
>   There he stood. His face composed itself. He was about to roar when, lying among the black sticks and straw under the cliff, he saw a whole skull— perhaps a cow's skull, a skull, perhaps, with the teeth in it (*Jacob* 10).

Images of large heads and lost maternal figures appear in both Woolf and Mansfield's texts, and similarly, this "[c]lean, white, wind-swept, sand-rubbed" skull (*Jacob* 10) that Jacob discovers may itself have an origin in "Prelude." In "Prelude," however, this "skull" is found in a "primitive" and bloodied state. In this disturbing moment in Mansfield's story, Pat the handyman entertains the children of Kezia's rural neighborhood by chopping off a duck's head in front of them:

> "Come with me," he said to the children, "and I'll show you how the kings of Ireland chop the head off a duck."
>   [Kezia asks Pat] "Is it a real duck's head? One from the paddock?"
>   "It is," said Pat. [. . .] He loved little children ("Prelude" 44).

I would argue that the skull that Jacob finds might be a reimagined descendant of the headless duck described here, and that Pat himself is transformed into an altered, and less threatening, form in *Jacob's Room.*

In Mansfield's tale, the character "Pat" is said to "love little children," and this sentiment is also shared by Woolf's character, Mr. Steele, who is "[e]xasperated by the noise, yet loving children" (*Jacob* 9). While this similarity may suggest that the two figures are connected, there are also several differences between them—differences that concern ideas of physicality and sentiment. Pat, for example, is a strong, burly, and hairy handyman, while Woolf's Charles Steele is a middle-aged painter of pale-paintings. Thus, in my reading, Woolf has removed the corporeal threat to the children that is implied in Mansfield's text, by redesigning Pat as an older, painterly character. As she places the children in her novel under the watchful eye of Mr. Steele, Woolf trades Pat's tomahawk for Mr. Steele's paintbrush. The name "Steele" also redresses the physicality of Mansfield's character, as the original "Pat" (which evokes the meaning "to touch") is disassociated from a subtext of contact by being hammered into "Steele." In both texts, these male characters create an image to be viewed: Pat's beheading of the duck like "the kings of Ireland," and Steele's pale painting. There is, however an important distinction between their respective creations: the "image" that Pat offers is anything but "pale"—it is, of course, blood red.

In this interpretation, then, just as Woolf cleansed the bloody duck's head and turned it into the white skull that Jacob finds, she also removed the blood stain from the character of Pat, and recreated him as the inoffensive Mr. Steele. If Woolf has drained the blood from these images, however, there are still remnants to remind us of the connections between her symbolism and Mansfield's own. As Jacob picks up this skull, for instance, Woolf fore-shadows his early death, his close proximity to decay. Likewise, in "Prelude," Kezia herself is linguistically associated with the ill-fated duck, as Mansfield employs the term "lump" to describe them both. In the scene cited above, as Pat prepares to decapitate the duck, he hands a second duck to one of the children: "He nearly sobbed with delight when Pat gave the white lump into his arms" ("Prelude" 46). Used here to describe the helpless, innocent crea-ture, the word "lump" echoes Linda Burnell's vision of her children at the start of the tale, as there she "could not possibly have held a lump of a child" on her lap "for any distance" (11).

The connection with Kezia, which begins with this linguistic link, takes on a sinister shade as Pat prepares the duck for death:

> Pat grabbed the duck by the legs, laid it flat across the stump, and almost at the same moment down came the little tomahawk and the duck's head flew off the stump. Up the blood spurted over the white feathers and over his hand. [. . .] "Watch it!" shouted Pat. He put down the body and it began to waddle—with only a long spurt of blood where the head had been; it began to pad away without a sound towards the steep bank that led to the stream. . . . That was the crowning wonder ("Prelude" 46).

As the headless duck waddles away, it recalls the "big naked" baby's head with a gaping bird's mouth, of which Kezia's mother had dreamed. Linda's fears of the baby bird's needs are confronted here as the hungry mouths of her dream are silenced by the decapitation of the duck. Later, the hunger of her own children will also be silenced, as they sit down to feed upon the body of this duck, presented that evening for dinner. That Linda's children, and Kezia in particular, are associated with the beheaded duck, suggests an interesting subtext at work in this scene. Linda's chil-dren must not only feed themselves, but also feed on themselves, in order to survive.

Mansfield's association of Kezia with the duck evokes a complex reading of "Prelude," both through the death of the duck and its later consumption. In the scene above, Linda's anxiety over "feeding" her children is "silenced" by the sacrifice of the duck, but Kezia's own, previously unnamed dread finds voice in this moment:

But Kezia suddenly rushed at Pat and flung her arms round his legs and butted her head as hard as she could against his knees.

"Put head back! Put head back!" she screamed (46).

Kezia's scream articulates her fear of "IT," of rushing and swelling animals, as her own identification with the duck is made manifest. Aware of her mother's desire to silence her children, in this scene Kezia symbolically battles against this silencing. As both she and Linda are shown to "hate" objects that rush at them, Kezia enacts a revolt against her mother, by transforming herself into just such a rushing thing, as she "suddenly rushed at Pat."

I argued above that Woolf felt Mansfield's texts were "corrupted" by sentiment, and that her own desire to avoid such "corruption" seems to have informed *Jacob's Room*. By cleansing the blood from Mansfield's imagery, Woolf perhaps attempted to remove the stain of sentiment from her own novel. In the passage above, for example, Kezia's scream is positioned as a fight for her life. In *Jacob's Room*, motifs from this pivotal scene also surface, but there they are stripped of such emotions. Unlike Kezia, who shouts at the duck's death, Jacob is calmed by the skull he finds: "He was about to roar when [. . .] he saw a whole skull—perhaps a cow's skull, a skull perhaps with the teeth in it" (10). In this scene, I would argue, Mansfield's story again functions as a "prelude" to *Jacob's Room*—for it is here that we find the body that belongs to Jacob's newfound skull. This skull is a remnant of the duck that the Burnell's enjoy for dinner. Perhaps. The skull that Jacob finds, though, is not clearly identified by Woolf: it is a cow's skull to Jacob, a sheep's jaw to Mrs. Flanders, but not, it seems, a duck's skull. Is the body to which this skull was once joined, then, to be found elsewhere in Mansfield's story? Might it be the skull of the ram who "has horns and runs for you," the ram of which Kezia is frightened? The disembodied, clean, white skull that Jacob finds could be seen as a remnant of the bloodied and enormous rushing creatures in Mansfield's text. If so, the duck's head that caused Kezia's scream in "Prelude" reappears in *Jacob's Room* as a nonthreatening, and even calming, influence: Jacob does not "roar" *because* he sees the skull. The life and death struggle of Kezia is depicted in "Prelude" by the horrific vision of the walking, decapitated duck. This horror is emptied out of Woolf's version of this scene, and death itself depicted as a mere novelty: a skull washed up on shore, its clean white bone showing no traces of its bloodied past.

Jacob's Room: Homage to the Lost Brothers

In the passages I examined above, the indebtedness of Woolf's *Jacob's Room* to Mansfield's "Prelude" raises questions about the literary relationship between these two writers. In *Jacob's Room,* Woolf refigures images and tropes from Mansfield's work, and in doing so devalues these tropes as overly sentimental. Throughout her text Woolf points to the danger of relying on "cheap realities" to portray one's artistic vision. Can Mansfield be seen as Woolf's "precursor," because Woolf appears to have reworked and overwritten the opening of "Prelude" in her novel? Such a Bloomian reading of *Jacob's Room* calls into serious question Gilbert and Gubar's alternative paradigm of "shared" literary influence among women writers: Woolf's bitter response to Mansfield's sentimentality in this work indicates that their relationship was less than "nurturing." Indeed, it does seem as though the animosity *and* the affection between them surfaced and informed their published texts. The equivocal nature of Woolf's negotiations of Mansfield's influence therefore could also be accounted for by Bloom's formulation: in his view such ambivalence would be a necessary psychic defense against one's precursor.

For Woolf, however, these feelings evolved not only in defense *against* Mansfield's greater success, but also *in sympathy with* Mansfield's own reaction to a personal tragedy. This more complicated reading of their relationship, and of the resulting connections among their texts, is informed by a sad and coincidental misfortune that each of these women underwent: both Woolf and Mansfield suddenly and unexpectedly lost a brother.[21] These biographical events, I suggest, no less than any defensive "psychic response," inflected both "Prelude" and *Jacob's Room.* Just as Mansfield had resolved in writing "Prelude" to compose "something nostalgic" to be dedicated to the memory of Leslie, Woolf's own novel contains images connected to her late brother, Thoby. As the critic Robert Kiely states in his essay "*Jacob's Room:* a Study in Still Life," "[t]he parallels between Jacob Flanders and Thoby Stephen are as obvious as the fact that *Jacob's Room* is a work of fiction, not a biography. The Cambridge education, love of literature, visit to Greece, intention to study law, even the awkward good looks and tendency to be tongue tied they have in common" (Kiely 207). As Kiely points out, however, *Jacob's Room* does not function as a biography of Thoby Stephen in a traditional sense, but rather as a sublimation or fictionalization of his loss. Similarly, "Prelude" (which Mansfield had first envisioned concluding with the birth of a boy who would "represent" Leslie) is itself a rendering of a present informed by impending tragedy. The choice of the title points to this project: the story is a "Prelude," a trope that inevitably suggests the future that will follow it.

In writing "Prelude," Mansfield sought to portray a past reimagined through the present, a nostalgia for that which is lost. The textual and linguistic similarities between *Jacob's Room* and "Prelude," moreover, indicate that Woolf found inspiration in her friend's attempt to give voice to her loss. As Woolf searched for "a new form for a novel" during the long months of typesetting "Prelude," she was perhaps moved to employ that "new form" to address her own brother's death. As Sydney Janet Kaplan notes, although "Mansfield wrote [. . .] that she intended [the story] to end with his birth, her final version in 'Prelude' did not include that birth. Her brother is the absent center, the son whose meaning to his parents is still incipient, in potential" (Kaplan 111). Thus, despite her original intention to memorialize Leslie, Mansfield's story ends before the birth of a brother.[22] Woolf's novel, by contrast, follows Jacob to his end. As this difference between the texts suggests, while there are many similarities between "Prelude" and *Jacob's Room,* each is finally the product of a separate artistic vision. Mansfield's story remains fixed in the past, with Leslie still, as Kaplan notes, "incipient, in potential." Woolf's Jacob, however, ventures onto university, adulthood, and finally death. Thus, if the opening pages of *Jacob's Room* recreate, reimagine, and rewrite portions of "Prelude," any analogy between the texts ceases abruptly when Jacob leaves his childhood behind. As if bidding a hasty farewell to the nostalgic children's world of Mansfield's tale, Woolf states suddenly that: "Jacob Flanders, therefore, went up to Cambridge in October, 1906" (*Jacob* 29).

As Jacob grows up and moves away from home, Woolf creates a distance between him and the reader: we will never know any more about Jacob's inner life than we have discovered on the beach in Cornwall. Instead, Jacob is seen through the eyes of other characters, to each of which he appears quite differently. For Mrs. Norman on the train to Cambridge, Jacob is "indifferent, unconscious" (*Jacob* 30). Mrs. Durrant finds him "extraordinarily awkward" yet "so distinguished looking" (*Jacob* 61), and her daughter Clara sees Jacob as "too good—too good" (*Jacob* 63). The inability of the text to portray Jacob definitively thus enacts the loss that Woolf seeks to describe. The pathos of the novel is derived not from Jacob's death per se, but from the ineffability of his life. Although attempting to recreate his character, to remember Jacob, Woolf's novel simultaneously argues that it is impossible to recall someone after their death, since they cannot be truly "known" in life.

In pointing to the fallibility of memories, Woolf also acknowledges being drawn to them: "But something is always impelling one to hum vibrating, like the hawk moth, at the mouth of the cavern of mystery, endowing Jacob Flanders with all sorts of qualities he had not at all [. . .] what remains is mostly a matter of guess work. Yet over him we hang vibrating" (*Jacob* 73). Woolf's admission here of the inability of writers to accurately depict any person or remembrance points to a haunting connection between *Jacob's Room* and "Prelude": both works sought to take on this impossible task. In *Jacob's Room,* I would argue, Woolf acknowledges Mansfield's own attempt to memorialize her lost brother, and employs Mansfield's tale as a "prelude" to her own.

While the first chapter of *Jacob's Room* revises scenes from Mansfield's story, this textual dialogue is, as I noted, broken when Jacob goes to Cambridge in October of 1906. The date that Woolf chose to define this break in the novel is itself important, for it was in fact one month later, in November of 1906, that her own brother Thoby had died. By looking back toward Mansfield's tale, therefore, Woolf allowed its sentimentality and sense of impending doom to foreshadow her own very personal account of loss: having once gone off to Cambridge, Thoby Stephen, like Jacob, never came home again. Before continuing with any comparison of Thoby and Jacob, however, I should note that similar as their stories may be, Jacob is not, of course, purely a fictionalization of Thoby. Indeed, Jacob may also be associated with Mansfield's brother Leslie. Unlike Thoby, Jacob does not die of typhoid fever; Jacob, like Leslie, dies in the war. Through such intimate connections with "Prelude," I suggest, Woolf's novel can be read not only as an attempt to overwrite Mansfield's story, but also, in a sense, to *fulfill* it.

As I noted above, Mansfield originally planned to end her story with the birth of a brother. She did not, finally, use this as the conclusion of "Prelude." Thus the tale that was to be a memorial to Leslie does not actually contain a character to "represent" him at all. Instead, as Kaplan suggests, through the characters of Kezia, Beryl, Linda, and Mrs. Fairfield, Mansfield's story explores the "female life cycle" (Kaplan 117). Woolf's novel, on the other hand, looks directly at the life of the male child who will die tragically young. In this way, *Jacob's Room* proceeds from the point that Mansfield's "Prelude" avoided: the boy becomes a man, the man dies in the war. If one accepts this possibility, a reductive interpretation of *Jacob's Room* as a psychic battleground for Woolf's anxiety and indebtedness toward Mansfield must be incomplete. Although Woolf's text does display the kind of overwriting of her "precursor" that Bloom's paradigm of influence describes, her fulfillment of Mansfield's project also evinces the "shared generosity" that Bloom decries as evidence of "weakness." Similarly, the "nurturing" muse scenario that Gilbert and Gubar posit is itself subverted by Woolf's deconstruction of the sentimentality of Mansfield's text in *Jacob's Room*. In fact, the intricate nature of the connections between these two works is further complicated by their respective conclusions, as the loss that each writer sought to describe is finally confronted quite differently.

The final scene in "Prelude" functions as a shift in the text, a broken moment, which is offered to the reader as such through Kezia's thoughts. As Kezia sits in front of the dressing table mirror, Mansfield avoids depicting the self-reflection that this scene might be expected to symbolize. Instead, Kezia forces her calico cat to peer into the glass: "'Now look at yourself,' she said sternly" ("Prelude" 60). Mansfield thus disallows a moment of self-realization for Kezia by substituting the cat's reflection for her own. Nonetheless, in this scene Mansfield also reinforces the hazards of peering into the mirror, for "[t]he calico cat was so overcome by the sight that it toppled over backwards and bumped and bumped on to the floor" ("Prelude" 60).

Although Mansfield does not allow Kezia to pause for self-reflection, the child is nevertheless shown to sense the danger implicit in doing so:

> And the top of the cream jar flew through the air and rolled like a penny in a round on the linoleum—and did not break.
>   *But for Kezia it had broken the moment it flew through the air,* and she picked it up, hot all over, and put it back on the dressing-table.
>   Then she tiptoed away, far too quickly and airily. . . . (60, my emphasis)

The broken lid is portrayed as an illusion, Kezia's mirage while sitting in front of the mirror. The "heat" that this vision produces, more importantly, foreshadows the tragedy that will befall the Burnell family: something will break, something will fall, but not now, not yet. By avoiding her own image in the mirror, Kezia thus denies the heat that her fear and illusion have created; she "tiptoed away, far too quickly and airily. . . ." ("Prelude" 60).

Thus, the story that was originally to end with the birth of a brother, instead concludes with this tableaux of anxiety and avoidance. Might Kezia's refusal to face herself therefore hint at Mansfield's own need to "tiptoe" away from a confrontation with the loss of Leslie? If so, this pattern is repeated throughout "Prelude," as Mansfield walks away from an exploration of her brother's death, both by concentrating on a tale of four women and by removing all trace of Leslie from her story. Even so, Mansfield did not deny the weakness that this avoidance implied: Kezia, we are told, moves away "*far* too quickly and airily . . ." ("Prelude" 60, my emphasis). By passing this judgment on Kezia's actions, Mansfield might in fact be engaging in a critique of her own story, suggesting that she too has shied away "far too quickly" from her original intention to memorialize her brother.

The conclusion of Woolf's novel *Jacob's Room* may also enact a critique of Mansfield's "Prelude." Here, Woolf restores and confronts the very horror of death from which Mansfield had "tiptoed" away. In the final scene of the novel, Mrs. Flanders and Jacob's friend, Bonamy, face the loss of Jacob. This confrontation brings about a curious revelation for Bonamy. Jacob's death, so far from having devastated Bonamy's world, seems instead to have had no tangible impact at all. Jacob, as Bonamy marvels, "'left everything just as it was'" (*Jacob* 176). Despite his realization, the emotional significance of Jacob's absence is voiced by Bonamy as, standing by the window, he cries "'Ja-cob! Ja-cob!'" (*Jacob* 176). As this moment recreates Archer's cry on the beach in the first chapter, Woolf indicates an important connection between the two scenes. The earlier shout of "'Ja-cob! Ja-cob!'" (*Jacob* 8) had the effect of darkening Mr. Steele's painting, and it also called forth a series of breaks in the text: to Mr. Steele's "horror" a cloud appeared over the bay; Mrs. Flanders rose; the reader entered Jacob's consciousness; the painting was left incomplete. The "horror" that Mr. Steele perceives earlier in the text, then, becomes by the end of the novel the "horror" that informs Bonamy's cry. Thus, the reader discovers that Woolf's portrait of Jacob, like Mr. Steele's painting, will remain unfinished.

In the first chapter, Woolf abruptly shifts from this indication of the ultimate inadequacy of art to depict life, to an exploration of Jacob's consciousness. In the conclusion of the novel, however, Woolf returns to confront this observation. Just as Mr. Steele's painting is interrupted, and therefore incomplete, Jacob himself cannot be portrayed adequately. Indeed, as Mrs. Flanders exclaims, there is "'[s]uch confusion everywhere!'" (*Jacob* 176). By thus addressing this confusion, this horror of failure, Woolf may be commenting on the inadequacies in Mansfield's "Prelude," and in her own novel. Both of these works attempt, in part, to pay homage to a brother now dead; but as I have argued, Mansfield was unwilling to explore that loss fully in her text. Like Kezia, perhaps, she could not gaze upon her own reflection for long. While Mansfield and Kezia tiptoe away, however, Woolf, Bonamy, and Mrs. Flanders stay put and face their tragedies. Bonamy, like Kezia, "turns away" from the window out of which he cries, but he is unable to escape the horror of death by doing so. Instead he and Mrs. Flanders are faced with further evidence of Jacob's absence: "'[w]hat am I to do with these, Mr. Bonamy?' She held out a pair of Jacob's old shoes" (176). In these concluding lines, then, Woolf attempts to give voice to the tragedy that Mansfield had cautiously avoided in "Prelude." Unlike Mansfield, Woolf does not tiptoe away from her loss, she cannot in fact *go* anywhere: the shoes are empty.

A final connection between Jacob and Kezia may again demonstrate the complex dialogue between their creators' visions. Kezia creates surprises for her grandmother, filling empty matchboxes with stones and flowers, and hastily, but lovingly, composing the "picture" inside. Jacob, on the other hand, organizes carefully arranged boxes, labeling the insects he collects with "a very fine pen" (23). For Woolf perhaps, Mansfield's "Prelude" was like Kezia's matchboxes; beautiful, but hastily prepared. Nevertheless, the affinities between *Jacob's Room* and "Prelude" indicate that Woolf was deeply indebted to Mansfield's tale, even if she complained of its "cheap realities." Just as Jacob is shown to correct the work of earlier insect collectors, because they were "sometimes wrong" (23), in *Jacob's Room* Woolf attempted to rework Mansfield's tale, choosing her own "very fine pen" to do so.

The differing artistic visions that these two closely connected tales articulate must ultimately disallow any oversimplified reading of Woolf and Mansfield as

either spiritual sisters or psychic rivals. Woolf may have revisited and reimagined motifs from Mansfield's review of *Night and Day* and "Prelude" in the first
chapter of *Jacob's Room,* but her novel also appears to fulfill what "Prelude" had
begun. By continuing the story from which Mansfield had tiptoed away, Woolf
confronts the loss that both texts sought to explore. The difficulty of explicat-
ing their complex relationship in literary terms is perhaps matched only by the
difficulty that Woolf and Mansfield had understanding it in personal terms: by
the time *Jacob's Room* was published, their friendship was at an end. This dissolution might, of course, be read as a "psychic defense" between literary rivals.
More prosaically, though, it may have been the understandable result of the
physical distance between them: as Mansfield's illness progressed she was spend-
ing nearly all her time abroad.

Jacob's Room was published in October of 1922, and, just over two
months later, Katherine Mansfield was dead. Upon hearing of her death
Woolf wrote in her journal, "Katherine has been dead a week and how far
am I obeying her 'do not quite forget Katherine' which I read in one of her
old letters? Am I already forgetting her?" *(DVW* 2:225–6).[23] As this diary
entry continues, Woolf seems very far indeed from forgetting Mansfield:

> It is strange to trace the progress of one's own feelings. Nelly said in her sen-
> sational way at breakfast on Friday "Mrs. Murry's dead! It says so in the
> paper!" At that one feels—what? A shock of relief?—a rival the less? Then con-
> fusion at feeling so little—then, gradually, blankness & disappointment; then
> a depression which I could not rouse myself from all that day *(DVW* 2:226).

As Woolf's conflicting responses of relief, rivalry, blankness, disappointment, and depression gradually unfold, I am reminded of the danger of
confining my interpretation of the connection between her and Mansfield
to any single cause or sentiment.

Woolf's envy of Mansfield was an important and undeniable aspect of
their association, yet other, more generous, feelings also informed her response to Mansfield's death. In this same diary entry, for example, Woolf reflects on the effect of this loss upon her own writing: "When I began to
write, it seemed to me there was no point in writing. Katherine wont read
it. Katherine's my rival no longer. More generously I felt, But though I can
do this better than she could, where is she, who could do what I can't!"
(DVW 2:226). One and a half years later, Woolf would deny this reading of
Mansfield as a different but equal writer. Then she noted in her diary: "if
she'd lived, she'd have written on, & people would have seen that I was the
more gifted—that wd. only have become more & more apparent" *(DVW*
2:317). As this reassessment of their relative skills suggests, Woolf's sense of
Mansfield's worth was far from resolved.

In a diary entry of January 1923 soon after Mansfield's death, Woolf offered another, rather complex and intricate account of her relation to Mansfield:

> What happened was, I suppose, faultfindings & perhaps gossip. She never answered my letter. Yet I still feel, somehow that friendship persists. Still there are things about writing I think of & want to tell Katherine. If I had been in Paris & gone to her, she would have got up & in three minutes, we should have been talking again. Only I could not take the step. The surroundings—Murry & so on—& the small lies & treacheries, the perpetual playing & teasing, or whatever it was, cut away much of the substance of friendship. One was too uncertain. And so one let it all go (*DVW* 2:227).

Thus, in Woolf's view, her relationship with Mansfield was informed by a variety of circumstances, the "surroundings" of their lives. The "faultfinding" and "small lies" she writes of coexisted with feelings of friendship, and the importance of "things about writing." Through *Jacob's Room*'s subtle and peculiar fulfillment of "Prelude," moreover, Woolf's responses to "whatever it was" between them surface repeatedly in her work.

The variety of Woolf's textual negotiations of Mansfield confirms that their association should not be interpreted simply as a battle for supremacy, or as a nurturing "garden" of shared sisterhood. By turns mutually admiring and dismissive, the two are perhaps best understood as collaborators, if at times unwilling ones, in the creation of a new kind of fiction. As Woolf concludes in the diary entry above: "Yet I have the feeling that I shall think of her at intervals all through my life. Probably we had something in common which I shall never find in anyone else" (*DVW* 2:227). Their shared sensibilities and artistic differences, their love of writing, their respective losses, and their literary collaborations, all combined to inform their highly individual, if mutually indebted, texts. There is then no one paradigm for influence that accounts for all of these variables. Just as the cloud passes over the bay, belying the accuracy of Steele's painting, so the complex lives and the inscrutable relationship of Woolf and Mansfield cast their shadow on would-be interpreters of their works. Their intricate texts defy attempts to reduce or confine them through formulas and theories.

Such reductive theories, in fact, may themselves be seen to negotiate the past in the way that Woolf's Jacob responds to his "predecessor" Kezia. Mansfield suggests through her rendering of Kezia's anxious dreams and reveries that this child has inherited the fears of her elders. Later, in turning away from the mirror, Kezia refuses to confront this dilemma. Through the character of Jacob, on the other hand, Woolf addresses the hazards of accepting received wisdom: as Jacob looks out the window, the text questions "[w]as it to receive this gift from the past that the young man came to the window and stood there, looking out across the court?" (*Jacob* 45). This "gift," like the paradigm of influence itself, provides a meaning for the past. A simplified, schematic rendering, it leaves the reader feeling, like Jacob, "satisfied; indeed masterly; [. . .] the sound of the clock conveying to him (it may be) a sense of old buildings and time; and himself the inheritor" (*Jacob* 45).

If Woolf's novel suggests the allure and satisfaction of feeling oneself as an inheritor, it simultaneously points to the pitfalls of such a legacy. The window at which Jacob receives "this gift from the past" will later in the novel be witness to the articulation of his death, through Bonamy's scream "'Ja-cob! Ja-cob!'" (176). Like Kezia's inability to face the future, Jacob's unwary acceptance of "old buildings and time" corresponds to the denial of the intricacies of literary influence that current models evince. To force the convoluted relations of writers' lives and textual debts into the constraints of such theories, is to be like Kezia, shying away from the complexities of reality. These reductive paradigms, that is, ask us to tiptoe away from the mirror, and return like Jacob, dangerously, to the window, satisfied with an inheritance of meanings from the past.

Chapter Five ❦

Ghost Story

Intertextual Hauntings: Virginia Woolf, Katherine Mansfield, and Thomas Hardy

In the previous chapter, I argued that Virginia Woolf's novel *Jacob's Room,* written during Katherine Mansfield's lifetime, could be read, in part, as a complex response to Mansfield and her works. After Mansfield's death in 1923, however, Woolf's writing offers evidence of another kind of negotiation, as she confronted the loss of her friend, "that strange ghost" (*DVW* 2:317), Katherine Mansfield. The intricate nature of this struggle is illustrated by a moment in Woolf's *Mrs. Dalloway,* in which Woolf places Mansfield's words into the mouth of one of her characters. In this scene, the fictional Doris Kilman pleads pathetically: "Don't quite forget me" (*Dalloway* 201). This phrase echoes Mansfield's own, as written in a letter to Woolf in June 1917: Mansfield's note ends "& don't quite forget Katherine" (*CLKM* 1:324). That Woolf was aware of these words *as* Mansfield's is clear: she had remarked on them in her diary shortly after Mansfield's death (*DVW* 2:226). Why, I wonder, might Woolf have employed Mansfield's plea in *Mrs. Dalloway,* and, more important, why would she have given those words to the self-righteous Miss Kilman to voice?

In the context of the novel, Miss Kilman's "[d]on't quite forget me" comes too late. Elizabeth Dalloway, whose affection Miss Kilman longs for, has at this point already "forgotten" her, and like "some dumb creature who has been brought up to a gate for an unknown purpose [. . .] stands there longing to gallop away" (*Dalloway* 200–1). When, in the course of the novel, Elizabeth does "gallop away" for "an unknown purpose," Woolf portrays her leaving as a moment of agony for Miss Kilman, who is "stricken once, twice, thrice by shocks of suffering. She had gone. [. . .] Elizabeth had gone. Beauty had gone, youth had gone" (201). As Woolf then depicts the abandoned Miss Kilman "blunder[ing] off" (201) in despair, one wonders what relationship this character has to the "ghost" whose words she voices.

The character of Miss Kilman can, of course, be read in many ways. She is, for example, shown throughout the text to be a counterpart to Clarissa Dalloway: Miss Kilman and Clarissa both vie for the love of Clarissa's daughter Elizabeth, and while Miss Kilman is a religious activist, Clarissa herself often feels "like a nun" (42). Both characters are also depicted as loving other women. Clarissa considers that "she could not resist sometimes yielding to the charm of a woman [. . .] she did undoubtedly then feel what men felt" (46–7). Similarly, Miss Kilman loves Elizabeth "without jealousy" and fantasizes about her as "a fawn in the open, a moon in a glade" (205). However, Clarissa and Doris Kilman are repeatedly portrayed as opposites in Woolf's text. As the character of Peter Walsh recalls, Clarissa was "[l]ovely in girlhood" (46), but Miss Kilman is by contrast "[h]eavy, ugly, commonplace" (190). Again, early on in the novel, Woolf draws another distinction between these characters, as Clarissa considers "how poor [Miss Kilman] was" and "how rich" Clarissa herself is (16). Later, Miss Kilman reflects that she "did out of her meagre income set aside so much for causes she believed in; whereas [Clarissa] did nothing, believed nothing" (190).

If Clarissa and Miss Kilman thus illustrate differences in cultural status and religious belief, their sexual preferences also suggest an underlying sympathy between the two characters. Clarissa believes that in another life "she would have loved Miss Kilman! But not in this world. No" (17). The distance between Clarissa and Miss Kilman is thus tempered by a subtext of mutual, but guarded, sympathy. Is it possible, then, if we consider this character in light of her articulation of Mansfield's words, that her relation to Clarissa may be interpreted as more than a study of cultural and social difference? Is the lost and forgotten Miss Kilman a ghost of the writer, Katherine Mansfield? Doris Kilman's shabby dress, her cleverness, her poverty, and her commonness (*Dalloway* 16), might all be seen to connect her with Mansfield, but what might this reading of her suggest about Woolf's sense of Mansfield at this time? Could it be related to the "unknown purpose" that causes Elizabeth to "gallop away"? If Miss Kilman is linked in some way to Woolf's perception of Mansfield, her character provides a very confusing portrait; Woolf depicts Kilman with both condescension and sympathy. Moreover, if Woolf was giving voice to Mansfield's words through this character ("[d]on't quite forget"), she did so to evoke a moment of loss, of pathos: Miss Kilman will be forgotten. But what of Katherine Mansfield? Soon after Mansfield's death, Woolf questioned in her diary "[a]m I already forgetting her?" (*DVW* 2:226). The reappearance of Mansfield's words in *Mrs. Dalloway* suggests that Woolf was far from doing so.

In the years 1921 to 1922, however, as their friendship had begun to dissolve, Mansfield is referred to much less frequently in Woolf's letters and journals. Indeed, Mansfield's name is but rarely mentioned in Woolf's papers after her death in early 1923. Could this sharp decrease in Woolf's references to Mansfield demonstrate that Woolf was attempting to "forget" her lost friend during this period? If so, did this wish to "forget" inform the novel that Woolf composed at this time? Perhaps, that is, Elizabeth's "unknown purpose" in leaving Miss Kilman behind originated in Woolf's own "longing" to be free of Mansfield's ghost. Such an interpretation would explicate not only Elizabeth's purpose, but also the "delight" she experiences upon "galloping" away from Miss Kilman. In this reading, Woolf's sense of "relief" upon hearing of Mansfield's death (*DVW* 2:226) is re-enacted by the character of Elizabeth: "did Elizabeth give one thought to poor Miss Kilman who loved her without jealousy, to whom she had been a fawn in the open, a moon in a glade? She was delighted to be free" (*Dalloway* 205).

This interpretation of Elizabeth's emotions as related in some way to Woolf's own raises further questions as *Mrs. Dalloway* concludes. Elizabeth Dalloway's freedom from a demanding relationship with the surrogate maternal figure of Kilman does not ultimately guarantee her independence. Although in the passage I examined above Elizabeth distances herself from Kilman, Elizabeth is not "free" in any sense by the end of the novel. Instead, the character that influences her has merely been replaced. As the novel concludes, Elizabeth, having forgotten Miss Kilman, is firmly at her father's side: "Richard was proud of his daughter. [. . .] That did make her happy" (*Dalloway* 296). Elizabeth's journey in *Mrs. Dalloway,* I would argue, from a mother/muse toward an alignment with a paternal mentor, may parallel Woolf's own, perhaps unconscious, movement in the writing of this novel. Woolf, that is, while striving for freedom from the influence of Mansfield, "galloped away," by turning her thoughts to a writer whom she associated with her father. As the name of Katherine Mansfield begins to vanish from Woolf's private papers, that of another writer appears more and more frequently: that of the novelist Thomas Hardy.

As I described in chapter two, Hardy had a long and complicated relationship with Woolf's father, Leslie Stephen. Woolf's own connection with Hardy began in early 1915, as she wrote to thank him for the poem "The Schreckhorn," which had recently been published in Hardy's volume *Satires and Circumstances:*

Dear Mr Hardy,
    I have long wished to tell you how profoundly grateful I am to you for your poems and novels, but naturally it seemed an impertinence to do so. When however, your poem to my father, Leslie Stephen, appeared in *Satires*

and Circumstances this autumn, I felt that I might perhaps be allowed to thank you for that at least. That poem, and the reminiscences you contributed to Professor Maitland's Life of him, remain in my mind as incomparably the truest and most imaginative portrait of him in existence, for which alone his children should always be grateful to you.

But besides this one would like to thank you for the magnificent work which you have already done, and are still to do. The younger generation, who care for poetry and literature, owe you an immeasurable debt, and in particular for your last volume of poems which, to me at any rate, is the most remarkable book to appear in my lifetime. I write only to satisfy a very old desire, and not to trouble you to reply (*LVW* 2:58).

This letter, profuse in its praise of Hardy's poems, illustrates that Woolf's sense of Hardy was interwoven with thoughts of her father, and with her own "immeasurable debt." Furthermore, it suggests that the publication of "The Schreckhorn" had in some way validated Woolf's "very old desire" to voice this "profound" gratitude to Hardy. For Woolf, the appearance of Hardy's "truest and most imaginative portrait" of Stephen not only produced a sense of entitlement, seen as she offers Hardy her "impertinent" opinions of his works, but also allowed her to articulate her "immeasurable debt" and "gratitude" to him.

In concluding her letter to Hardy, Woolf states that she does not want to "trouble [him] to reply," but he did so shortly afterwards:

Dear Mrs. Woolf:

I am much pleased to hear that you like the lines I wrote in recollection of your father, & that the imperfect picture I gave of him as editor, in Professor Maitland's book, brought him back to you. He had a peculiar attractiveness for me, & I used to suffer gladly his grim & severe criticisms of my contributions & his long silences, for the sake of sitting with him.

As to what I am doing now, I often wonder what he would say to it. I find that most of the present-day critics read it very superficially, & often miss one's intention, in a way that he certainly never did (*CLTH* 5:76).

As in Woolf's letter above, the point of reference here for Hardy is the person of Leslie Stephen. In response to Woolf's compliments, Hardy offers her another "portrait" of her father: "his grim & severe criticisms," "his long silences," and his skill at understanding "one's intention." This correspondence demonstrates, therefore, that thoughts of Stephen informed Woolf's association with Hardy from the beginning. She came to know Hardy through his relationship with Stephen, and she was reminded of her father by reading Hardy's "imaginative portraits" of him.

For Woolf, the figure of Thomas Hardy thus became aligned with memories of her father, and, as I noted above, her interest in Hardy grew steadily after Mansfield's death. I would argue, moreover, that Woolf's movement from a connection with Katherine Mansfield toward her sense of "debt" to Thomas Hardy is echoed in the novel she composed during this period. As Elizabeth Dalloway travels from a maternal influence to a paternal one, her fictional transition may be informed by Woolf's own, parallel journey. This movement in *Mrs. Dalloway,* however, carries with it several interpretative dilemmas for the reader. Firstly, one may question the very nature of a movable indebtedness. Was Mansfield, for example, replaced as a literary "precursor" when Woolf's interest in Hardy grew? Did Woolf forsake a mother/muse for a patriarchal mentor? Or does neither of these influence scenarios sufficiently account for the Mansfieldian and Hardinian echoes that reverberate throughout *Mrs. Dalloway?*

The Return of Thomas Hardy:
Woolf's Intertextual *Voyage*

In the previous chapter, I touched on the notion of intertextuality in order to account for some aspects of the relation between Jacob in *Jacob's Room* and Kezia in "Prelude." I believe that it is a useful tool for reading many of the textual difficulties that arise in *Mrs. Dalloway* as well. Indeed, the intertextual view of meaning itself as derived from dialogues among texts, and demonstrated by shifting textual surfaces with indeterminate significance, may be the best way to account for the variety of writings that surface in Woolf's works. Intertextual theory, as critics Jay Clayton and Eric Rothstein explain, maintains that "the intersection of textual surfaces in a literary word can never be circumscribed, is open to endless dissemination" (Clayton and Rothstein, "Figures" 19). One could well argue that Woolf's novels are best understood through the very openness of such intertextual readings, as the strength of her texts lays, finally, in their textual complexity. In this chapter, I will employ aspects of intertextuality and influence theory to suggest ways of reading Woolf's textual negotiations of the literary ghosts of her past.

As I argued above, Woolf's association with Thomas Hardy was informed from the start by his relationship to her father. While Woolf's struggle with Hardy's legacy as both a novelist and a patriarchal figure surfaces in *Mrs. Dalloway,* which she wrote in the years 1922 to 1924, there is also evidence that Hardy's work was of interest to her much earlier. In a letter to Lytton Strachey in December of 1912, for instance, Woolf mentions that she is reading *The Return of the Native,* "a novel by Thomas Hardy" (*LVW* 2:15). Woolf's reading of Hardy's text thus coincided with her rewriting the chapters leading to the death of the character Rachel Vinrace in her first novel, *The Voyage Out.* As I have demonstrated, such tracings of possible "original" sources of meaning are employed in studies of influence to ground the literary allusions that a critic reads in a given text. If, that is, one found echoes of Hardy's *Native* in Woolf's *The Voyage Out,* and then discovered that Woolf was reading *Native* in 1912, one would feel justified in asserting that the earlier text informed the later.

In his essay "The Alphabet of Suffering," Jay Clayton argues that such reliance on traceable literary sources is useful mainly if one wants to "connect" a given writer to a specific tradition of enquiry (42). In the previous chapter, for instance, I demonstrated that portions of Woolf's texts have been utilized to align her both with a revolt against patriarchy (Marcus, "Thinking Back Through Our Mothers"), and with a utopian politics of shared sisterhood (Hawkes, "Woolf's Magical Garden of Women"). Clayton maintains that the limitations of such pointed readings are exacerbated by the refusal of some critics to declare their particular biases. As he asserts: "Literary history, within an intertextual frame, becomes situating a text within the zones of force that alter and are altered by it. [. . .] These histories must be acknowledged to be partial and specific—oriented to particular tasks, with particular readers in mind" ("Alphabet" 57). With Clayton's warning "in mind," let me clarify the "zone" of my inquiry into the (possible) relationship of Woolf's *The Voyage Out* and Hardy's *The Return of the Native.* As always in this study, I hope to open up and complicate interpretations of these works, to attempt to account for the dialogue I sense between them, and to engage creatively with those connections that I propose.

As I shall argue, Woolf's responses to Hardy's work can be read in many ways. Hardy's relation to Woolf's father, and her own ambivalent response toward both men, may promote a reading of the connections between her texts and Hardy's as a symptom of her "anxiety of influence." Intertextual theory, however, allows me to avoid such author-based interpretations, as it produces readings of those textual connections as intertextual intersections instead. Roland Barthes' argument, for example, highlights the final anonymity of the sources that inform the reader's reading, as he states that: "the citations which go to make up a text are anonymous, untraceable, and yet already read" ("Work to Text" 160). In an intertextual sense, then, the similarities between Woolf's work and Hardy's are not related to the personal history of either writer, but are a surfacing of the "already read" motifs of which Barthes writes.

What are the allusions to *The Return of the Native* that I sense in Woolf's *The Voyage Out?* Well, for a start, the title of Woolf's first novel may be an early expression of her indebtedness to Hardy's work. The original version of this text, with the working title *Melymbrosia,* appears to have been begun in 1907.[1] The work did not bear the name *The Voyage Out* until after Woolf's extensive revisions in the winter of 1912 to 1913 (Heine 402 and 450–1). As Woolf's major revision of the novel thus coincided with her reading *The*

Return of the Native, could this change in its title indicate a debt to Hardy? Does Woolf's novel, that is, enact her attempt to "voyage out" as Hardy's own work "returns"? Certainly, a similar theme of "journey" is employed in both novels, as the main character in each is portrayed as a traveler. *The Voyage Out* charts the progress of the fictional young English woman, Rachel Vinrace, through her passage "out" toward adulthood, as she leaves her father, crosses the ocean, and falls in love. Hardy's novel, by contrast, explores the impact of the return of the traveler Clym Yeobright to his mother's home, in his "native" Egdon Heath. Woolf's novel, then, may respond to Hardy's on the level of motif; the themes of journey, home, and familial loyalties that appear in *The Return of the Native* are also explored in her text. Is *The Voyage Out,* however, necessarily connected to *The Return of the Native* just because both address similar concerns? One way of considering such an argument would be to examine the changes that Woolf made to her novel after she read Hardy's *Native.*

As Elizabeth Heine notes in "Virginia Woolf's Revisions to *The Voyage Out"* (1990), one difference between *Melymbrosia* and the later *The Voyage Out* is the language that Woolf uses to describe Rachel's dream visions, the "tunnels in Rachel's nightmare" and her "fevered dream" (Heine 433). Heine states that in *Melymbrosia* "both dreams have tunnels but only the earlier one has a wall that 'dripped with wet'" (Heine 433). Woolf, Heine explains, later inserted this detail into Rachel's second "fevered dream" as well. Similarly, the image of drops sliding down the wall of the tunnel appeared only in Rachel's second dream in the original text of *Melymbrosia.* In Woolf's revision, this image was added to Rachel's earlier nightmare as well. Heine also notes that in an apparent effort to link these dreams more closely by enhancing the likeness of their imagery, Woolf made a further change: she replaced the phrase "dripped with wet" to "oozed with damp" in both passages. As Heine records, this substitution "could have occurred [. . .] sometime between April 1913 and early 1915" (Heine 433), that is, after Woolf had read *The Return of the Native.*

If the timing of this revision strengthens my interest in Woolf's reworking of these two dreams, I am also intrigued by the trope Woolf used to connect these passages: Woolf's language here echoes that found in a scene in Hardy's novel. As *The Return of the Native* draws to a close, the character of Thomasin walks through a rainstorm at night across Egdon Heath, with her child in her arms. Hardy portrays Thomasin's journey over the heath as follows: "Sometimes the path led her to hollows between thickets of tall and dripping bracken, dead, though not yet prostrate, which enclosed her like a pool. When they were more than usually tall, she lifted the baby to her head, that it might be out of the reach of their drenching fronds" (37:22). As the novel progresses, Thomasin is shown to survive her trek in the rain, but two other characters, Eustacia and Damon, drown on the heath that same night. Hardy thus provides different fates for these figures, but he also indicates a connection among them. The language that Hardy employs to describe the weir in which Damon and Eustacia die, links their watery deaths with the "drenching" by the "dripping bracken" that "enclosed" Thomasin "like a pool." "Shadwater Weir," in Hardy's description, "had at its foot a large circular pool. [. . .] The sides of the pool were masonry" (37:227). Hardy thus creates symmetry among the obstacles that face his characters, by using the same word "pool" to describe them.

The importance of this water imagery becomes clear as each of the three characters respond differently to the "pool" before them. While connecting these characters through his repetitive troping, Hardy also foretells the eventual fates of his three main figures in these confrontations. In particular, in these two scenes, Hardy draws a distinction between Thomasin and Eustacia and the nature of their respective imaginations: "To [Thomasin] there were not, as to Eustacia, demons in the air, and malice in every bush and bough. The drops which lashed her face were not scorpions, but prosy rain; Egdon in the mass was no monster whatever, but an impersonal open ground. Her fears of the place were rational, her dislikes of its worst moods reasonable" (37:23). In this context, then, the futures of both Thomasin and Eustacia are signaled by their respective "readings" of the heath itself. Eustacia, who sees "demons in the air," will finally meet her death on the heath, while Thomasin's more rational "fears of the place" are rewarded with survival.

Thus the characters' "readings" of the heath, and the pools it contains, are indicative of their eventual fates. This idea is echoed in Hardy's description of those who face the weir. Damon, like Eustacia, misreads the danger he confronts, as "without showing sufficient presence of mind even to throw off his great-coat, he leaped into the boiling caldron" (37:227). Damon's characteristically rash decision, combined with his misjudgment of the pool's danger, will cost him his life. On the other hand, the "native" of the heath, Clym Yeobright, is linked with Thomasin in this passage through his relatively rational approach to the danger at hand. Clym, Hardy tells us, "[b]ethink[s] himself of a wiser plan" (37:227) of rescue than Damon's. Clym's connection to Thomasin is further strengthened as the same character, Diggory Venn, rescues them both: Venn guides Thomasin to safety across the heath, and he extracts Clym from the weir. Later Venn, by raising his lantern "aloft" as he stands in the pool, is also associated with Thomasin, who "lifted her baby to the top of her head" in order to ensure its survival against a similar "drenching."

The repetition of the words "pool," "drench," "drip," and "dead" thus function within the climax of Hardy's novel to point to the destinies of his characters, and their relation to each other within the text. The (re)appearance of these tropes in Rachel's nightmare, and her later fevered dream in Woolf's *The Voyage Out,* signals a variety of (inter)textual connections between this novel and Hardy's *Native.* The first passage in which these images surface occurs early in Woolf's novel, soon after Rachel is kissed by Mr. Dalloway on their journey across the ocean. Rachel later falls asleep and is visited by a frightful dream:

> She dreamt that she was walking down a long tunnel, which grew so narrow by degrees that she could touch the damp bricks on either side. At length the tunnel opened and became a vault; she found herself trapped in it, bricks meeting her wherever she turned, alone with a little deformed man who squatted on the floor gibbering, with long nails. His face was pitted and like the face of an animal. The wall behind him oozed with damp, which collected into drops and slid down. Still and cold as death she lay, not daring to move.[2]

Both Rachel's nightmare and Thomasin's journey across the heath, therefore, contain several similar motifs. Just as Thomasin follows a path in which she becomes surrounded by tunnel-like "dripping bracken" that "enclose" her, Rachel also "walk[s] down" a "long" and "narrow" "tunnel." If I read these passages as connected, the "damp bricks" that Rachel encounters in her dream are, perhaps, a refiguring of the "masonry" walls of the weir on Egdon Heath, or, again, of the "tall and dripping bracken" that surround Thomasin on her long walk.

A further link between these texts can be seen in Rachel's strange meeting in her dream-tunnel. "At length," Woolf writes, Rachel reaches a "vault" and becomes "trapped." She finds herself "alone with a little deformed man," with a face "pitted" and like "an animal." Thomasin has a corresponding encounter, as "[a]t length" she "reach[es] a hollow," and "discern[s] through the rain" (37:23) an equally strange figure: "lurid from head to foot" (37:24), the reddleman, Diggory Venn. Upon waking herself from her nightmare, Rachel laid "still and cold as death." Here again there is a semblance between Woolf's language and Hardy's own. If the water and tunnel imagery suggested a link between Woolf's Rachel and Hardy's Thomasin, this scene hints at Rachel's possible connection to Eustacia: when extracted from the weir Eustacia's body is "dead" and "cold" (37:230) and "lay there still in death" (37:232).

While this examination of the similarities in these two passages suggests an important, if enigmatic, relationship between them, a close reading of Rachel's later dream further problematizes their (possible) connection. In this section of Woolf's text, Rachel, newly engaged to Terence Hewet, contracts a fatal fever and is confined to her bed. There, her earlier nightmare returns but appears to have been reimagined: "Rachel again shut her eyes, and found herself walking through a tunnel under the Thames, where there were little deformed women sitting in archways playing cards, while the bricks of which the wall was made oozed with damp, which collected into drops and slid down the wall. But the little old women became Helen and Nurse McInnis after a time [. . .]" (*Voyage* 353). As I noted above, it is possible to read Rachel's dreams as a partial refiguring of both Thomasin's walk and Eustacia's death in *The Return of the Native*. If I continue with such a reading, then the change of details in this later fevered vision provides further evidence of Woolf's negotiation of Hardy in this novel.

By relocating Rachel's "tunnel" "under the Thames," for example, Woolf implicitly denies a connection between that tunnel and the "tall" bracken that "enclosed" Thomasin on Egdon Heath. Thus, this change may illustrate Woolf's desire to refute Hardy's text as the source of the imagery in Rachel's dreams. Indeed, in Woolf's late revision of her novel, she had replaced the phrase "dripping with wet" (which may have originated in Hardy's "dripping bracken") with the words "oozed with damp" (Heine 433). Furthermore, the "little deformed man" of the earlier nightmare becomes "little deformed women" "playing cards" here. When I read this passage as an instance of Woolf's denial of Hardy's influence, I also find that the "little deformed man" is no longer an image of Diggory Venn; Woolf transforms him into several "little deformed women." As a result, the only echo of Venn in Rachel's later dream is the card playing of these women, as this recalls Venn's own fateful game of dice, which provokes the climax of Hardy's novel.

Woolf's removal of the "deformed man," who seemed tied in some way to Venn, could also strengthen a reading of these dreams as somehow related to Woolf's father. Indeed, as I noted in chapter two, "Venn" was the surname of Leslie Stephen's mother, and this character has much in common with the real Stephen. If Woolf had seen a likeness between her father and Diggory Venn, would her replacement of the reddleman-like "deformed man" with the later "deformed women" indicate a negation of her father? Would such a denial of indebtedness to the "lurid" reddleman of Hardy's text also be a disavowal of her own (paternal) ancestry? Then again, as Leslie Stephen's mother, Jane Venn was part of the matriarchal line of Woolf's family. Does this suggest that while Hardy uses the name "Venn" for his "deformed" reddleman, Woolf, in Rachel's later dream, reassociates "Venn" with her own female ancestry, by transforming him from a deformed man into deformed women?

As such varied readings illustrate, historical and biographical sources offer exciting tools for the reader, by providing a context in which to interpret difficult passages and possible literary allusions in a given text. However, if a reading of Rachel's dreams as a response to Hardy is persuasive, there are nonetheless many other ways of unpacking the imagery Woolf employs in those scenes. Within the context of Woolf's novel, for instance, the change from the "little deformed man" to the later "little deformed women" could also be said to re-enact Rachel's gender-inflected psychological journey. The first nightmare in the tale takes place as Rachel is still in the care of her father, on board the ship, but the later dream occurs under the watchful eyes of two women: Helen and Nurse McInnis. By replacing the "deformed man" with the "deformed women," Woolf may signal Rachel's movement from a difficult paternal influence to an equally difficult (surrogate) maternal one.

Another possible interpretation might emphasize that Rachel's earlier nightmare occurs soon after her first kiss, while her later dream takes place during an illness begun as her fiancé, Terence, "was reading Milton aloud, because he said the words of Milton had substance and shape" (*Voyage* 347). As critic Jane Marcus asserts, Woolf saw the figure of Milton as a "ferocious male patriarch," "the patriarchal God and the patriarchal father" (Marcus, "Niece" 128). Indeed, in Woolf's *A Room of One's Own,* it is the narrator's attempt to seek out "the manuscript of one of Milton's poems" that leads her to be barred from the Oxbridge library (7). Woolf's critique of Milton's power continues as *A Room of One's Own* concludes, as the narrator calls for the women who hear her to "look past Milton's bogey," in order to ensure that "the woman poet" can be born (117).

Marcus argues that Woolf's need to slay the "ghost of Milton's bogey" ("Niece" 128) arose from a specific desire to revolt against patriarchy, a revolution enabled by the financial legacy of Woolf's aunt Caroline ("Niece" 118). As Woolf herself described, this inheritance from Caroline Stephen "unveiled the sky to me, and substituted for the large and imposing figure of a gentleman which Milton recommended for my perpetual adoration, a view of the open sky" (*Room* 39). If *The Voyage Out* was informed by Woolf's sense of the destructive power of Milton, then Rachel's illness and eventual death may not be a response to Hardy, but, rather, could be connected with Rachel's listening to Milton's poem. In this reading, the earlier dream that visits Rachel after she accepts Richard Dalloway's kiss is a foreshadowing of the danger that will accompany her surrender to men. By the time Rachel's dream returns, her fate is sealed: Rachel's willingness to be taught the words of Milton signals her complicity in the male domination that appears to cause her fatal illness.

This interpretation is strengthened by the poem that Terence reads to Rachel, which inscribes patriarchal images of conquest. In these verses, "Sabrina" "the virgin pure" is located as: "the daughter of Locrine,/ That had the sceptre from his father Brute" (cited in *Voyage* 347). Rachel's encounter with this "brutish" Miltonic father combined with her inability to escape his message of male domination (in her dream, she is "trapped") thus leads to her death. Woolf, moreover, locates this struggle with "the father" in the wet, narrow, and vagina-like tunnel, which ends in a "vault" whose walls, like those of a womb, "ooze with damp." By doing so, Woolf may point to Rachel's "fever" as an inevitable symptom of her burgeoning womanhood. Entrapped in a woman's body, but living in a patriarchal culture, Rachel will necessarily sicken and die.

As I noted earlier, Jay Clayton suggests that source hunting, like that which uncovers Woolf's uncomfortable relation to "Milton's bogey," is useful only if one wants to "connect" a given writer to a specific tradition of enquiry ("Alphabet" 42). If I read Rachel's death as a result of her battle with a Miltonic patriarchy, I could locate Woolf's novel as a point in the articulation of feminist struggle. As Clayton further asserts, however, this reliance on traditional textual sources (such as Hardy or Milton) in the reading of images and motifs may serve to limit our understanding of a given text. For, as he states "[t]he anonymous and traditional make up the intertextual web, just as much as do allusions to canonical texts" ("Alphabet" 40). Such "anonymous and traditional" tropes in a text, he argues, function like stock footage: archetypes that are part of every reader's storehouse of images.

Read in this way, the passages from Woolf's *The Voyage Out* and Hardy's *The Return of the Native* are "connected" only insofar as each relies on a similar set of "anonymous" motifs of tunnels, dampness, bricks, deformities, and dripping enclosures. In keeping with Barthes' account of intertextuality, such images can have no "meaning" in themselves, but are "inscribed" on the reader as the "space" upon which their "unity" is organized. Clayton, however, suggests an alternative interpretation. His reading seeks to fuse traditional influence methodologies, which rely on locating biographical and historical allusions, and the anonymous and untraceable quotations that theorists of intertextuality claim are at work in all texts. In Clayton's view, both kinds of readings are valid, and frequently overlap. In my examination above, for example, I located both historical and archetypal sources for the "tunnel" and other images in Woolf and Hardy's texts. For Clayton, the very existence of what he calls this "double determination" of motifs allows for a "more comprehensive map of affiliation" ("Alphabet" 56–7). In the pages that follow, I will make use of this notion of double-determination and explore readings of Woolf's texts as inflected by historic, biographic, and archetypal sources. In doing so, I will attempt to account for the (inter)textual repetition of tropes that I encounter, and to map their (possible) historical, biographical and (inter)textual affiliations.

Textual Negotiations:
The Mayor, Mrs. Dalloway, The Times, and The Athenaeum

In his essay "Interpretation and Undecidability," intertextual critic Michael Riffaterre argues that a "proper interpretation" (Riffaterre 227) can be found for any given text, if the reader is alert to the "guides" within that text. As Clayton and Rothstein explain, for Riffaterre, "[a]mbiguity, obscurity, undecidability, indeterminacy, unreadability, ungrammaticality—all these exist only as a stage in the reading process and serve to alert the reader to the presence of an intertext that will resolve the work's difficulties" ("Figures" 24). For Riffaterre, then, all texts have a correct and proper intertext, which can be employed by the competent reader to resolve the difficulties and ambiguities encountered in the reading process. Clayton and Rothstein maintain that this particular technique of intertextual reading functions spatially as a "resegmenting of literature, allowing a reading of the words of one text as 'part' of another text in a single unit of meaning" ("Figures" 24). In *Mrs. Dalloway*, I suggest, just such a moment of Riffaterrian "ambiguity" and "difficulty" occurs when a "violent explosion" on Bond Street signals the passing of a "motor car" (19). Within this fictional car, nestled in its "dove-grey upholstery," the reader encounters an image whose meaning is difficult to decipher: a "face of the very greatest importance" (19).

The ambiguity of this passage lies in the fact that, thanks to Woolf's refusal to disclose the identity of this "important" figure, both the reader of this scene and the characters within it remain unsure as to whom this face belongs: "[w]as it the Prince of Wales's, the Queen's, the Prime Minister's? Whose face was it? Nobody knew" (20). The first time I read Woolf's *Mrs. Dalloway*, I had difficulty making sense of this passage. Why, I wondered, had Woolf refigured a moment from Hardy's *The Mayor of Casterbridge* in her novel? To me, that is, the procession of the "unknown important person" in *Mrs. Dalloway* was familiar, as it re-enacted a similar scene in Hardy's novel. This sensation of familiarity that Clayton terms intertextual "uncanniness" is, in his view, a function of "the intertextual web." As he explains, "[e]ach text is haunted by the others, the earlier by the later, the later by the earlier. This uncanny afterlife constitutes, in part, the felt life of each text. Intertextuality is a ghost effect" ("Alphabet" 54). As Clayton might predict, in my reading of *Mrs. Dalloway* the unnamed "Royal Personage" of *The Mayor of Casterbridge* had found just such an intertextual "afterlife." It seemed to me that the ghost of this character visited Clarissa and Septimus in Bond Street, haunting this scene in Woolf's text. Could this "uncanny" haunting indicate that *The Mayor of Casterbridge* is the intertext of *Mrs. Dalloway*?

To answer this question, I should first define the "uncanny" that Clayton discusses; although he retrieves this trope from Freudian discourse, he employs it differently from Freud. According to Freud, the "uncanny" is: "in reality nothing new or alien, but something which is familiar and old-established in the mind and which has become alienated from it only through repression" (Freud XVII: 241). Freud thus theorized the uncanny as a psychic response that attempts to alienate and repress feelings and images.

Clayton's intertextual "uncanny," on the other hand, is part of "the felt life of each text." It is, therefore, not situated within the psyche of the reader, but in the text itself. My own sense of the "uncanny" likeness of these scenes in *Mrs. Dalloway* and *The Mayor of Casterbridge* confirms Clayton's reading of this phenomenon. The "repression" of *The Mayor of Casterbridge* as the source of the "face of the very greatest importance" was not being enacted in my "psyche"—I was fully aware of the allusion. Instead, as Clayton's account would suggest, this "repression" appeared to exist within the text itself.

Having sensed this repressed debt in Woolf's novel, I chose to explore my supposition that her text was "linked" in some way to Thomas Hardy. In order to do so, I attempted to locate a historical connection between Woolf and Hardy: I went to the library. There, among piles of collected letters, journals, notebooks, and biographies, I found what Clayton might term "a canonical origin" ("Alphabet" 40) for the affiliation I sensed. Alongside the evidence of Woolf and Hardy's correspondence and references to each other in their notebooks, journals, and essays, there was an interesting footnote: when Woolf went to Hardy's home in Dorchester in July of 1926 (her only recorded meeting with Hardy), she brought along a copy of one of Hardy's novels for him to autograph—*The Mayor of Casterbridge* (*DVW* 3:99).

In the section that follows, I will seek to interpret this fact and its place in the complex relationship between Woolf and Hardy. In order to ground the (inter)textual connections that I posit, I will also explore a range of possible contexts in which to read Woolf's *Mrs. Dalloway.* Is this novel best understood, for example, as a Riffaterrian intertext of *The Mayor of Casterbridge,* as a textual negotiation of Katherine Mansfield's death, or as an enactment of Woolf's indebtedness to Hardy? Indeed, is it in Kristevan terms all of these and more, "open" as it must be to "endless dissemination?" I will address these questions by returning to an examination of Woolf's relation to Thomas Hardy, and her thoughts on his novel, *The Mayor of Casterbridge.*

In the years 1919 through 1924, Woolf frequently mentioned the name of Thomas Hardy in her letters, journals, and essays. Beginning in January of 1919, when she compared Lytton Strachey's work to Hardy's in her diary ("Thomas Hardy has what I would call an interesting mind [. . .] but not Lytton" [*DVW* 1:238]), such references often contain praise of his work. As I noted in chapter one, in April of 1919, Woolf wrote in her essay "Modern Novels" that all writers should "reserve our unconditional gratitude for Mr. Hardy" (189). When Woolf later revised this essay for collection in *The Common Reader* (1925), she added the following comment on influence and indebtedness: "We know only that certain gratitudes and hostilities inspire us; that certain paths seem to lead to fertile land, others to the dust and the desert; and of this perhaps it may be worth while to attempt some account" ("Modern Fiction" 185). As Woolf's later essay continues, however, it seems that despite her call for "unconditional gratitude" for Hardy, she makes no attempt to "account" for his influence upon her work. Instead, she turns to an assessment of James Joyce's *Ulysses*.

In her critique of *Ulysses*, Woolf states that although she admires the "brilliancy," "sordidity," and "originality" of Joyce's language, she feels that as a novel it "fails to compare" with "The Mayor of Casterbridge" ("Modern Fiction" 191).[3] As she concludes this comparison, Woolf admits to "fumbling rather awkwardly" to explain why "a work of such originality" has failed. She then suggests that her dissatisfaction with *Ulysses* and other modern novels is the result of the limits imposed by the traditional novel form: "it is possible to press a little further and wonder whether we may not refer our sense of being in a bright yet narrow room, confined and shut in, rather than enlarged and set free, to some limitation imposed by the method as well as the mind. Is it the method that inhibits the creative power?" ("Modern Fiction" 191).

Here, Woolf blames the "confining" and traditional "method" of novel-writing for the weakness of contemporary works, and this passage may thus foretell her later desire to create "a new form for a novel" (*DVW* 2:13). As discussed in chapter four, this project began in earnest with her preparations for *Jacob's Room* in January of 1920.[4] However, the argument that Woolf employs in the 1924 essay "Modern Fiction" to protest against the limitations of tradition is itself evidence of her indebtedness to the very method she denounces. Although Woolf claims that the traditional method is a "narrow" and "confining" room from which the writer yearns to be "set-free," this same method produced Hardy's *The Mayor of Casterbridge,* for which, she insists, "we" must "reserve our unconditional gratitude."

Woolf's essay thus combines both her praise of Hardy and her denouncement of the traditional structures that he employed. If this ambivalent assessment can be read as a kind of "cover" for Woolf's indebtedness to Hardy, there is also a possible circumstantial reason for her reference to Hardy here. Only shortly before Woolf first published "Modern Novels" in 1919, she had also accepted a somewhat different assignment from Bruce Richmond at *The Times:* he asked Woolf to write a posthumous survey of Thomas Hardy's work. As Richmond wrote in his letter to Woolf, he hoped that such an essay would not be needed for some time (Hardy being still alive), but he asked, "would you be ready with an article on Hardy's novels whenever the evil day comes?" (cited in *DVW* 2:126n). Woolf mentions her preparations for this Hardy article many times in the years 1920 and 1921. In her diary on November 25, 1921, for example, she notes, "[b]ut I wake in the night & think that I haven't written Hardy; & I shall open my paper & find him dead—So we go on" (*DVW* 2:145).

Although Hardy was to survive until January of 1928, when Woolf's posthumous essay on his work was finally published in *The Times Literary*

Supplement, her diaries in the intervening years provide ample evidence of her preoccupation with Hardy's impending death and her own unpreparedness for it.[5] Woolf's composition of a premature eulogy for Hardy, interestingly enough, places her in a continuum with other writers in this study who prepared "textually" for the deaths of influential figures in their lives. Just as Hardy had written "The Schreckhorn" for Leslie Stephen and the bitter epitaphs for George Moore and G. K. Chesterton, and Murry the poem "To T.H." for Hardy, Woolf engaged in a similar undertaking. Might this suggest that such a premature textual "slaying" of a literary rival is a necessary enactment of their "anxiety of influence"? This is one possible reading. I should also note, however, that while Hardy and Murry wrote their rivals' poetic epitaphs of their own accord, Woolf was assigned the task of eulogizing Hardy. Should this difference in the impetus for composing these works inform the way they are read?

In previous chapters I have explored an interpretation of the posthumous poems written by Hardy and Murry as a "working out" of their "anxiety of influence." Woolf's composition of the Hardy survey, however, does not seem to fit into this Bloomian paradigm. The writing of this article, so far from resolving any anxiety Woolf might have felt toward Hardy, seems instead to have refocused his influence upon her. As Woolf engaged in this study of Hardy's novels, her earlier indebtedness to him, as suggested by my reading of Rachel's dreams in *The Voyage Out,* had apparently resurfaced: evidence of Woolf's resurgent interest in Hardy can be found throughout her private papers of this time. As I noted previously, in the years 1918 through 1920, Woolf's journals and letters contained scores of references to Katherine Mansfield and her works. From 1921 to 1926, however, Mansfield's name was, as it were, "replaced" with that of Thomas Hardy. Furthermore, although Woolf's references to Hardy prior to 1921 were often couched in terms of praise, admiration, and gratitude, after her completion of a final draft of this posthumous article in January of 1922, Woolf's papers voice a more ambivalent response to Hardy.

In October of 1922, for example, Woolf recounted E. M. Forster's less than flattering impression of Hardy in a letter to her friend Janet Case: "Thomas Hardy is [. . .] alas, a very vain, quiet, conventional, uninteresting old gentleman. [. . .] It's all disillusioning—but perhaps at 82 one rots a little" (*LVW* 2:559). Woolf claims here that Hardy's faults, as told to her by Forster, are "disillusioning," but she nevertheless recorded them both in this letter to Case and in her diary. There, she writes: "Hardy is perfectly ordinary, nice, conventional, never says a clever thing. [. . .] How am I to dress this for the Obituary?" (*DVW* 2:204). The dating of this letter and diary entry is itself of interest: as Woolf twice records the image of Hardy as uninteresting, old, and conventional, she was beginning to work on her next novel, *Mrs. Dalloway* (*DVW* 2:307). Throughout the course of writing this book, moreover, Woolf used her journal to chronicle her difficulties with Hardy and his work. Woolf describes him during this period as old, as "rotting," as conventional, but also as "sacred" (*LVW* 3:281), and as a "great man" (*LVW* 3:202). Does Woolf's rather sudden ambivalence toward Hardy indicate an unconscious literary debt to him? One that she was attempting to "repress"? Or was she, perhaps, truly disillusioned by Forster's impressions of Hardy, and frustrated at how to "dress" this uninteresting old man up "for the Obituary?" Moreover, did this newly equivocal response to Hardy find its way into Woolf's writings of this time? Does her work enact an attempt to settle her "immeasurable debt" to Hardy's novels? In order to address such questions, I will examine Woolf's references to Hardy and his works during the course of composing *Mrs. Dalloway*.

Woolf's posthumous survey of Hardy's work was tentatively completed and put aside until the "evil day" in 1928. However, she employed some of the knowledge she had gained in her study by including Hardy in her essay "How It Strikes a Contemporary," published in the April 5, 1923, edition of *The Times Literary Supplement*. In the unsigned article, Woolf discusses the confusion and lack of focus she finds in "contemporary" critical practice. Within this argument she asserts:

> Great Critics, if they are not themselves great poets, are bred from the profusion of the age. There is some great man to be vindicated, some school to be founded or destroyed. But our age is meagre to the verge of destitution. There is no name which dominates the rest. There is no master in whose workshop the young are proud to serve apprenticeship. Mr. Hardy has long since withdrawn from the arena.[6]

As in her earlier essay, "Modern Novels," Woolf harks back to "Mr. Hardy"'s work as a high point when discussing the relative poverty of imagination in her "age." Here, Woolf does not appear to regret his "withdrawal" from the "arena" of writing per se, but from the role of "master" in a "workshop" of "apprenticed" younger writers. Woolf's critique thus implies that without "some great man" like Hardy to "be vindicated" or "destroyed," her contemporaries are consequently "destitute."

In keeping with her newly ambivalent response to Hardy, Woolf's article ostensibly praises his work while simultaneously portraying him as already gone: Woolf states that Hardy has "withdrawn from the arena." Hardy himself reacted strongly against this anonymously written dismissal of his current work, to which his friend Vere Collins had alerted him. In a letter to Collins on April 7, Hardy remarks: "the curious blunder in the Literary Suppt. [. . .] ought to be corrected," and points further to the disgrace of "making that statement about a writer, who as you remark has pubd [sic] 3 vols. of new verse within 10 years—one of them only last year" (*CLTH* 6:190).

Woolf's declaration of Hardy's retirement in this essay could be read as a further example of her desire to "slay" her presumed precursor. However, a letter that Woolf wrote to Hardy shortly after the publication of this article problematizes this interpretation. Despite Woolf's recent assertion of Hardy's "withdrawal" from literature, she wrote to him to ask for a contribution to the literary magazine *The Nation and Athenaeum.* Woolf made this request on behalf of her husband Leonard, who had recently been named the magazine's Literary Editor.[7] Having first asked for a submission, Woolf then went on to flatter and cajole Hardy into agreement, stating "[t]here is, of course, no other writer who could give the paper the distinction that you could give it. [. . .] Please excuse me if I bother you in making this request. I cannot help thanking you once more for the profound and increasing pleasure which your writings give me" (*LVW* 3:37). Interestingly, Woolf's letter reads much like those John Middleton Murry wrote to Hardy during his tenure as editor of *The Athenaeum.* Here, as Woolf remarks upon "the distinction" that Hardy's work would "give the paper," I am reminded that the poems that Hardy had contributed to *The Athenaeum* during Murry's editorship greatly aided its circulation. The once prosperous magazine, however, began to fail when Murry was forced by his wife's illness to resign. At this time, then, the newly amalgamated *The Nation and Athenaeum,* with Leonard Woolf at its helm, once again needed a turn in fortunes.

While Hardy had helped Murry's career by his frequent contributions to *The Athenaeum,* he was not quite so willing to offer his work to the Woolfs. His response to Virginia's request was as follows:

> It was a pleasure to see the name subscribed to your letter, as being that of the daughter of one who influenced me in many ways when I was a young man. [. . .] As for your kind suggestion that I should contribute something, alas I have fallen into the sere & yellow leaf, & fear I am unable to undertake writing now. [. . .] But there are plenty of young pens available, & I shall, just the same, take much interest in the paper (*CLTH* 6:196).

In this letter to Woolf, Hardy once again returns to write of his memories of Leslie Stephen and the "influence" he had on Hardy. These recollections did not help his daughter in obtaining Hardy's contribution, however. Hardy refused, politely, to submit anything to *The Nation and Athenaeum.* But why would Hardy do so? Perhaps the language of his letter lends a clue. Hardy likens himself here to the doomed Macbeth ("the sere and yellow leaf" [5:3:23]), and his reference to the "young pens" available to Woolf must be ironic in light of his earlier protest against the anonymous statement that he had "withdrawn from the arena." Indeed, Hardy's intriguing wording of this letter causes me to posit a hidden meaning in his refusal: perhaps Hardy knew that Woolf herself was the author of the unsigned "How it Strikes a Contemporary" and was now enjoying his subtle revenge.

In any case, Woolf was unsuccessful at securing a contribution from Hardy for Leonard's magazine, and turned her attentions elsewhere. She now began reworking her story "Mrs. Dalloway on Bond Street," which had "branched into a book" tentatively entitled *The Hours* (*DVW* 2:207). In her diary of this period, Woolf's thoughts about the "design" of this piece are frequently mentioned. In June of 1923, for instance, Woolf notes that the "design is so queer and masterful," and that October she boasted that "the design is more remarkable than in any of my books." Again, in January of 1924, she confirmed that "I think its the design that's good this time" (*DVW* 2: 248,272,289).[8] Importantly, however, Woolf's emphasis on the structure of her novel coincides with numerous references to Hardy and his work in her private papers.

In a diary entry of March 1924, for instance, Woolf remarks on George Moore's dismissal of Hardy's work in *Conversations on Ebury Street*.[9] Woolf notes that "Moore ought to [have] been smacked on the bottom for talking about Hardy as he did" (*DVW* 2:296). Later that same year, she sent Hardy a copy of The Hogarth Press edition of Leslie Stephen's *Early Impressions* (1924), for which Hardy then wrote to thank her. "In the nebulous disguise of The Hogarth Press," Hardy wrote, "I recognize the daughter of my old friend Leslie Stephen, & I send this line of thanks to her" (*CLTH* 6:255). Thus, while Woolf was articulating her ambivalent responses toward Hardy, in her journal the ghost of Leslie Stephen was still continuing to inform their correspondence. Did this equivocal "paternal" association between Woolf and Hardy complicate or "haunt" the novel that she composed in these years? Does Hardy's novel *The Mayor of Casterbridge* (which Woolf had praised as so "high" an "example" of fiction, that no modern novel could "compare") have what Jay Clayton terms the intertextual "ghost effect" on *Mrs. Dalloway*? And what of Woolf's preoccupation with the "design" of her work? Does this relate to her call in "Modern Fiction" for a "new method" to replace the limiting structure that Hardy's own works followed? In order to explore some possible answers to these questions, I will take a look at the connections I sense between *Mrs. Dalloway* and *The Mayor of Casterbridge*.

Uncanny Likeness:
Mrs. Dalloway and *The Mayor of Casterbridge*

As I noted above, Woolf praised *The Mayor of Casterbridge* as incomparable, and had taken a copy of the book with her to Maxgate for Hardy to autograph soon after the publication of her own *Mrs. Dalloway*. If, as this episode suggests, Woolf was seriously intrigued by Hardy's novel, I find myself similarly intrigued by the variety of textual links between these works. Both *Mrs. Dalloway* and *The Mayor of Casterbridge* contain a scene of a "royal procession," in which a figure of "great importance" remains unnamed. In both works this procession foreshadows the eventual fates of the main characters. There are further similarities to be found: both novels make use of the return of a long lost love to propel the main character into crisis; both texts contrast a mentally stable character with another, unstable figure; the main characters of each struggle for the affections of a daughter named Elizabeth (Elizabeth-Jane in *The Mayor of Casterbridge*); both end with the tragic death of the mentally unstable character, and in each text these deaths occur as the other, saner figure attends a party.

The opening sequences of both works relate an early choice, made by the main characters, regarding marriage. These youthful decisions will in turn become a central source of sorrow and regret for these figures. In the first chapter of *The Mayor of Casterbridge*, for instance, the origin of Michael Henchard's later troubles is conveyed. Henchard, having had far too much to drink at the Weydon Priors Fair, auctions his wife Susan to the highest bidder. He boasts: "I'll sell her for five guineas to any man that will pay me the money" (*Mayor* 34). A sailor takes up Henchard's offer and leaves the fair with Susan and Henchard's young daughter, Elizabeth-Jane. As the plot of this novel is related chronologically, Henchard's rash act is seen to propel the narrative that follows. In contrast, Clarissa Dalloway's tale is given to the reader in flashback.

Woolf's novel begins as the middle-aged Clarissa leaves home to purchase flowers for a party. The beauty of the morning soon "plunges" her back into a sea of memories. It recalls to Clarissa her eighteenth year, and her earlier love, Peter Walsh. Her first thoughts are of a summer at Bourton: "What a lark! What a plunge! For so it had always seemed to her, when, with a little squeak of the hinges, which she could hear now, she had burst open the French windows and plunged at Bourton into the open air. How fresh, how calm, stiller than this of course, the air was in the early morning; like the flap of a wave; the kiss of a wave; chill and sharp [. . .]" (*Dalloway* 3). While Henchard's story is, as I noted, relayed in a linear time sequence, Clarissa's early years are presented to the reader through memories. The effect of this narrative difference is clear: Hardy's omniscient narrator imparts seemingly reliable information about an event in the life of the fictional Michael Henchard, but Clarissa's life story, as conveyed through memory, is thus figured by Woolf as unreliable, changeable, and insecure.

If at first Clarissa recalls her time in Bourton as "a lark," as "fresh," "calm," and "still," for example, the instability of her narrative is illustrated as she begins to recall a conversation with Peter Walsh. Suddenly, her happy thoughts and reminiscences become clouded and "solemn":

[. . .] and yet (for a girl of eighteen as she then was) solemn, feeling as she did, standing there at the open window, that something awful was about to happen; looking at the flowers, at the trees with the smoke winding off them and the rooks rising, falling; standing and looking until Peter Walsh said, "Musing among the vegetables?"—was that it?—'I prefer men to cauliflowers"— was that it? (3–4)

As this shift destabilizes her pleasant memories, Clarissa begins to question the veracity of her recollections: "was that it?" "was that it?" While the narrator of *The Mayor of Casterbridge* is constructed as a fount of relevant detail, the details of Clarissa's own narrative are offered to the reader as insecure. Due to this structure, the beginning of *Mrs. Dalloway* calls attention to the very act of narration, and in doing so subtly blurs the distinction between writer, character, and narrator. The openings of these two novels thus differ sharply in narrative methodology. Nevertheless, both relate a choice made early in the lives of these characters that they are forced to address in the course of the novel. Moreover, both Woolf and Hardy rely on the surprising return of their main characters' long-lost loves, in order to provoke a confrontation with the past.

In Hardy's novel, this "returning love" takes the form of the character of Susan, who arrives in the town of Casterbridge some twenty years after being sold by Henchard. Unbeknownst to Susan, Henchard had sworn off "strong liquor for the space of twenty-one years" (*Mayor* 39) on the day following the auction of his wife, and spent many years in search of his wife and child. Upon discovering that they had "emigrated" (40), however, Henchard gave up his search and moved to "Casterbridge, in a far distant part of Sussex" (40). In the intervening years he has prospered, and by the time of Susan's return, he is the Mayor of the city. Meeting the now-powerful Henchard for the first time in twenty years, the widowed Susan is unsure of how she and her daughter Elizabeth-Jane will be received. Henchard, however, seems anxious to make reparations for the past: "I have thought of this plan: that you and Elizabeth take a cottage in the town as the widow Mrs. Newson and her daughter; that I meet you, court you, and marry you, Elizabeth-Jane coming to my house as my step-daughter. The thing is so natural and easy that it is half done thinkin o't" (63). As this passage implies, Henchard is both glad of the opportunity to make amends to his wife, and eager to ensure that doing so will cause him no embarrassment. In this way, Susan's arrival in Casterbridge is located as a moment of crisis for him. Susan's return allows Henchard to seek redemption for his sins, but her knowledge of his secret past provokes his fear of social downfall.

In *Mrs. Dalloway*, Woolf also employs the return of a long-lost love to create a moment of crisis for Clarissa. Like Susan's return to Casterbridge,

Peter Walsh's appearance after many years in India shocks and surprises Woolf's central character. As Clarissa sits "mending her dress" (61) for that evening's party, Peter unexpectedly arrives. In a further demonstration of the unreliability of Clarissa's memory, she momentarily cannot recall his name:

> Now the door opened, and in came—for a single second she could not re-member what he was called! so surprised she was to see him, so glad, so shy, so utterly taken aback to have Peter Walsh come to her unexpectedly in the morning! (She had not read his letter.) "And how are you?" said Peter Walsh, positively trembling; taking both her hands; kissing both her hands. She's grown older, he thought, sitting down. I shan't tell her anything about it, he thought, for she's grown older (59–60).

Like Hardy's Michael Henchard, Clarissa Dalloway has "grown older" by the time of her re-encounter with the past, and the arrival of a visitor provokes a sense of yearning and regret for both Clarissa and Henchard. While Hen-chard had promptly conceived of a plan to redress those regrets, however, at this point in Woolf's novel Clarissa can do nothing to lessen her remorse: "[n]ow I remember how impossible it was ever to make up my mind—and why did I make up my mind—not to marry him?" (61–2). In both *Mrs. Dalloway* and *The Mayor of Casterbridge*, then, the return of a lost love pre-cipitates a crisis of regret for the main characters, forcing them to confront their earlier choices.

There are, however, as least as many differences between the early chap-ters of these novels as there are parallels: for one, Henchard is a man and Clarissa is a woman. Furthermore, Hardy's text employs a traditional narra-tor, while Woolf presents the reader with an unreliable narrative scheme. Other dissimilarities surface as these novels continue: the final result of Susan's arrival in Casterbridge is Henchard's destruction, but although Peter's return is painful to Clarissa, it does not lead to her death. Indeed, by the close of Hardy's novel, Henchard will lose his fortune, his family, and his social status, but the conclusion of *Mrs. Dalloway* finds Clarissa's family in-tact and her social standing secure. I will argue, however, that these differ-ences in the relative fates of Woolf and Hardy's characters are themselves evidence of a connection between the two novels. An examination of the roles of the secondary characters in each of these works will help to develop this argument.

In both *The Mayor of Casterbridge* and *Mrs. Dalloway*, important sec-ondary characters are introduced in relation to the main characters. In her "Introduction" to the Modern Library Edition of *Mrs. Dalloway*, Woolf used the term "double" to describe the association between the characters of Sep-timus and Clarissa (vi). I would suggest that Hardy similarly locates Donald

Farfrae, the "Scotchman" in *The Mayor of Casterbridge,* as a "double" of Michael Henchard. As both texts thus rely on a structure of doubled characters, might this likeness hint at deeper connections between them? Woolf's purpose for this "doubling" in her text was clear, as she noted in her diary: "I adumbrate here a study of insanity & suicide: the world seen by the sane & insane side by side—something like that" (*DVW* 2:207). In Woolf's conception of the novel, then, Septimus and Clarissa were to be seen "side by side."

Similarly, in Hardy's *The Mayor of Casterbridge* the character of Farfrae can readily be seen as a foil against which the relative success (and sanity) of Henchard is gauged. When Farfrae and Henchard first meet, for example, Henchard is the most powerful man in Casterbridge. As Mayor and a successful corntrader, the prosperous Henchard takes a strong liking to Farfrae, offering the young stranger a position as manager on his farm. Although Farfrae calmly replies that he is "only passing through" (67), Henchard is convinced that Farfrae should stay in Casterbridge. Later, on the day of Farfrae's planned departure, Henchard pleads fervently with Farfrae to take the job, exclaiming, "hang it, Farfrae, I like thee well!" (75). These scenes illustrate a clear difference between the characters of Henchard and Farfrae. Henchard's "sudden liking" and vehement regard for a total stranger is depicted as an inappropriate overreaction, particularly when it is met with Farfrae's cautious and bemused reply, "I never expected this—I did not!" (75).

This distinction between Henchard's hasty and emotional reaction and Farfrae's more reasonable response also foreshadows the future destinies of both these characters. Farfrae, by virtue of his more rational nature, will eventually usurp Henchard's position as Mayor, corntrader, Lucetta's lover, and Elizabeth-Jane's protector. Similarly, the rash decision that Henchard makes in hiring Farfrae is merely one in a series of characteristically precipitous acts that lead to his final self-destruction. Just as he sold his wife, and lived to regret it, the same impulsiveness propels Henchard to: dismiss Farfrae through jealousy though "his heart sank within him" when it was done (109); throw his daughter Elizabeth out of his house for her courtship with Farfrae (136); blackmail Lucetta into an engagement (178); and, for fear of losing his daughter, tell the returning Captain Newson that she is dead (151).

In this way, the charting of Henchard's "fall" is the framework of *The Mayor of Casterbridge.* The rashness and emotional instability that he evinces from the beginning of the novel are shown to be the flaws that lead him to a tragic end. Furthermore, Donald Farfrae plays a role in almost all of Henchard's rash acts. Through his courting of Henchard's daughter, his overshadowing of Henchard as a corn trader, his wooing of Lucetta, and his later marriage to Elizabeth-Jane, Farfrae's success in Casterbridge, when seen alongside Henchard's failures, evokes a pathos that would not be felt without his presence. In Hardy's novel, then, the character of Farfrae functions not only as a gauge by which to measure Henchard's success and sanity, but also as a catalyst for tragedy. As Henchard accepts Farfrae with open arms, it seems, he is also opening himself to his tragic fate.

Unlike Henchard and Farfrae, in Woolf's *Mrs. Dalloway* the "doubles" Clarissa and Septimus never meet. Nevertheless, through their joint presence on Bond Street as the "face of the very greatest importance" drives by, their mutual interest in the sky-writing plane that hovers over both of them in Regent's Park, and their dual associations with the psychiatrist Sir William Bradshaw, Woolf allows them to circle each other throughout the text. Just as Hardy encourages the reader to see Henchard and Farfrae in terms of each other, Woolf's "design" for *Mrs. Dalloway* promotes a similar reading for the relationship between Clarissa and Septimus.

As Woolf noted in her 1928 "Introduction" to *Mrs. Dalloway,* however, this "doubling" of Clarissa and Septimus was not part of her original design for the novel. There she stated: "Of *Mrs. Dalloway* then one can only bring to light at the moment a few scraps, of little importance or none perhaps; as that in the first version Septimus, who was later intended to be her double, had no existence; and that Mrs. Dalloway was originally to kill herself, or perhaps merely to die at the end of the party" (198). Here Woolf suggests that this "scrap" of information is "of little importance," but I would argue that it offers a most exciting context for reading her novel. Like Hardy's tale, which ends with Henchard's death soon after his daughter's wedding party, Woolf's first version of *Mrs. Dalloway* would presumably have charted the crises and downfall of Clarissa, and concluded as she dies "at the end of the party." Thus, in composing her original drafts of *Mrs. Dalloway* Woolf would have found herself creating a novel that followed the same Aristotelian tragic codes upon which *The Mayor of Casterbridge* was structured. By bringing the character of Septimus into "existence," however, Woolf overturned the original tragic design she had envisioned for her novel: Hardy's Henchard dies, but Woolf's Clarissa lives.

As I have illustrated, in *The Mayor of Casterbridge* Farfrae functions as a catalyst for the main character's demise, and lends pathos to Henchard's tale through his relative success. Septimus, like Farfrae, is a "double" of the main character, but he fulfils a very different purpose: Septimus dies, but Farfrae lives. Like Henchard, Clarissa believes herself to be a tragic figure ("[s]omehow it was her disaster," Clarissa thinks [282]). In the context of Woolf's novel, however, it is not Clarissa but Septimus who plays the tragic role. If *Mrs. Dalloway* thus overturns a traditional tragic structure by allowing Septimus to die in place of Clarissa, I would argue that this "original fate" nevertheless haunts Clarissa in the text. Near the end of the novel, Clarissa considers: "[b]ut that young man had killed himself. Somehow it was her disaster—her disgrace" (282). As Clarissa's first destiny would have echoed Henchard's, Woolf's later addition of the character of Septimus serves a dual purpose. When I recall Woolf's essay "Modern Fiction," it appears to me that Clarissa's survival responds to the demands Woolf outlined there. By allowing Clarissa to live, that is, Woolf deconstructs the traditional "method" that she called a "limitation" to modern writers. Simultaneously, she creates a new "design" for a novel that will not fail to "compare" to *The Mayor of Casterbridge*. I therefore read Woolf's revision of Clarissa's fate as an attempt to compose a novel that would both critique and equal *The Mayor of Casterbridge*.

In Woolf's first version of the novel, as I argued above, the character of Clarissa was very like that of Henchard; having made some early mistakes, she would become a prosperous, socially acceptable figure whose re-encounter with the past led to death. By following such a "method," Woolf had not only employed a traditional tragic form, but also the same form upon which *The Mayor of Casterbridge* was based. Woolf's later "design" for *Mrs. Dalloway* not only breaks with the narrow and confining "method" of earlier novels, but also represses her indebtedness to them. In doing so, moreover, it forestalls comparison with Hardy's work. While such a reading of Woolf's "design" for the novel is supported by her "confession" of its original structure, it is further confirmed by the dating of the "Introduction" in which this admission appeared. Although *Mrs. Dalloway* came out in 1925, Woolf did not publish this singular explanation of the novel's first version until just after Hardy's death, in early 1928. Might Hardy's passing have reminded Woolf of her debt to his novel? If so, was this "Introduction" written as a salve for Woolf's guilty conscience, as it hints at *Mrs. Dalloway's* indebtedness to the past?

If the displacement of the fates of Woolf's "doubles" provides some indication of the influence of *The Mayor of Casterbridge* on *Mrs. Dalloway,* the nature of their connection is best explored through a reading of a scene that appears to occur in both texts. In Hardy's novel, the arrival of an unnamed "Royal personage" is a pivotal plot moment. It signals Henchard's final public humiliation and usurpation by Farfrae, and it points the way to Farfrae's success and Henchard's demise. In the author's "Preface" to *The Mayor of Casterbridge,* Hardy details the emphasis he placed on this episode: "The incidents narrated arise mainly out of three events [. . .] in the real history of the town called Casterbridge and the neighbouring country. They were the sale of a wife by her husband, the uncertain harvests which immediately preceded the repeal of the Corn Laws, and the visit of a Royal personage to the aforesaid part of England."[10] Hardy's inclusion of this "visit of a Royal personage" in his "Preface" confirms its importance to the novel's structure. The events Hardy mentions here comprise the three gravest errors of Henchard's life: the sale of Susan, his wife; the loss of his business due to his reliance on a weather prophet; and his public humiliation on the day of the royal visit.

As the entire city of Casterbridge gathers to witness the arrival of the Royal personage, they are also present at the tragic climax of Henchard's fate. At the head of the crowd, the new Mayor Farfrae, Henchard's former lover Lucetta, and his daughter Elizabeth-Jane look on with mortification, as the mentally unstable Henchard halts the "Royal carriage" in its procession: "There were a few clear yards in front of the Royal carriage, sanded; and into this space a man stepped before anyone could prevent him. It was Henchard. He had unrolled his private flag, and removing his hat he staggered to the side of the slowing vehicle, waving the Union Jack to and fro" (*Mayor* 232). As "Farfrae with Mayoral authority" seizes Henchard and tells him "roughly to be off," Henchard resists momentarily. Then "by an unaccountable impulse" Henchard "gave way and retired" (232). Here, Henchard's humiliation is complete: in the course of the novel, he will never recover his family, his dignity, or his sanity.

While Hardy thus employs this event as climatic, the similar scene in *Mrs. Dalloway* is placed at the beginning of the novel, and serves as an introduction to Clarissa's "double," Septimus. In this episode, an anonymous male hand draws down the curtain on the window of a "dove-grey" car. As this happens, both Clarissa and Septimus look on from opposite sides of Oxford Street:

> Mrs. Dalloway, coming to the window with her arms full of sweet peas, looked out with her little pink face pursed in enquiry. Every one looked at the motor car. Septimus looked. Boys on bicycles sprang off. Traffic accumulated. And there the motor car stood, with drawn blinds, and upon them a curious pattern like a tree, Septimus thought, and this gradual drawing together of everything to one centre before his eyes, as if some horror had come almost to the surface and was about to burst into flames, terrified him. The world wavered and quivered and threatened to burst into flames. It is I who am blocking the way, he thought. Was he not being looked at and pointed at; was he not weighted there, rooted to the pavement, for a purpose? But for what purpose? (21)

Septimus is then dragged away by his embarrassed wife, but, like Hardy's Henchard, he resists momentarily. At length, however, he concedes to her demands and crosses the street. While Henchard demonstrates a rather pathetic patriotism in front of the Royal carriage as he waves his "Union Jack to and fro," in *Mrs. Dalloway*, Clarissa is also shown to experience a sense of national pride; the royal vehicle recalls to her "the majesty of England, the enduring symbol of the state" (23). Thus, an unnamed Royal personage, a mentally unstable character blocking the Royal carriage, a crowd of interested onlookers, and symbols of the state are found in both novels. If the symmetry of these scenes draws my attention, however, I find even greater interest in the subtle differences that they evince. In *The Mayor of Caster-bridge,* for example, it is Henchard who shows mental instability, blocks the path of the Royal carriage, is stared at by onlookers, and forced away from the street. In *Mrs. Dalloway,* on the other hand, the secondary character, Septimus, takes on this role.

While Henchard stops the Royal carriage in its tracks, he does so with a specific purpose: he plans to upstage his rival Farfrae. Woolf's character Septimus, by contrast, only imagines that he is "blocking the way" and that it is he who is "looked at and pointed at" because of his terror and paranoia. In fact, as Woolf makes clear, it is not Septimus who has stopped the car, or at whom the crowds stare. The chauffeur has momentarily alighted, and people on the street consequently gather to look at the stationary vehicle. Thus, while in *The Mayor of Casterbridge* Henchard's actions are shown to have a purpose, the entire royal episode in *Mrs. Dalloway* is figured as an illusion for Septimus, a misreading. Standing in the street, he believes he does so "for a purpose? But for what purpose?" (21). The ambiguity and uncertainty of Septimus' hallucination recalls critic Michael Riffaterre's account of inter-textual obscurity and undecidability. As Riffaterre maintains, an encounter with such a textual difficulty is a sign that points the competent reader to an intertext that will resolve it. In other words, Septimus' uncertainty in this passage suggests that, within the context of *Mrs. Dalloway,* he cannot know his "purpose" for "blocking the way" of the Royal car. Riffaterre's work, though, allows me to propose that Septimus' "purpose" in this scene *can* be located in the intertext from which it is derived. If I propose *The Mayor of Casterbridge* as this intertext, I can posit that Septimus' lost "purpose" is found in Henchard's need to upstage Farfrae, in the scene that Septimus un-knowingly re-enacts. In this intertextual reading, Septimus' uncertainty is only "resolved" by locating his "purpose" in Henchard's desires in *The Mayor of Casterbridge.* Thus, while the "ghost" of Henchard "haunts" and informs the actions of Septimus, his mad intertextual counterpart, the "meaning" of those actions have, for Septimus, been seemingly lost in the intertextual web.

In Hardy's text, the characters in the novel know the Royal personage, al-though he remains unnamed by the narrator: Hardy has Farfrae speak to him and Lucetta shake his hand (233). In *Mrs. Dalloway,* however, "nobody knew whose face had been seen" (20). Like Septimus' lost purpose, then, the am-biguous identity of this Royal figure in Woolf's novel could also have its ori-gin in *The Mayor of Casterbridge.* As Hardy does not identify this figure, this information is unavailable to Woolf's characters; like any other "readers" of Hardy's novel, they can only guess whose face is inside the Royal carriage. These connections between the two passages could also suggest a further, psy-choanalytic reading of *Mrs. Dalloway.* The loss of both Septimus' purpose and the name of the Royal figure, that is, may be evidence that the "familiar" and true source of this passage has been "alienated" and "repressed." In this reading, Woolf "represses" *The Mayor of Casterbridge* as the origin of the ambiguity of this Royal figure. Refusing to acknowledge her debt to Hardy, Woolf attempts to justify the uncertainty over this figure's identity. Woolf's characters, the narrator claims, cannot name him because "a male hand drew the blind and there was nothing to be seen" (*Dalloway* 119). In this way, Woolf could be said to anticipate and disallow a reading of her novel as informed by Hardy's. If Woolf was denying her text's connection to *The Mayor of Casterbridge* here, a similar refutation of Hardy's novel can be seen in Septimus' misreading of the street scene.

As Septimus stands staring at the car, he begins to hallucinate, and this hallucination can be read as a "haunting" of Woolf's text by the repressed figure of Henchard. Such an interpretation, moreover, explicates the language Woolf uses to depict Septimus' vision: it is evidence of her own denial of indebtedness to Hardy. For Septimus, Woolf writes, it is "as if some horror had come almost to the surface and was about to burst into flames" (*Dalloway* 21). But what "horror"? What was about to "burst into flames"? If I read these words as Woolf's refusal to acknowledge Hardy's "influence," it seems that in this moment of lost purpose, Septimus voices the writer's own fear of discovery. In this scene, that is, Woolf evacuates Septimus' purpose (which might link him to Henchard) in order to avoid acknowledging her use of a Hardinian vision. To do so, she suggests that Septimus' sense of "blocking" and being "looked at" are merely symptoms of his paranoia. Thus "the horror" of Woolf's debt to *The Mayor of Casterbridge,* which had "come almost to the surface" is successfully "repressed," but at the cost of Septimus' sanity: the world now "wavered and quivered" and "terrified him."

I suggested earlier that Woolf created the character of Septimus in an attempt to overturn the traditional, tragic strategy employed by Hardy in *The Mayor of Casterbridge*. If this were so, it would further explain Septimus' "haunting" by the ghost of Henchard in this Royal scene. Septimus, that is, was conceived and sacrificed on the altar of Woolf's repressed indebtedness to Hardy. In *The Mayor of Casterbridge,* Henchard's destiny is one of rags to riches to rags to death, but Woolf chose to disallow that punishing end for Clarissa. Instead, she created the character of Septimus, who serves as a martyr for Clarissa's own salvation, as is evidenced by his final words "I'll give it you!" (*Dalloway* 226). Clarissa's sense of guilt upon hearing of Septimus' suicide is a further "difficulty" that is hard to contextualize. This guilt, however, can be explained via the intertext of *The Mayor of Casterbridge,* or again, through a psychoanalytic interpretation of Woolf's negotiations of Hardy.

In the midst of her party, Sir William Bradshaw tells Clarissa of Septimus' death. Although she has never met Septimus, Clarissa feels an unaccountable responsibility for him: "[b]ut that young man had killed himself. Somehow it was her disaster—her disgrace. It was her punishment" (282). To account for Clarissa's guilt, one can look back to her intertextual counterpart, Henchard. Clarissa, it seems, is haunted by his fate, which was to be her own in Woolf's first version of the novel. Clarissa's ability to escape death thus leads her to face the remorse of a fortunate survivor. Indeed, despite Woolf's attempt to ground Clarissa's guilt within the context of *Mrs. Dalloway*, ["[s]he had schemed; she had pilfered. She was never wholly admirable" (282)], this sudden self-criticism is out of character and unconvincing. Does the difficulty of this passage then, signal a further "surfacing" of Woolf's debt to Hardy? Clarissa's remorse, that is, while confusing when read as a response to the death of a stranger, does make sense as an inscription of Woolf's own guilt. If this is so, then this passage may contain a further admission. Here, perhaps, Woolf confesses to the "not wholly admirable" "scheme" of "pilfering" from Hardy's novel, and, moreover, discloses her reason for doing so: "She had wanted success" (282).

Although this biographically centered reading of Woolf's novel seems to fly in the face of intertextual theory, it is nevertheless one that Woolf herself promoted as a way of understanding her work. As Woolf notes in her 1928 "Introduction" to *Mrs. Dalloway:* "Books are the flowers or fruit stuck here and there on a tree which has its roots deep down in the earth of our earliest life, our first experiences. But here again to tell the reader anything that his own imagination and insight have not already discovered would need not a page or two of preface, but a volume or two of autobiography" (198). The "volumes" of Woolf's "autobiography" are now available in the form of her letters and journals, and these do indeed offer "insights" about the "roots" and sources of her "experiences," and the "books" that "flowered" from them.

The difficulty for the reader who would explore these biographical "roots," however, is that of surmising the relative "significance" of one experience over another. Does it matter, for instance, that after finishing *Mrs. Dalloway*, Woolf postponed a trip to visit Hardy at Maxgate several times? Or that she wrote to her friend Janet Case in September of 1925, saying "and so, though Thomas Hardy has asked us to come and see him (this is a boast) we don't do it; and I'd rather see Janet, as I hate great men" (*LVW* 3:202)? As I noted earlier, Jay Clayton asserts that such determinations of the "meaning" of a source are necessary only if one wants to connect a writer to a "specific tradition" of "enquiry." By linking Woolf's reluctance to meet Hardy with her repressed "anxiety of influence," for example, I can locate her as a later poet battling with ambivalence toward her presumed precursor.

In fact, such a reading explicates both Woolf's hatred of "great men," of which she wrote to Janet Case, and the nervousness surrounding her impending meeting with Hardy, which Woolf admitted in the following letter to Vita Sackville-West:

About coming—I'm dashing off, you'll be amused to hear, on my chronic visit to Hardy. [. . .] I shall only stay one day and drink one cup of tea, and be so damned nervous I shall spill it on the floor, and what shall I say? Nothing, but arid nonsense. Yet I feel this is a great occasion. Here am I approaching the immortal fount, touching the sacred hand: he will make all of us [. . .] seem transparent and passing (*LVW* 3:281).

Woolf's ambivalence toward Hardy, as illustrated by these two letters (she "hates great men" yet thinks of Hardy as "the immortal fount") could be read as evidence of her anxious negotiations of his influence.

In Woolf's later recounting of her meeting with Hardy, however, the "anxiety" that she anticipated feeling was not experienced by her, but by Hardy himself: "So we got up & signed Mrs H's visitors books; & Hardy took my L[ife's] Little Ironies off, & trotted back with it signed, & Woolf spelt Wolff, wh. I daresay had given him some anxiety" (*DVW* 3:100). Here, as Woolf recounts the "anxiety" that Hardy felt upon signing her book, I must recall that this recording of Hardy's feelings is itself a textual rendering, composed by Woolf herself. If I read the passage with this in mind, Hardy's nervousness, as depicted by Woolf, could be a "projection" of her own sensations. Indeed, Woolf's "anxiety" seems much more clearly signposted in the passage, as having brought a copy of *The Mayor of Casterbridge* for Hardy to autograph, she instead had him sign a different one of his works (fittingly entitled *Life's Little Ironies).*

As Woolf concludes this recollection of her visit with Hardy, his own parting words to her produce a further ambiguity. "'They've changed everything now,' he said. 'We used to think there was a beginning & a middle & an end. [. . .] Now one of those stories came to an end with a woman going out of a room.' He chuckled. But he no longer reads novels" (*DVW* 3:101). Within the context of Woolf's diary entry, the "story" to which Hardy refers may be Aldous Huxley's "Half-Holiday."[11] The exact reference is unclear, however, as "Half-Holiday" ends with a man, not a woman, leaving a room, and later in the entry Hardy suggests that he does not remember Huxley's story. This uncertainty over the text of which Hardy spoke allows me to posit a different novel as the object of Hardy's critique. Perhaps here Hardy refers to Woolf's own *Mrs. Dalloway,* which ends with Clarissa entering a room. Is it possible that Hardy was slyly criticizing Woolf's design for *Mrs. Dalloway,* its overturning of his preferred "method" with its clearly defined beginning, middle, and end? The ambiguity with which Woolf surrounds this incident disallows a definitive answer. While it is clear that Hardy was quite knowledgeable about current literature (despite Woolf's claim that he "no longer reads novels"), there is no evidence that he read *Mrs. Dalloway.* Thus, as ever, the curious reader must be satisfied with pondering the possibilities.

Katherine Mansfield: The Ghost in *Mrs. Dalloway*

Such biographical sources as these diary entries may therefore suggest Hardy's influence on Woolf, enticing readers to see her texts as a negotiation of her indebtedness to him. But there are, of course, other ways of interpreting her works. Roland Barthes' account of intertextuality, for instance, insists that "to try to find the 'sources' and 'influences' of a work is to fall in with the myth of filiation" for the author himself is "no longer the origin of his fiction, but a fiction contributing to his work" ("Work to Text" 160–1). If this is so, wouldn't a reading of *Mrs. Dalloway* as an ambitious and anxious response to *The Mayor of Casterbridge* dramatically limit its potential meaning(s)? In an attempt to reopen the possibilities, and to problematize some of the interpretations that I have proposed above, I turn now to a very different reading of *Mrs. Dalloway*.

Before re-entering her party at the end of *Mrs. Dalloway*, Clarissa has a strange, voyeuristic vision: "She parted the curtains; she looked. Oh, but how surprising!—in the room opposite the old lady stared straight at her! She was going to bed" (283). Clarissa continues to watch, and finds it "fascinating" that "[s]he was going to bed" while people are "laughing and shouting in the drawing-room" (283). Like Clarissa, I suggest, the reader experiences a similar sense of fascination and wonder here, as the voyeurism Woolf depicts becomes two-sided: Clarissa watches the old lady, who in turn "stared straight at her!" (283). In this passage, Woolf's blurring of the distinction between Clarissa's consciousness and the voice of the narrator leads to confusion. Because the words "she" and "her" are repeated here, a dialogue is seemingly enacted between Clarissa and the "old lady." As each is in her bedroom, gazing upon the other, the words that follow could arguably originate in the thoughts of either woman: "[s]he was going to bed," "[c]ould she see her?," "[s]he pulled the blind now" (283). This enigmatic passage, moreover, raises questions aside from those of narrative strategy. Who, the reader may ask, is this old lady, and what has she to do with Clarissa? Are the windows out of which each stares like two sides of a mirror? Does Clarissa, for whom "the sheet was stretched and the bed narrow" (70), see herself as the old lady in that mirror, in bed alone despite people "laughing and shouting" below (283)?

Perhaps instead this old lady is an echo of the abandoned Miss Kilman. In an earlier passage, Clarissa herself links the two characters: "Clarissa had often seen her. [. . .] Somehow one respected that—that old woman looking out of the window, quite unconscious that she was being watched. There was something solemn in it—but love and religion would destroy that, whatever it was, the privacy of the soul. The odious Kilman would destroy it. Yet it was a sight that made her want to cry" (191–2). As I suggested earlier, the

character of Miss Kilman can be associated with Woolf's memories of
Katherine Mansfield, whose words Miss Kilman voices. While Mansfield,
dead at thirty-four, never became old, Woolf nevertheless described Mansfield in her illness as "crawling about the room like an old woman" (*DVW*
1:216). Furthermore, the trope "the privacy of the soul" that Clarissa believes Miss Kilman will destroy is, like Kilman's "[d]on't quite forget me," a
reiteration of Mansfield's own words. In the same diary entry that contains
the image of Mansfield as an "old woman," Woolf also noted that "[i]llness,
[Mansfield] said, breaks down one's privacy so that one can't write" (*DVW*
1:216). Could this old woman, then, "going to bed," be another refiguring
of Katherine Mansfield?

In this passage, as in the later one that also contains the mysterious "old
lady," the complicated narrative structure Woolf employs poses interpretative
difficulties. Nevertheless, I will posit some possible explanations for Clarissa's
condemnation of Kilman here, and her association of Kilman with the "old
woman." First, while it is Clarissa who "had often seen" the "old woman"
through the window, she blames "love and religion" along with the "odious
Miss Kilman" for the destruction of the "privacy of the soul." Is it not instead
the voyeuristic Clarissa who invades the old woman's privacy? If I reassert that
the old woman is a shadow of Mansfield, then, according to this passage, hers
is a "soul" "quite unconscious of being watched." Could this act of "watching,"
then, be a metaphor for literary influence? Does this scene enact the dynamics
of indebtedness, as the later poet gazes upon the "old," who is in turn "unconscious of being watched"? If so, literary influence is envisioned as destructive
here, invading the privacy of the precursor's soul, and leaving it "destroyed."

In this moment, Clarissa projects her invasion of the old woman's "privacy" onto Kilman, and perhaps by creating Kilman as a Mansfield-like
character, Woolf herself enacted a similar projection. Woolf, that is, watched
the ailing Mansfield through the window of memory, and by inventing fictional representations of Mansfield in *Jacob's Room* and *Mrs. Dalloway*, in-
vaded and destroyed the "privacy" of Mansfield's soul. As the passage
continues, however, Woolf seems to insist that Mansfield's destruction was
no one's fault but her own: "[t]he odious [Mansfield-like] Kilman will destroy it" (191). Thus, in this complex scene, Woolf appears to both accept
and reject Mansfield's influence—to gaze upon Mansfield's soul with "respect," and then to depict her as self-destructive. Indeed, the difficulty of
Woolf's negotiation of Mansfield's influence is further illustrated by the sudden (and unaccountable) surfacing here of Clarissa's sorrow: "[y]et it was a
sight that made her want to cry" (192).

Interestingly, when this same "old lady" appears later in Woolf's text,
Clarissa's reaction to her is quite different. Once this woman whom Clarissa
has watched "many times before" stares "straight at her," the blinds are closed,

and Clarissa turns her thoughts to Septimus. Earlier, Clarissa had regarded both Septimus' death and the sight of the woman as sorrowful, but now "[s]he felt glad he had done it": "There! the old lady had put out her light! the whole house was dark now with this going on, she repeated, and the words came to her, Fear no more the heat of the sun. She must go back to them. But what an extraordinary night! She felt somehow very like him—the young man who had killed himself. She felt glad he had done it; thrown it away" (283).

Within this intricate prose, I suggest, are images of literary influence and indebtedness best understood not within the context of *Mrs. Dalloway,* but rather in the "intertextual web" of Woolf's own biography, as related in letters, journals, and essays. As the mysterious "old lady" puts out her light, that is, I see not only Woolf's desire to confront Mansfield's death, but also her need to break free of her literary debts to both Mansfield and Hardy.

Woolf's letters and journals are central to such an interpretation of her novel. As I have demonstrated, several of *Mrs. Dalloway's* narrative difficulties can be resolved (partially) by reading Woolf's private responses to Mansfield and Hardy as possible "intertexts" of the novel. Like the "unknown purpose" behind the actions of both Elizabeth and Septimus, the ambiguous nature of the "old woman" is also explained by an intertextual reading that takes into account such biographical sources. As the old lady stares "straight back," for instance, I can locate Woolf's own need to cease her voyeuristic "watching" of Mansfield's "soul." Here, this lost friend, whom Woolf described as an "old woman crawling about the room," is finally confronted and put to bed. When the blind is shut, moreover, Mansfield's influence upon Woolf is depicted as gone: "the old lady had put out her light." This lack of inspirational "light," however, inscribes no fear. Instead it invokes a cry of freedom, a relief from the "heat" that this light had given: "Fear no more the heat of the sun." Turning away from the darkened window, Woolf, in this reading, has conquered her indebtedness to Mansfield. Curiously, however, the drawing of this blind recalls the earlier scene in which "a male hand drew the blind" (*Dalloway* 19) on the window of the Royal motor car. As this first "pulled blind" appears during an episode informed by *The Mayor of Casterbridge,* I question to whom that "male hand" belongs. In composing *Mrs. Dalloway,* perhaps, Woolf not only attempted to "draw the blinds" on Katherine Mansfield, but also upon a male figure to whom she was equally indebted: Thomas Hardy.

As I noted earlier, Clarissa is shown to experience an unaccountable sense of guilt upon hearing of Septimus' suicide. Later however, and with no contextual explanation, Clarissa suddenly "felt glad he had done it" (283). I have argued that Clarissa's remorse is suggestive of Clayton's account of the intertextual "ghost effect," or of a Bloomian strategy of psychic defense against literary debt. Clarissa's sudden "gladness," I think, can be similarly accounted for. Woolf, by replacing Clarissa's death with that of Septimus, had overturned not only the traditional tragic structure that she had originally conceived for her novel, but, more specifically, the Hardinian genre of the tragic novel. In this way, a second triumph over influence is suggested in this scene from *Mrs. Dalloway:* by killing Septimus rather than Clarissa, Woolf had also slain her indebtedness to Hardy. Perhaps that is why "[s]he felt glad he had done it" (283).

In the previous chapter I noted that among Woolf's reactions to the death of Katherine Mansfield were the thoughts: "a shock of relief," and "a rival the less" (*DVW* 2:226). After attending Thomas Hardy's funeral in January 1928, Woolf wrote a similar consideration of the impact of his death on her own career:[12] "Yesterday we went to Hardy's funeral. What did I think of? Of Max Beerbohm's letter [of praise for the Common Reader], just read; or a lecture to the Newnhamites about women's writing. At intervals some emotion broke in" (*DVW* 3: 173).[13] Woolf goes on to describe the funeral ceremony, and the dinner that followed, and recounts Lytton Strachey's opinion of the "great man's novels" as "the poorest of poor stuff" (*DVW* 3:174). Afterwards, however, she returns to the thought of her own work, noting: "Over all this broods for me, some uneasy sense, of change & mortality, & how partings are deaths; & then a sense of my own fame—why should this come over me?" (*DVW* 3:174). Why indeed? In this chapter I have offered ideas of literary influence and indebtedness as possible contexts for understanding some difficult passages in Woolf's texts, and as an explanation for their "uncanny" similarity to the works of both Mansfield and Hardy. The theory of intertextuality, however, maintains that the meaning of a text is always another text. The "death of the author" is thus propounded as a method for steering clear of biographical sources (such as the journal entries I have relied upon) as origins for "meaning" within a given text.

Clayton and Rothstein explain that theorists of intertextuality promote the notion that biography is irrelevant to "meaning within a text." "Influence," they note, "depends on the lives of the authors, and in our accounts of these lives, incident should illustrate character and character determine incident. During the last half-century or more, however, critics have split being from doing—character from incident—as the autonomy of the text has gained adherents" ("Figures"14). Yet one must wonder, are not biographies, autobiographies, journals, and letters themselves texts, with their own "autonomy" as such? Does not their existence as texts grant them a place in the "intertextual web" of signs and quotations, which may then be organized as "meaning" upon the reader? I would insist that as the lives of figures from the past are always only available as text, they must be considered as within the realm of available intertext.

In Virginia Woolf's novels, one often finds images and tropes that she also employed in her private papers. In this way, her letters and journals must be seen as intertexts in the "resegmenting of literature," which allows for the "reading of the words of one text as 'part' of another text in a single unit of meaning" ("Figures" 24). This is not only true for the contemporary reader. Woolf herself noted in her diary on the day she had completed *Mrs. Dalloway:*

> (It strikes me that in this book I *practise* writing; do my scales; yes & work at certain effects. I daresay I practised Jacob here,—& Mrs D. & shall invent my next book here; for here I write merely in the spirit—great fun it is too, & old V. of 1940 will see something in it too. She will be a woman who can see, old V.:—everything—more than I can I think. But I'm tired now) (*DVW* 2:319–20).

Woolf's novels allude in complex ways to the texts of both Mansfield and Hardy, and can thus be read as responding to them as fellow writers, as friends and as rivals. In the passage above, however, she tells of another intriguing "influence" upon her work. Here, Woolf proposes her own journal as a future intertext, upon which the "old V. of 1940" will be able to inscribe meanings "unseen" by the present "V." By describing her current words as part of a later work as yet unimagined, Woolf's language here proleptically echoes Clayton's explanation of intertextuality: "[e]ach text is haunted by the others, the earlier by the later, the later by the earlier[. . .] Intertextuality is a ghost effect" ("Figures" 54). If the "ghosts" of Mansfield and Hardy had informed Woolf's early novels, the Virginia Woolf of October 1924 imagined that the meaning of her current text would only be inscribed on the "old V. of 1940," who could "see everything." The haunting thus continues.

Chapter Six ❦

Ambivalence

Virginia Woolf's Biographies of Leslie Stephen

In October of 1924, in the same diary entry in which Virginia Woolf termed her journals a "practice" ground for her fiction, she also considered the "ghosts" that "slip between me & the page" (*DVW* 2:317). Among these was Katherine Mansfield, "that strange ghost [. . .] dragging herself across her room" (*DVW* 2:317). Here, Woolf contemplates Mansfield's "gifts" but ultimately dismisses them as inferior to her own, noting that "if she'd lived, she'd have written on, & people would have seen that I was the more gifted—that wd. only have become more & more apparent" (*DVW* 2:317). Later in the same entry, Woolf also reflects on another literary "ghost" in her life: Thomas Hardy.

In this passage, Woolf portrays Hardy like she did Mansfield: as a diminishing figure whose importance to her had dwindled. She introduces this thought by discussing her own increasing fame, remarking, "[s]o very likely this time next year I shall be one of those people who are, so father said, in the little circle of London Society which represents the Apostles, I think, on a larger scale [. . .] just imagine being in that position—if women can be. Lytton is: [. . .] not perhaps Hardy" (*DVW* 2:319). Woolf then considers her own relation to Hardy, stating, "[n]othing very exciting, even as a boast not very exciting now. H[ardy] remembers your father: did not like many people, but was fond of him; talks of him often. Would like to know you. But I cant easily fit into that relation; the daughter grateful for old compliments to her father" (*DVW* 2:319). Interestingly, these rather lukewarm reassessments of Mansfield and Hardy coincide with Woolf's completion of *Mrs. Dalloway*. Might Woolf's view of these two writers have been altered by that recent achievement? As I have argued, Woolf's earlier novels were informed by her relationships with Mansfield and Hardy. If this is so, could it be that the composition of *Mrs. Dalloway* had enabled Woolf to resolve her indebtedness to these two "ghosts"?

In this same journal entry, Woolf further asserts that she had "exorcised" a "spell" through writing *Mrs. Dalloway*.[1] I would argue that, in truth, what she exorcised was her sense of debt toward Mansfield and Hardy. Woolf's reflections of October 17, 1924, therefore, can be read as a narrative of her struggles with literary influence. In these lines, Woolf contemplates both Mansfield and Hardy and their previous importance to her life and work, but portrays them as fallen idols, rather less "gifted" and less "exciting" than she had formerly believed them. Once she has laid these spirits to rest, however, Woolf identifies another, whose influence continues to "slip between [her] & the page." She reflects upon the success of *Mrs. Dalloway*, fearing that this "feat" will be hard to follow, and this anxiety about her accomplishments leads her to thoughts of another literary figure: "I see already The Old Man," her father Leslie Stephen (*DVW* 2:317).[2]

Here, Woolf mentions her father while writing about her discomfort with her own success. Is this evidence, then, of her struggle with Stephen's "ghost"? As I noted above, Woolf claimed that she did not "easily fit into" the relation of "the daughter grateful for old compliments to her father" (*DVW* 2:319), but into what relation with Stephen did she "easily fit"? To me, this excerpt suggests that although Woolf had exorcised the ghosts of Mansfield and Hardy, she was as yet unable to confront her feelings toward her father, or his influence upon her writing. After portraying him as "The Old Man" in her journal, Woolf concludes that some day all these considerations will be seen differently, by the "old V. of 1940" who can see "everything" (*DVW* 2: 320). In this chapter, I will attempt to chart that change in vision by examining the various images of Leslie Stephen that Woolf created throughout her life. The "old V. of 1940" did see differently, and in the following pages I will examine the mutable nature of that vision. Woolf's need to define and redefine her feelings toward her father and his literary legacy casts its shadow over much of her work. From her earliest work to her last, the influence of Leslie Stephen can be seen, and by targeting such moments I hope to offer a necessarily fragmented narrative of this most powerful force upon Woolf's voice.

In the previous chapter I noted that Woolf proposed a relationship between autobiography and fiction in her 1928 "Introduction" to *Mrs. Dalloway*. There, she stated that in order for a reader to understand fully the author's intentions, they would need "not a page or two of preface" but a "volume or two of autobiography" (198). Thus, in her view, the author's personal history was an important source for locating meaning within a text. As she "practised" her writing in her journals, Woolf considered one as the workshop for the other, in which she would "do [her] scales; yes & work at certain effects" (*DVW* 2:319). The intertextual link that Woolf promoted between her fiction and her diaries can be used to suggest a range of possible "meanings" within her works. Nevertheless, any strict reliance on Woolf's "autobiography" as the primary origin for her fictional works would also serve to limit the potential readings of those texts. Indeed, by concentrating on Woolf's personal writings as a starting point for the "meanings" found in her novels, a prior intertextual source might be ignored: Woolf's journals were themselves informed by the memoirs and biographies of others. In the following pages I will look at the role that Woolf's interest in biography played in her texts. For reasons I shall suggest below, Woolf intertwined this literary form with thoughts of patriarchy, of canonical status, and, perhaps most importantly, with memories of her father.

Leslie Stephen's own association with the genre of biography arose from his work as editor of the *Dictionary of National Biography,* which was published between 1885 and 1902. This dictionary was designed to be the chief biographical reference work for the United Kingdom, written both for general readers and academics; in all it contained about 38,000 articles. It was an awesome undertaking. Woolf's biographer, Lyndall Gordon, goes some way toward explaining Stephen's decision to leave his position at *Cornhill* magazine in 1882 and begin his tenure on the *DNB*. In Gordon's view, Stephen threw himself into this daunting editorial task as a result of the failure of his philosophical study *The Science of Ethics.* "It was with this book," Gordon notes, "that he had hoped to establish himself as a speculative philosopher and it had been his disappointment at its reception which had led him, in 1882, to accept the publisher, George Smith's suggestion that he compile the biographical dictionary, that was, ironically, to make his name" (L. Gordon 25). Gordon suggests here that Stephen's role as editor of the *DNB* was indeed to "make his name" during his lifetime. This change in Stephen's role in literary history is therefore doubly ironic: unable to "make his name" as a philosopher, he did so by promoting the "names" of others. The appearance of another troublesome legacy in the same year, however, ensured that his name did not die with him: in 1882, his daughter, Virginia, was born. Thus, while Stephen attained a degree of renown in his own era by memorializing the famous dead in the *DNB,* one century on the source of his posthumous fame has changed. For most contemporary readers, Leslie Stephen is best remembered (if at all) as Virginia Woolf's father. Stephen's role as biographer in turn influenced his daughter's writing career, thus resulting in his current, tangential place in literary history.

Gordon argues that Stephen used his work on the *DNB* as an escape from his failures, but Stephen himself seems to have had high hopes for the project. In his announcement of the *DNB* in 1882, for example, Stephen asserted: "A biography written with a single eye to giving all the information presumably desirable by an intelligent reader may be not only useful, but also intensely interesting, and even a model of literary art."[3] This "model of literary art," begun in the year of his daughter's birth, was to have a major impact upon Virginia throughout her childhood. As Phyllis Rose observes in her biography of Woolf: "[f]or the next ten years, this enormous project of writing and editing was being conducted in, was to some extent dominating, the house in which Virginia Woolf was growing up" (Rose 4). The young Virginia took a great interest in her father's work, and soon began to write her own childish "journals" and "newspapers." In February of 1891, for example, Virginia and her brother Thoby created *The Hyde Park Gate News,* a collection of stories, poems, and articles later "published" weekly by them.[4] An article, which appeared in this "newspaper" in December of 1893, hints at the young Virginia's view of her father.

During that month, Leslie Stephen had been elected President of the London Library, a prestigious appointment in which, as Stephen later noted, he had "succeeded Tennyson, who succeeded Houghton, who succeeded Carlyle; so that the position has hitherto been respectable. It amused me because the first proposal was to elect Gladstone. Somebody then proposed me" (cited in Maitland 416). Virginia's article in *The Hyde Park Gate News* reported this newsworthy story as follows: "We think that the London Library has made a very good choice in putting Mr. Stephen before Mr. Gladstone as although Mr. Gladstone may be a first-rate politician he cannot beat Mr. Stephen in writing" (cited in L. Gordon 16). Aside from the pride in her father that Virginia's editorial displays, it also serves another purpose: in this short piece the young Virginia creates a "portrait" of her father. In this early specimen of her writing, that is, the biographer's daughter tries her hand at her father's work, by depicting her subject "Mr. Stephen."

Virginia's interest in writing thus grew while surrounded by the copy, the proofs, and the piled papers that represented her father's distillation of the lives of 378 great men.[5] Stephen himself took note of the intensity with which his daughter was attracted to all things literary, remarking in a letter to his wife Julia: "[s]he takes in a great deal & will really be an author in time."[6] Stephen was only half right in this assessment of his daughter's potential. Though Virginia did indeed "take in a great deal," her publication of the weekly newspaper illustrates that far from becoming an author "in time," his daughter was, in fact, already one. Moreover, just as her publication of this childish journal foretold Woolf's later career, the early portrait of her father that appeared there anticipates a recurring theme in her mature works. Alongside Woolf's later endeavors as critic, essayist, and novelist, she enacted another role as well. Woolf became the biographer of her father, the biographer.

Virginia's first true biographical portrait of her father was begun in 1904, shortly after Stephen's death from cancer that February. Both Virginia and her Aunt Caroline, Leslie's sister, had been asked to offer guidance to Frederic Maitland, Stephen's biographer.[7] The reasons behind Virginia and Caroline being chosen as family representatives on this work are themselves intriguing. Caroline Emelia Stephen had become known in certain circles for her religious books, which related her personal experiences of God through the Quaker faith. In addition to this, through her niece Katherine Stephen, principal of Newnham College, Cambridge, Caroline was frequently called upon to speak to female students on the topics of religion and charitable works.[8] As a result, Caroline, or "Nun" as she was called in the family, became something of an eccentric literary figure about Cambridge: living alone, writing religious treatises, and befriending and influencing a new generation of female scholars. Caroline's literary status, and familiarity with her brother Leslie's Cambridge connections, thus made her an obvious choice for assisting Maitland. Virginia, by contrast, seems to have been offered this responsibility for therapeutic purposes: soon after her father's death Virginia underwent a second nervous breakdown. This was a much more severe attack than the one she had suffered following her mother's death, and in order to help speed her recovery, Virginia was sent to visit Caroline in Cambridge. Caroline soon realized that rather than rest, what her niece needed was to be engaged in an activity that would distract and occupy her. Thus, in 1904, Virginia assisted in compiling and contributing to Maitland's biography of her late father.

The contributions of both Virginia and her Aunt Caroline to this volume, however, raised tensions in the family. As Jean Love remarks in *Virginia Woolf: Sources of Madness and Art:*

> Virginia's role in Maitland's biography was to read and abstract the family letters and to write a brief account of her father from the family's perspective. Virginia wanted the task for reasons other than the work involved; she was apprehensive that "Nun" [Caroline] would write about him from her particular biases. Virginia [. . .] wanted to assist Maitland in order to dispose of "Nun's" theories about him (Love 313).

In her essay "The Niece of a Nun," Jane Marcus argues that Caroline Stephen had reason enough for her biased view of her brother. Leslie, as Marcus asserts, was unable to "comprehend the value of a woman's life if it did not revolve around marriage and motherhood," and thus considered Caroline's life as a failure ("Niece" 122). Marcus maintains that Stephen held his sister's mysticism and Quaker faith in contempt, and notes that in his *Mausoleum Book* he dismissed Caroline's texts as "little." There, he stated that his sister "became an invalid, though make[s] a few pathetic little attempts to turn her really great abilities to some account" (*Mausoleum Book* 55).

Marcus argues that in opposition to the reverential tone that Maitland took toward his subject, Stephen, Caroline wanted to write a candid "warts and all" portrait of her brother. Caroline's emphasis on "truth-telling in biography," as Marcus suggests ("Niece" 119), caused problems for her niece. "[Caroline]," Marcus argues, "struggled with Maitland (and the young Virginia) to no avail over the prettified portrait of Leslie Stephen that neglected to sketch in his temper and his emotional bullying of women" ("Niece" 119). Virginia at last prevailed against her aunt's preferences. Her contribution to Maitland, therefore, holds a threefold interest. This reminiscence was Virginia's first work written for publication, it is her earliest recorded posthumous assessment of her father, and it is informed by a conflict over truth-telling in biography that Virginia would return to consider in many of her later works.

Because Virginia was unwilling to relate unpleasant truths about her father, the resulting tone of her piece in Maitland is noticeably cautious and sentimental, and begins as follows:

> My impression as a child always was that my father was not very much older than we were. He used to take us to sail our boats in the Round Pond, and with his own hands fitted one out with masts and sails after the pattern of a Cornish lugger; and we knew that his interest was no "grown-up" pretence, it was as genuine as our own; so there was a perfectly equal companionship between us (cited in Maitland 474).

This image of a domestic idyll that the young Virginia offers to Maitland's readers is subtly destabilized as the piece continues. If at first Virginia describes her father as an "equal companion," later in the piece she paints a much more daunting paternal figure.

In the following passage, for example, Virginia recalls Stephen's method of teaching literature to his children: "At the end of a volume my father always gravely asked our opinion as to its merits, and we were required to say which of the characters we liked best and why. I can remember his indignation when one of us preferred the hero to the far more life-like villain" (cited in Maitland 474). The language Virginia employs here—"gravely," "required," "indignation"—leads me to wonder whether this description depicts the same man earlier referred to as a "playmate" and an "equal." The two images are not easily reconciled, and are further complicated by another consideration: although Virginia portrays her father as both a playmate and a grim and donnish teacher, she never mentions him here as a writer. Stephen's interest in literature is noted in her contribution only in so far as it relates to his voracious reading habits and his ability to recite poems from memory. He "loved reading aloud," she writes, his "memory for poetry is wonderful [. . .] and [he] shouted Mr. Henry Newbolt's 'Admirals All' at the top of his voice" (cited in Maitland 475–6).

Virginia's ostensible purpose in contributing to Maitland was to provide a private view of the public man, but she seems rather to have avoided the personal in her account of Stephen. She does not, for instance, mention the painful effects that the deaths of his first wife, Minnie, his second wife, Julia, and his stepdaughter, Stella, had upon her father. Nor does she describe Stephen's suffering during his long, slow death from cancer. Instead, Virginia chooses to provide Maitland's readers with a list of Stephen's favorite books. In this way, Wordsworth, Scott, and "Miss Austen" are the figures of importance in this piece, replacing, as it were, the familial names of Minnie, Julia, and Stella. With the distanced voice of an impartial observer, she concludes her recollection by offering this deathbed image of her father: "[d]uring his last illness he read French books by the score" (cited in Maitland 476). Her contribution to Maitland's biography of Stephen therefore raises several questions. Why, for instance, did Virginia place such emphasis on her father's reading here, while ignoring his career as a writer? Why, in what was to be a private view of Stephen, did she neglect to speak of the personal tragedies that affected his life?

As I noted earlier, Susan Stanford Friedman argues that such choices on the part of an author may be read as evidence of their negotiations of desire and denial (Friedman 173). The terms that Virginia chose to describe her father, that is, allowed her to ignore the private and hurtful side of his nature. Thus, Virginia's "desire" to avoid the painful "truth telling" that her Aunt Caroline had wanted, made her not only "deny" her father's "emotional bullying of women," but also her difficulty with him as a writer. In this way, Virginia's contribution to Maitland could be symptomatic of her uncomfortable relation to her father's literary legacy. Unfortunately, such a reading promotes Stephen as yet another influence for Virginia to negotiate. I argued previously that the reductive nature of influence theory cannot sufficiently account for all the levels of intertextual connection that Woolf's texts evince. Indeed, in my view, it is the changing and fluid character of Woolf's negotiations of desire and denial, rather than any static scheme of battle with a single precursor, which informs and "haunts" her texts. Her struggle with her father's legacy was similarly mutable. As Jane Marcus notes, for instance, while in 1905 Virginia took on the role of "her father's champion against Caroline's negative view of her brother," in later texts Virginia herself "criticizes her father for the same faults Caroline had seen" ("Niece" 122).

Thus, in her more mature works Virginia would explore more fully the darker side of Stephen's nature, but in 1905 she was quite content with her portrait of him in Maitland. In a letter to Violet Dickinson written in February of that year, Virginia noted with pride Fred Maitland's praise of her contribution:

> As I can make my boasts in public, I must send a line to say that I have heard from Fred Maitland, and he says my thing is "beautiful. Really it is beautiful, and if this were a proper occasion I would write a page of praise. But of course I know that this is not what you would like and I can only say that what you write is just what your father would have wished you to write" (*LVW* 1: 180).

Here, Maitland assumes that "praise" "is not what" Virginia "would like," but by publicizing her "boast" to Violet Dickinson, Virginia demonstrates her intense gratification at Maitland's approbation. The pride Virginia took in his letter, moreover, may be specifically linked to Maitland's mention of her father. As Maitland suggests, Virginia wrote "just what [her] father would have wished [her] to write." More to the point, through Virginia's work on Maitland's life of Stephen, her thoughts of biography, of truth-telling, and of the beauty of her own writing, had now become entangled with the figure of her father.

In the years following her father's death, Virginia maintained a strong interest in what she termed "the art of biography" ("Sterne" 86). As a frequent reviewer for *The Times Literary Supplement,* she often critiqued newly published biographies, and in these articles discussed her own, changing sense of this literary form. A central theme in these essays, as in her dealings with her Aunt Caroline, is that of "truth-telling" and its place in biographical works. In August of 1909, for example, Virginia reviewed *The Life and Times of Laurence Sterne* by Wilbur Cross, and there remarked on the difficulty of writing a writer's life: "[i]t is [. . .] a wise precaution to limit one's study of a writer to his works; but, like other precautions, it implies some loss" ("Sterne" 86). As her critique continues, Virginia argues that to ignore the personal history of a writer is also to deny that "between dawn and sunset, he shows the same point of view as that which he elaborates afterward with a pen in his hand" ("Sterne" 86). Ironically, though, Virginia herself had chosen not to "elaborate" on Stephen's writing career, or on the tragedies that informed his "point of view," in her contribution to Maitland.

Later in this article on Sterne, however, Virginia retracts this argument, and offers instead a valid reason for employing such "precaution." As she describes the difference between biography and fiction, Virginia asserts that it is far less dangerous to tell the truth about a fictional character than it is to detail the failings of a historical figure. "One of the objects of biography," she notes, "is to make men appear as they ought to be, for they are husbands and brothers; but no one takes a character in fiction quite seriously"

("Sterne" 87). To "make men appear as they ought to be," then, was, at least in part, Virginia's view of the role of the biographer. Here she emphasizes that this cautious approach is needed, for such men are "husbands and brothers," and, I would add, fathers. Virginia's "biography" in Maitland had employed a similar "precaution," portraying her own father as he "ought to be": a companion, a teacher, and an avid reader. Indeed, this image was so cautious that, as Maitland remarked, it was just what Stephen would have wished her to write. Thus, while Virginia notes the difficulty of the biographer's task in this article, she also suggests the inability of biography to tell the truth. But, as she remarks, such precautions are not necessary in fiction, as "no one takes a character in fiction quite seriously." In this statement, I locate an origin for Virginia's later "representations" of her father: aware of the difficulty of "truth-telling" in biography, she turned instead to depicting Stephen in fictional form.

Absurd Portraits: Virginia and The Learned Man

Woolf's fictional portraits of her father are found throughout her works. In 1911, for example, she wrote another review of a biography for *The Times Literary Supplement* in which there appears a very Stephen-like figure. The article, entitled "The Duke and Duchess of Newcastle-upon-Tyne," begins with the following passage:

> Someone has probably written a story in which the hero is for ever thinking about the dead. It troubles him that people think of them so little. [. . .] Becoming obsessed by the idea, he spends his life in reading, volume after volume. He discovers that great men had uncles and aunts and cousins. He dives after them, so to speak, and rescues them by the hair of their heads. It is another form of philanthropy.[9]

The "hero" that Virginia describes in this review is "obsessed" with the dead and "spends his life reading" about "great men." As this occupation calls to mind Stephen's work on the *DNB,* this "heroic" figure might also hint at Virginia's developing sense of her late father. Here, the character about whom "someone has probably written" "rescues" great men from obscurity "by the hair of their heads." Through such actions, Virginia clearly aligns this imaginary figure with the preservation of a patriarchal history. The language that she employs here, moreover, qualifies the hero's efforts as slightly absurd: he is "obsessed"; "it troubles him that people think of [the dead] so little"; "he dives after them"; he "rescues them by the hair of their heads." Here then, the "art of biography" is depicted as a slapstick struggle to save great men from obscurity. Is this the way that Virginia viewed her late father's work? Phyllis

Rose argues that at the time of Stephen's death he "had imprinted on the mind of his youngest daughter a heroic impression of literary activity" (Rose 5). In the passage above, however, Virginia clearly evacuates any sense of heroism from this figure's biographical endeavors: this "hero" is a patriarchal philanthropist, an absurd character "obsessed" with "great men."

If this "obsessed" figure is a caricature of Leslie Stephen, it is quite unlike the heroic figure that Rose claims the young Virginia admired. This figure may, therefore, indicate a change in Virginia's sense of Stephen, both as a writer and as a daughter. Virginia's image of Stephen as an absurd character, that is, could articulate both her awe of her father's literary accomplishments, and her anger at the philosophy behind his rescue of "great men": Proud of her heritage as a child of Sir Leslie, Virginia was nevertheless uncomfortable with being the daughter of a patriarch. Indeed, when this character is read as a depiction of Stephen, it suggests a further difficulty in Virginia's perceptions of him: Leslie Stephen was not the only one who was "obsessed" by the dead. In the years to come Virginia herself would return, like the figure in her article, to read her father's own "volumes" attempting again and again to "dive after," "rescue," and define him in her works.

In November of 1916, for example, soon after what would have been her father's eighty-fourth birthday, Virginia, now Virginia Woolf, wrote an article in *The Times Literary Supplement* that bore the name of Stephen's own collections of essays.[10] Woolf's "Hours in a Library" discusses the relative strengths and weaknesses of contemporary, and what she terms "classic," literature. Woolf's essay opens with a description of another recognizable figure. Here, she writes of an elderly, "learned man" that is contrasted with another, the youthful "true reader":

> We conceive a pale, attenuated figure in a dressing-gown, lost in speculation, unable to lift a kettle from the hob, or address a lady without blushing, ignorant of the daily news, though versed in the catalogues of the second-hand booksellers, in whose dark premises he spends the hours of sunlight—a delightful character, no doubt, in his crabbed simplicity, but not in the least resembling that other to whom we would direct attention. For the true reader is essentially young. He is a man of intense curiosity; of ideas; open minded and communicative ("Library" 565).

Woolf's conception of a "pale attenuated" "learned man," I would argue, provides another fictionalized rendering of Leslie Stephen. Here, this elderly figure "lost in speculation" is not portrayed as a ridiculous hero of patriarchal history, but rather as "delightful" and "simple." Nevertheless, he, like the "obsessed hero" of her earlier essay, is irrelevant to Woolf's modern world. As Woolf asserts, although the "learned man" is "versed in the catalogues of the second-hand booksellers," the future belongs to the youthful "true reader," and it is to this "other" that one should direct "attention."

If this "learned man" *is* associated with Stephen, what is the role of the young "open-minded" reader who is his opposite? Did Woolf perhaps align herself with this youthful "true reader"? If so, an interesting negotiation may be taking place in this passage. By entitling her essay "Hours in a Library," Woolf here compares her studies with those of her father. This older "learned" figure "searches through books to discover some particular grain of truth upon which he has set his heart" ("Library" 565). The "true reader," "on the other hand, must check the desire for learning at the outset," for such knowledge "is very apt to kill what it suits us to consider the more humane passion for pure and disinterested reading" ("Library" 565). In contrast to the "true reader," the "learned man" is a "crabbed" relic of the past, ultimately undeserving of attention. If I align Stephen with this "crabbed relic" and Woolf with the passionate "true reader," an interesting reading of this article emerges: while Woolf's "learned" father had sought "some particular grain of truth upon which he ha[d] his heart set," she, as a "true reader," is able to remain open-minded, and to engage in what she terms "the more humane passion for pure" reading (565). This argument becomes difficult to maintain as the essay continues, however; soon the distinction between the "learned man" and the "true reader" becomes blurred.

In the next passage, Woolf offers a list of works "that someone has read in a past January at the age of twenty" (565). The "Elizabethans," "Webster," "Browning," "Shelley," "Spenser," and "Congreve," are all mentioned alongside "Miss Austen," "Meredith," "Ibsen," and "Shaw" (565). Woolf then argues "we have all, at one time or another" (565) composed such reading lists of "great writers." She concludes that by doing so, "[w]e are fighting under their leadership, and almost in the light of their eyes. So we haunt the old bookshops" (565). Here then, Woolf implies that the readers of this essay and its author, as well as the "true reader" and the "learned man," have all converged into "we." "We" compose lists; "we" "fight" under the "leadership of "great writers"; and "we" all become like the "learned man," as we "haunt" "old bookshops."

Thus, Woolf suggests in this passage that the very act of "listing," of reading the "classics," not only transforms the young reader, but all of us, into a likeness of the "learned man." Like the twenty-year-old she describes, that is, Woolf argues that she and her readers can never engage fully in what she calls "pure" and disinterested reading. Woolf claims that, having read the works of the "greatest writers," our reading becomes "contaminated." In this essay, therefore, Woolf proclaims that the act of learning, of reading the classics, destroys the ability to read in a "pure" "humane" way, as it forces the reader into battle, "fighting under their leadership." In Woolf's view, "our"

"Hours in a Library" serve to overturn our youthful "open-mindedness," rendering us instead as worshippers of the great writers of the past. This same passage, moreover, also illustrates Woolf's revised sense of her father's role as biographer. Woolf's earlier essay portrayed the figure of an "obsessed man" "rescuing" the past as slightly absurd. Here, though, the Stephen-like "learned man," the young "true reader," and "we" are all seen by Woolf as victims of literary tradition; of the lists "we have all at one time or another" created. In this essay, therefore, canonization, the listing and retrieval of the past as exemplified by Stephen's work on the *DNB,* is promoted not as a peculiar profession, but as something in which "we" all engage. If Woolf's earlier caricature of her father shows him as single-handedly rescuing the stories of great men, here Woolf presents "the learned man" as just like the rest of us: subject to the ideologies of an exclusive literary canon.

In this piece, then, Woolf argues that "we" all, at one time or another, have conscripted to fight under the leadership of "the classics." More to the point, her own difficult relation to the "great writers" of the past is demonstrated here, as she remarks on the exclusivity of the "lists" "we" all create. These are, she notes "curious documents, in that they seem to include scarcely any of the contemporary writers" (565). Later, she offers a warning about this exclusion, arguing that those who do read contemporary works "come from adventuring among new books with a far keener eye for the old. [. . .] We shall find, probably, that some of the great are less venerable than we thought them. Indeed, they are not so accomplished or so profound as some of our own time" (566). Here, Woolf asserts that the reading of "new books" enables readers to demystify the "classics." The conclusion of her essay, on the other hand, maintains the near-heavenly significance of the literature of the past. These works, she argues, offer "some consecration" that "descends upon us from their hands which we return to life, feeling it more keenly and understanding it more deeply than before" (566). As Woolf employs the image of the "descending" "consecrating" hand of the "classics," her hierarchical troping once again demonstrates her ambivalent relation to influences from the past.

This essay, then, ostensibly discusses the relative strengths of "old" and "new," of "young" and "learned" readers, of canonical and noncanonical works. Throughout the piece, however, Woolf's arguments are propounded and retracted, reading lists offered, and deconstructed, and characters defined as opposing and then elided. At first attempting to promote the importance of contemporary texts, by the end of the article Woolf sanctifies the classics, as she kneels beneath the "great hand" descending. Furthermore, this blessing from the past comes at the conclusion of an article written on her father's birthday and entitled "Hours in a Library," one that begins with the Stephen-like figure of the "learned man." Could the contradictions and concerns of the essay thus be informed by Woolf's negotiations of her father? Was Stephen a rescuer of patriarchy, or, like the rest of "us," a victim of its traditional, canonical lists? Woolf's ambivalence toward her father's legacy, as seen in these essays, ensured that this conflicted vision of him would continue to haunt her later texts as well.

Lady Georgina and Women's Language

As the examples above illustrate, Woolf's portraits of her father often appeared alongside her discussions of patriarchal exclusion and canonical status. However, in one essay that Woolf published in March of 1920, she confronts these issues without creating a Stephen-like character to voice them. The piece, entitled "A Talk about Memoirs," is nevertheless useful for understanding Woolf's later depictions of her father. In it, Woolf offers a dialogue between two women, "Ann" and "Judith," trying to discuss literature while embroidering. As the piece begins, the character of Ann suggests that she and Judith "can talk about the Greeks," but soon abandons this idea, remarking that she prefers memoirs, and there "is not a single memoir in the whole of Greek literature" ("Memoirs" 216). This observation causes Ann to confess that at times "the mere thought of a classic is repulsive" to her ("Memoirs" 216). The character of Judith concurs, adding:

> *Judith:* [. . .] But I can't embroider a parrot and talk about Milton in the
> same breath.
> *Ann:* Whereas you could embroider a parrot and talk about Lady Geor-
> giana Peel?
> *Judith:* Precisely ("Memoirs" 216).

For me, Judith's reference to Milton recalls Jane Marcus' argument as discussed in the previous chapter. Marcus asserts that in Woolf's view, the figure of Milton was emblematic of patriarchal power and its implicit and explicit exclusion of women. As Marcus also notes, Woolf similarly viewed the Greek language as entwined with notions of male domination. For Woolf, Marcus argues, familiarity with this language was a prerequisite for obtaining access to other privileged forms of knowledge. Therefore, Marcus writes, "Woolf felt that not knowing Greek [. . .] meant no female intellectual aristocracy" ("Liberty" 92).

When read with Marcus' arguments in mind, Woolf's essay produces a dark rendering of these very concerns. More black comedy than satire, this piece suggests that while the women of her tale long to talk about literature (for there are "no gentleman present" ["Memoirs" 216]), they do not have the language to discuss "the Greeks." Like the "oil portrait of Uncle John"

("Memoirs" 216) that watches over them, the figure of "Milton" is similarly portrayed in this essay as an intruder on the women's space: as Woolf makes clear, Judith cannot "embroider a parrot and talk about Milton in the same breath," "[w]hereas," as Ann suggests, Judith "could embroider a parrot and talk about Lady Georgiana Peel" (216). When a conversation about Lady Georgiana's memoirs ensues, however, this work is itself depicted as an oppressive force. Far from providing a woman's language or a heroine with which Ann and Judith can sympathize, the memoir instead inscribes patriarchal themes of its own.

In fact, the story they discuss does not tell the tale of the Lady's life, but rather, the history of her father, Lord John: "*Ann:* Lady Georgiana Peel was born in the year of 1836, and was the daughter of Lord John Russell" (217). Ann continues her synopsis of the memoir and gives a short description of Lord John's encounter with the Queen. Judith then interrupts Ann with the question "[a]nd Lady Georgiana? *Ann:* Well there's not much about Lady Georgiana. She saw the Queen having her hair brushed, and went to stay at Woburn" (217). Like the embroidering of the "parrot," then, the reading of Lady Georgiana's memoirs is an enterprise that makes use of women's time while posing no threat to the patriarchal order. Unable to discuss the Greeks or Milton, Ann and Judith find no escape from male domination in the room over which their "Uncle John" keeps watch. The works of Lady Georgiana, to which they turn, are themselves filled with tales of great men, as the stories of "Lord John," "Charles Dickens," and the "Grosvenor boys" (217) are narrated there. At the end of Woolf's essay Ann and Judith are left, finally, with no language of their own. As Ann concludes "[h]ow splendid we should think it if it were written in Greek! Indeed, how Greek it all is!" (220).

These considerations of language, patriarchy, and biography that appear in the essays I have examined here continue to emerge in Woolf's later works. Often they are specifically aligned with thoughts of her childhood, and of her father. Soon after completing *Mrs. Dalloway,* for instance, Woolf connected these themes to Leslie Stephen in her journal. After creating a list of stories that she plans to write, Woolf remarks, "[s]hort ones—scenes—for instance The Old Man (a character of L.S.) The Professor on Milton—(an attempt at literary criticism) & now The Interruption, women talking alone. However, back to life. Where are we?" (*DVW* 3:3). Because of the order in which Woolf arranges these images here, "L.S." (Leslie Stephen), the Professor, and Milton seem to lead her to conceive a story about "The Interruption." This tale, as described here, will apparently depict an "interruption" of "women talking alone." Thus, an intrusive relation is suggested between the male figures she considers and these "women." As the patriarchal characters of L. S., the Professor, and Milton emerge, they disrupt the talk of these fictional women. Moreover, they also seem to obstruct the flow of

Woolf's own thoughts: "[w]here are we?," she questions. Perhaps I can offer a belated answer. Woolf was heading down a road upon which she would confront the themes of language, patriarchy, biography and autobiography, canonical status, and the interruption of women's discourse. Virginia Woolf was about to begin writing *To the Lighthouse.*

Paper Cut-Outs, Private Codes, and Patriarchy: Leslie Stephen and *To the Lighthouse*

In each of the texts I have examined in this chapter, I have uncovered evidence of Woolf's struggle with the figure of her father and the legacy of his work. As *To the Lighthouse* contains her most fully developed fictional portrait of him, it enacts a substantial and sustained attempt to negotiate his influence. Moreover, these earlier works are themselves reinterpreted in this novel; the words of those texts, that is, appear to resurface in *To the Lighthouse* with new and surprising meanings. If I return, for example, to Woolf's contribution to Maitland's biography of Stephen, I find there a reminiscence that will seem strangely familiar to those acquainted with *To the Lighthouse.* Recounting her father's habits, the young Virginia wrote, "[e]very evening we spent an hour and a half in the drawing-room, and, as far back as I can remember, he found some way of amusing us himself. At first he drew pictures of animals as fast as we could demand them, or cut them out of paper with a pair of scissors" (cited in Maitland 474). This image of Stephen's cut-out animals, I would argue, clearly prefigures an early moment in Woolf's *To the Lighthouse.* There, Woolf introduces the character of James Ramsay, a child who is "sitting on the floor cutting out pictures from the illustrated catalogue of Army and Navy stores" (*Lighthouse* 11). In Virginia's earlier account of her father's paper cutting, she states that this was done to "amuse" his children. In *To the Lighthouse,* however, James' paper cutting is framed by two observations that endow this activity with more serious meaning. Firstly, the reader is told that James "belonged, even at the age of six," to "a great clan" (*Lighthouse* 11). Then, soon after James is shown "cutting out pictures," the text asserts that he "had already his private code, his secret language" (*Lighthouse* 12).

This arrangement of images allows me to posit one possible reading of James' paper cutting and its relation to Woolf's reminiscences in Maitland. There, the young Virginia recalled the carefully cut and shaped figures that Stephen created for his children's amusement. In *To the Lighthouse,* on the other hand, James Ramsay's paper cut-outs are introduced alongside, and thus appear to be associated with, his entry into a "secret" society and his knowledge of a "private code." Moreover, as this passage continues, both this "secret language" and James' paper cutting are linked in his mother's thoughts with ideas of power and patriarchy. In Mrs. Ramsay's view, James' actions lend him an air of "uncompromising severity" "[. . .] so that his mother, watching him guide his scissors neatly round the refrigerator, imagined him all red and ermine on the Bench or directing a stern and momentous enterprise in some crisis of public affairs" (12). In *To the Lighthouse,* then, these cut-outs represent more than a childish amusement: they are ciphers, "a private code" that allows James access to the powerful role that Mrs. Ramsay envisions for him.

Soon, further connections (and distinctions) between Stephen and James develop in Woolf's text. While Stephen "drew pictures of animals and cut them out of paper," James cuts images drawn by someone else, out of a catalogue. The kinds of objects that they cut out are also dissimilar. As an account by another contemporary in Maitland tells us, Leslie Stephen was able to "cut out a series of animals—beautifully formed giraffes, bears, goats" (cited in Maitland 477). James, on the other hand, takes his scissors to pictures that his mother chooses: a refrigerator, a rake, and a gentleman in evening dress. Thus, in contrast to Stephen's wild animal figures, the images that James cuts are all in some way domesticated: objects of civilization.

In my reading, Woolf makes a further observation concerning power, authority, and patriarchy in her novel as this scene continues. James learns the skill of paper-cutting, which is linked in Mrs. Ramsay's thoughts to patriarchal forms of power, at his mother's knee. Furthermore, as he undergoes this instruction, James becomes overwhelmed with a desire to kill his father. Mrs. Ramsay has promised that James may go to the lighthouse "if it's fine tomorrow" (11). Soon after, Mr. Ramsay disagrees, insisting that "[. . .] 'it won't be fine.' Had there been an axe handy, or a poker, any weapon that would have gashed a hole in his father's breast and killed him, there and then, James would have seized it" (12). Why, I wonder, should James want to kill his father at the very moment he enacts what is, in Mrs. Ramsay's thoughts, a patriarchal task? Perhaps because, for James, paper-cutting is not an act of patriarchal allegiance, but is instead a revolt against it. Leslie Stephen, that is, had cut out wild animals, but James cuts out domestic images: the refrigerator, the rake, and the evening dress. As Mrs. Ramsay reflects, in doing so James, like all "young men," "parodied her husband" (29). James' domesticated paper cut-outs may thus be read as images of defiance: in creating them, James revolts against his father (whom he "parodie[s]") and against Mrs. Ramsay's complicity in teaching James this patriarchal skill. In James' thoughts, perhaps, this paper-cutting represents his need to cherish images of domesticity and to quietly defy patriarchal order. For Mrs. Ramsay, on the other hand, it is a skill that will afford her son access to power.

This connection between James' paper cutting and Stephen's own is strengthened by a note Woolf made in her journal just before beginning this novel, in which she discussed its specifically autobiographical origins. Here, Woolf summarizes the subject matter of *To the Lighthouse:* "This is going to be fairly short: to have father's character done complete in it; & mothers; & St. Ives; & childhood; & all the usual things I try to put in—life, death &c. But the centre is father's character" (*DVW* 3:18–9). As this excerpt outlines, the figure of Leslie Stephen was to be the center of Woolf's novel, and the character of Mr. Ramsay can indeed be read as a fictional portrait of him. In the scene that opens the novel, however, Woolf does not utilize her father's hobby of paper-cutting as a characteristic of Mr. Ramsay. Instead, she has his child, James, engage in this activity.

By forging this symbolic link between James Ramsay and her own father, Woolf establishes a convoluted system of patriarchy in her text. Paper-cutting (and the power to which it affords access) becomes a metaphor for a legacy that is passed from father to son via the complicity of the mother. This is confirmed by the opening passage of this novel, which implies that James learns his "secret language" and skills of patriarchy through his mother's guidance, with the scissors she has given him. James' resentment of this knowledge is apparent, but this too seems to be part of his journey toward manhood. Mrs. Ramsay imagines that James, clad in his ermine robes, will eventually be called upon to direct "stern" enterprises, and to intervene in public crises. Indeed, he must be prepared to do so if he is to succeed his father. It is this thought that enables Mrs. Ramsay to continue her instruction of her son, despite his obvious discontentment: "All she could do now was to admire the refrigerator, and turn the pages of the Stores list in the hope that she might come upon something like a rake, or a mowing machine, which, with its prongs and its handles, would need the greatest skill and care in cutting out" (29). Thus, "[a]ll" Mrs. Ramsay can do is "admire" her son's efforts to cherish the domestic, as she simultaneously steers him toward total dissociation from his maternal ties. These, as she acknowledges, "would need the greatest skill and care in cutting out." In Mrs. Ramsay's eyes, therefore, James is already aligned with a patriarchal order, which itself was reproduced in the structure of Woolf's own family. Like the "secret code" and "private language" that James learns, the men of the Stephen line also shared a discourse unavailable to women.

In her study of Caroline Stephen, Jane Marcus remarks on the careers of Leslie Stephen and his brother Fitzjames as follows:

Fitzjames literally "laid down the law" in his legal digests. [. . .] His legal language of controversy, argument, aggressive denunciation, and judgement [. . .] was male discourse of immense and ferocious authority. Even Leslie Stephen's essays were authoritative male discourse, argumentative and assertive. The *Dictionary of National Biography* is a patriarchal masterpiece in its exclusion of women and of men who did not fit the pattern of power. Sitting on the library shelves, the volumes of the DNB are a horizontal monument to phallocentric culture ("Niece" 119).

This "Language of Patriarchy" of which Marcus writes can be associated both with James Ramsay's secret language, and with the "uncompromising severity" of his demeanor. Because James learns this code at his mother's knee in the first pages of the novel, the early part of *To the Lighthouse* articulates the strange marriage of complicity and exclusion through which women imagined themselves to be of importance to the "phallocentric culture." The character of Mrs. Ramsay thus demonstrates Woolf's view of the role of women in a society filled with men in ermine robes: women were required to provide a safe domestic space in which to teach and encourage the development of patriarchal skills. As if to remind her readers of the distance such roles inscribed between men and women, Woolf points out that Mrs. Ramsay cannot understand men's language: "Mrs. Ramsay did not quite catch the meaning, only the words, here and there . . . dissertation . . . fellowship . . . readership . . . lectureship" (*Lighthouse* 22).

Jane Marcus suggests that the image of the lighthouse in this novel was itself connected with Woolf's concerns about language. In Marcus' reading, Woolf may have retrieved the trope from an essay written by her aunt Caroline. In that essay, entitled "Divine Guidance," Caroline Stephen wrote:

> Have you ever seen a revolving lighthouse at night from across the sea, with its steadfast light alternately hidden and displayed? [. . .]And have you considered how the very fact of its intermittency is the means by which it is recognised and its message is conveyed? It is a light given not to read by, but to steer our course by. Its appearances and disappearances are a *language* by which the human care that devised it can speak to the watchers and strugglers at sea (49).

Marcus maintains that this intermittent language of "human care" of which Caroline writes may be aligned in Woolf's novel with Mrs. Ramsay; she, more than any other character, identifies with the lighthouse's beam. If the paper cut-outs are a secret patriarchal cipher, whose meaning Mrs. Ramsay cannot understand, Marcus counters that Mrs. Ramsay herself communicates with a private "Morse code" ("Niece" 130). Thus, the male and female characters appear to employ different, gender-inflected discourses, and Woolf's text makes a clear distinction between these two languages.

The men in *To the Lighthouse* use their "secret code" to speak of their awards and achievements, of their "dissertations" and "lectureships." For Mrs. Ramsay, however, the language of the lighthouse is not one of personal merit. In her reveries, the lighthouse appears to communicate a peculiarly feminine, maternal language. It is a discourse of communion, embodied by Mrs. Ramsay, who finds "herself sitting and looking, sitting and looking, with her work in her hands until she became the thing she looked at—that light for example" (100–1). As the character of Mrs. Ramsay illustrates, in Woolf's text the lighthouse merges with ideas of maternity and femininity, becoming at last a beacon whose language is one of safety, a "course to steer by," as Caroline wrote. Thus, while Mrs. Ramsay cannot understand the "meaning" of the men's words, she can and does offer these men something: a domesticating, maternal, and pitying solace. Later, Mrs. Ramsay will reflect on the "sacrifices" that her husband "required" (30), and this passage provides further evidence of the distance Woolf inscribes between them. It is not only a language barrier that divides Mr. and Mrs. Ramsay in the text, but a difference in their respective powers.

Mr. Ramsay, in the early part of the text, refuses the trip to the lighthouse, "sheds" his acolyte Charles Tansley, and, later, disrupts the family dinner by "scowling," as one of their houseguests, Mr. Carmichael, requests another bowl of soup (148). Mrs. Ramsay, on the other hand, must placate James in his disappointment at the postponed trip, let Tansley know, subtly, that he has been "shed," and dispel the dinner's disruption by saying "promptly," "[l]ight the candles" (149). Thus Mr. Ramsay denies and disallows, while Mrs. Ramsay reaches, communicates, and sheds light. Mr. Ramsay's power in the text, like his patriarchal "academic jargon" (24), is shown to be derived from personal desires and ambitions. The maternal discourse of light that Mrs. Ramsay articulates, however, is communal: Mr. Ramsay cuts, but Mrs. Ramsay knits.

Despite the distinction Woolf makes between the languages used by the men and women in the novel, it is also clear that *what* Mrs. Ramsay knits, the thoughts and desires she most frequently communicates, are not her own, but those of her husband. In the passages above and in others, Mrs. Ramsay becomes the public voice of her husband's desires. By doing so, moreover, she is shown to lose track of her own thoughts: Woolf figures Mr. Ramsay as an interruption. Just as the image of Milton had interrupted the embroidery of Judith and Ann in Woolf's "A Talk about Memoirs," in *To the Lighthouse* Mr. Ramsay similarly intrudes upon his wife's domestic space. Indeed, Mr. Ramsay's first words in the text are an unwelcome disruption of Mrs. Ramsay's discussion with James: "'But', said his father, stopping in front of the drawing room window 'it won't be fine'" (12). Such surprise interruptions, moreover, appear to symbolize more than an invasion of the domestic sphere. In fact, I would argue that throughout the first third of the novel Woolf utilizes these intrusions to foreshadow Mrs. Ramsay's early death. This argument is strengthened by Woolf's repeated use of the words "sudden" and "interrupted" in this part of the text: "[b]ut here, as she turned the page, suddenly her search for the picture of the rake [. . .] was interrupted"; "[i]t suddenly gets cold"; "[b]ut this was suddenly interrupted" (*Lighthouse* 29, 35, 37).

In the first example above, the interruption depicted is linked both to Mr. Ramsay and to his wife's concern for him. Sitting in a room next door to the men, Mrs. Ramsay listens in and notices that the "gruff murmur, irregularly broken by the taking out of pipes and the putting in of pipes which had kept on assuring her, [. . .] had ceased" (29). No longer "assured," her thoughts of James and his future are halted. She is then confronted with a further "sudden" intrusion:

> Suddenly a loud cry, as of a sleep-walker, half roused, something about
> Stormed at with shot and shell
> sung out with the utmost intensity in her ear, made her turn apprehensively to see if anyone heard him (29).

As Mr. Ramsay shouts bits of poetry aloud, I am again reminded of Woolf's portrayal of her father in Maitland. There, Woolf recalled Stephen's habit of proclaiming Newbolt's "Admirals All," "at the top of his voice as he went about the house or walked in Kensington Gardens, to the surprise of nursery-maids and park-keepers" (cited in Maitland 476).

This resurfacing of Woolf's earlier portrait of her father may indicate a deliberate reassessment of her memories of him. As I noted previously, Stephen's routine of reciting poems aloud was depicted as an endearing eccentricity in Maitland, in keeping with Woolf's sanitized characterization of her father there. In *To the Lighthouse*, by contrast, Mr. Ramsay's shouts are frightening, and bear "the utmost intensity." These fictional outbursts are therefore located not only as a violation of Mrs. Ramsay's thoughts, but as a symptom of her husband's possibly dangerous mental instability. In her revised depiction of these episodes, moreover, Woolf not only reinterprets the actions of the "sleep-walker" father, but also takes note of the *re*-actions of the mother who listens. In this scene, Woolf emphasizes that Mrs. Ramsay's main concern is to know "if anyone heard him." Thus here, Woolf once again points to the complicity of Mrs. Ramsay in the patriarchal scheme. In keeping with her role as a protector of male tradition, Mrs. Ramsay's fear is not of her husband's possible madness, but of his being "found out."

These constant interruptions of Mrs. Ramsay's thoughts also serve as a reminder that all is not well, not complete, and that danger lies around each corner of this seemingly safe domestic space. Mr. Ramsay is "[s]tormed at by shot and shell" (31), while Mrs. Ramsay knits. Moreover, her need to knit together, and thus deny the threat of, these disruptions locates her as an ac complice to danger. Mrs. Ramsay, that is, allows her own thoughts to be intruded upon by her husband, so that she may intervene and maintain the patriarchal order of the family. But how do these episodes affect Mr. Ramsay? Rather than representing a cry for understanding, his outbursts appear to lead him into a state of solipsistic bliss. Later in this scene, for example, as he repeats his earlier cry of "[s]omeone has blundered !" (44), Mr. Ramsay attempts to "brush off" the gaze of Lily and Mr. Bankes. "[A]s if," Woolf writes, "he begged them to withhold for a moment what he knew to be inevitable, as if he impressed upon them his own child-like resentment of interruption, yet even in the moment of discovery was not to be routed utterly, but was determined to hold fast to something of this delicious emotion, this impure rhapsody of which he was ashamed, but in which he reveled" (44). In this passage, then, Mr. Ramsay is shown both to revel in, and to have a "child-like resentment" of, the disruption he creates. He has contradictory desires: he wants to be interrupted by Lily and Mr. Bankes, but would also like to "withhold" their inevitable intrusion. Ramsay's needs thus illustrate a further difference between him and his wife. While Mrs. Ramsay's thoughts are of making connections among people, Mr. Ramsay aches for psychological solitude, the "impure rhapsody" of a self-imposed limbo.

Woolf imbues this trope of interruption with further meaning as the novel continues. As Woolf recreates her father's image in *To the Lighthouse,* she uses these sudden intrusions to symbolize not only Mrs. Ramsay's early death, but also the goals that Mr. Ramsay will never reach. Because Woolf herself so clearly links Mr. Ramsay with her father, I would argue that these continuous interruptions are a metaphor for Stephen's own shortcomings. In this text, Woolf poeticizes Stephen as a man unable to attain his chosen destiny. The passage in which Mr. Ramsay considers his life, for example, may be a reminder of Stephen's work on the *DNB*: "his splendid mind had no sort of difficulty in running over those letters, one by one, firmly and accurately, until it had reached, say, the letter Q. He reached Q. Very few people in the whole of England ever reach Q. [. . .] But after Q? What comes next?" (56–7). While Mr. Ramsay is portrayed here as unsatisfied with his achievements, Leslie Stephen had similarly attested to disappointments in his own career. As Stephen commented in his autobiographical *Mausoleum Book:* "The sense in which I do take myself to be a failure is this: I have scattered myself too much. I think that I had it in me to make something like a real contribution to philosophical or ethical thought. Unluckily, what with journalism and dictionary making, I have been a jack of all trades" (93). Like Ramsay who cannot reach R, much less Z, Stephen was eventually forced to give up philosophy and the editorship of the *DNB*, allowing the final alphabetical volumes to be completed by his assistant Sydney Lee.[11] Thus, Ramsay's inability to see past "Q" may be a reference to Stephen's enforced retirement from a project to which he had devoted nearly twenty years of his life. However, as "R" is the first letter of "Ramsay," Mr. Ramsay's longing to get to R, to understand R ("R is then—what is R?" [57]), might represent more than Stephen's abandonment of the *DNB.* It might also symbolize his inability to make sense of himself. As Mr. Ramsay asks, "what is R?," his lack of self-knowledge recalls Stephen's own comments in the passage from the *Mausoleum Book,* cited above. There, Stephen, like the fictional Ramsay, evinces a hesitant and deprecatory perception of himself, as he qualifies his talents with the phrases "I think," "something like," and "jack of all trades."

Woolf's description of Mr. Ramsay's inability to get past "Q," I would argue, promotes this "interruption" as evidence of his failures. The reader is called on here to be as suspicious of Ramsay's achievements as is he, and led to believe William Bankes' statement that: "'Ramsay is one of those men who do their best work before they are forty.' He had made a definite contribution to philosophy in one little book when he was only five and twenty; what came after was more or less amplification, repetition" (41). In one of Woolf's later works, *Three Guineas* (1938), she proclaimed that the "boldest mission" of "Victorian sons and daughters" is to "cheat the father, to deceive the father, and then to fly from the father" (244). Is such a stance perhaps foretold in *To the Lighthouse,* through Woolf's insistence upon portraying Mr. Ramsay's shortcomings? If so, how successful was this novel in allowing Woolf, as a Victorian daughter, to complete the bold mission she describes?

If Woolf's intention in creating the fallible, antiheroic Mr. Ramsay was to cheat, deceive, and then fly from Leslie Stephen's legacy, this would suggest a striking similarity between her and Thomas Hardy: both writers struggled with Leslie Stephen's influence. In chapter two, I suggested that evidence of Hardy's indebtedness to Stephen could be found in Hardy's poem "The Schreckhorn." There, I argued that Hardy employed alpine language, characteristic of Stephen, in order to rewrite Stephen's literary legacy. It may be significant, then, that in *To the Lighthouse* Woolf also uses "mountaineering" terminology in one of her descriptions of Mr. Ramsay's thoughts:

> Feelings that would not have disgraced a leader who, now that the snow has begun to fall and the mountain-top is covered in mist, knows that he must lay himself down and die before morning comes, stole upon him, paling the colour of his eyes, giving him, [. . .] the bleached look of withered old age. Yet he would not die lying down; he would find some crag of rock, and there, his eyes fixed on the storm, trying to the end to pierce the darkness, he would die standing. He would never reach R (58–9).

Woolf's use of alpine imagery thus echoes the language used in Hardy's poem, which was, in her view, "incomparably the truest" portrait of her father "in existence" (*LVW* 2:58). Much as "The Schreckhorn" appears to commemorate Stephen while simultaneously denying him as a writer, in this passage Woolf's own language privileges Ramsay's failure and death over his accomplishments. As this scene makes clear, Mr. Ramsay is not a leader, but has feelings that would not have "disgraced" a leader, and though the word "disgraced" is negated here, it still manages to leave a strong impression on the reader. This disgrace inscribes a sense of impending disaster upon Ramsay's metaphoric expedition: Mr. Ramsay "knows that he must lay himself down and die before morning comes."

This passage continues with images of impotence and aging as Mr. Ramsay's eyes pale, leaving him with "the bleached look of withered old age." Thus, like Hardy before her, Woolf takes charge of Stephen's language of snow and expeditions, and employs these tropes to portray his powerlessness and his failure. She addresses, as did Hardy, the obstinacy that drives him, writing: "he would die standing" (55). Hardy had also imagined Stephen's eventual death in his poem, as the "eternal essence of [Stephen's] mind" merged with the "adamantine shape" of the Shreckhorn. There is a difference between these two portraits of Stephen, however: if Hardy had rendered Stephen as a muted "low voicing," Woolf leaves him straining "to pierce the darkness," not mute as Hardy had shown him, but blind. Perhaps then, by imagining Mr. Ramsay as unable to see, Woolf felt herself free to paint this disabled fictional father as she liked, with no fear of reprisal. As the passage in *To the Lighthouse* concludes, Woolf once again asserts the character's essential inadequacy: "[h]e would never reach R."

In this scene, Woolf appears to belittle the achievements of the fictionalized father, Mr. Ramsay. Nevertheless, this depiction of impotence is belied by the power that Ramsay is shown to wield throughout the novel. His friends and family are obedient to his silent demands, and his wife is figured as a willing slave to his needs. Mrs. Ramsay's own powers are displaced: she derives strength by giving voice to her husband's desires. Woolf thus inscribes a subtext of blame in the early part of the novel by locating this maternal figure as both the servant and the agent of male domination. Chapter six begins: "But what had happened?" "[s]ome one had blundered" (*Lighthouse* 51), and as this scene continues, it becomes clear that it is Mrs. Ramsay who has "blundered," through her covering of danger and her knitting together of interruption. Subtly, and cryptically, therefore, Woolf's novel suggests that Mrs. Ramsay is accountable not only for her own untimely death, but also for the desolation of the family she leaves behind.

There is, however, a lack of certainty that surfaces in the text's accusations of Mrs. Ramsay. As she sits thinking, Mrs. Ramsay realizes that "something had happened, someone had blundered. But she could not for the life of her think what" (52). Can the origin of Mrs. Ramsay's bewilderment here be located? As

I noted in the previous chapter, critic Michael Riffaterre argues that this kind of narrative ambiguity ("Interpretation" 227) can be read as a sign of intertextual debt. Looking at this passage with Riffaterre's argument in mind, I wonder which intertext, if any, can resolve Mrs. Ramsay's dilemma. Who is to blame for the "something" that had happened? If I search for an answer in the intertextual web of Woolf's own works, I find that a simple solution is elusive: the burden of responsibility for the various tragedies Woolf depicts in her texts is constantly shifting.

In *The Voyage Out,* for instance, who is to blame for Rachel Vinrace's death? Is it Terence, her fiancée, Helen, her surrogate mother, or Milton's poetry? Or is Rachel herself at fault, through her submission to male domination? Again, in *Jacob's Room,* is the loss of Jacob ascribed to Mrs. Flanders for sending him away, or to the patriarchal military machine for including him in its war? Or, are we to blame Jacob for believing himself to be the "inheritor" of a masculine legacy of power? In *Mrs. Dalloway,* too, there is a complex negotiation of accountability for Septimus' suicide. Here, as in *Jacob's Room,* the war is a suspect, alongside Sir William Bradshaw, Clarissa, and Septimus himself.

Far from resolving the narrative ambiguity found in Mrs. Ramsay's thoughts, Woolf's earlier novels appear to maintain that uncertainty, as they also exhibit unresolved mediations of blame. Perhaps, then, just as Mrs. Ramsay cannot "for the life of her" know "who had blundered," Woolf herself was unable to determine the agent of tragedy in her works. Cautiously ascribing guilt first to one cause or character and then another, the author of these texts enacts the very ambivalence to which her characters give voice. In the first half of *To the Lighthouse,* for example, Mrs. Ramsay's willingness to submit to the imperatives dictated by the men around her, to be a martyr to patriarchy, casts the blame for her early death upon her own head. Later in the text, however, the culprit has changed. Mrs. Ramsay may allow herself to be interrupted, but it is Mr. Ramsay who interrupts.

This transfer of reproach in the novel is first seen through the eyes of the character of Lily Briscoe. Lily's anger toward Mr. Ramsay is made clear as she thinks: "[h]e is petty, selfish, vain, egotistical; he is spoilt; he is a tyrant; he wears Mrs. Ramsay to death" (*Lighthouse* 43). As Lily engages in this silent tirade against Mr. Ramsay, I will pause to consider her role in the text. Woolf claimed that Mr. Ramsay is based in great measure upon Leslie Stephen. Lily Briscoe, on the other hand, may be informed by Woolf's own character. It is, after all, Lily who administers blame in the novel. In the scene above, for example, Lily's accusation that Mr. Ramsay "wears" his wife "to death," clearly ascribes the responsibility for Mrs. Ramsay's eventual loss to him. In the course of the novel, however, Lily's view of Mr. and Mrs. Ramsay's respective roles in this tragedy will change radically.

The death of Mrs. Ramsay in the central "Time Passes" section of *To the Lighthouse* calls forth a reassessment of the accusations of guilt found in the first third of the novel. The manner of her death is itself a "sudden interruption," and is predicted in the conclusion of a scene that I examined above. In that passage Mrs. Ramsay, upon hearing the voices in the other room cease, looks up "with an impulse of terror" (30) as her husband shouts aloud verse from Tennyson's *The Charge of the Light Brigade*. This "terror" falls upon Mrs. Ramsay while her husband is described as being like a "sleepwalker" (31). This moment thus prefigures Ramsay's stance in the central "Time Passes" section. This later scene provides the following image of Mr. Ramsay's reaction to his wife's death: "[Mr. Ramsay stumbling along a passage one dark morning, stretched his arms out, but Mrs. Ramsay having died rather suddenly the night before, his arms though stretched out, remained empty]."[12] Mrs. Ramsay's death thus fulfils the call for disruption that was anticipated in the first third of the text by the words "sudden" and "interrupted." In this central passage, the repetition of the phrases he "stretched his arms out" and his "arms though stretched out" similarly foreshadows events in the last section of the novel.

In this final third of the text, the emphasis shifts from Mrs. Ramsay toward a consideration of the empty outstretched arms of her husband. In fact, the last part of *To the Lighthouse* may be said to articulate Mr. Ramsay's longing for that emptiness to be filled. Moreover, as the focus of the novel changes, another transformation is suggested: once again it seems that it is Mr. Ramsay, and not his wife, who bears the responsibility for her death. Here, it is Lily Briscoe who does the accusing. Long after the tragic deaths of Mrs. Ramsay, Prue, and Andrew, Lily returns to the Ramsays' house in the Hebrides. While there, she thinks back over the past and sees in it a single villain—Mr. Ramsay: "That man, she thought, her anger rising in her, never gave; that man took. She on the other hand would be forced to give. Mrs. Ramsay had given. Giving, giving, giving she had died—and had left all this" (231–2). These thoughts thus echo Lily's earlier prophecy that Mr. Ramsay would "wear" his wife "to death," and they illustrate that Lily has continued to envision him as responsible for Mrs. Ramsay's loss. But suddenly, and unaccountably, the object of her anger is redirected, as Lily realizes: "[r]eally, she was angry with Mrs. Ramsay. With the brush slightly trembling in her fingers she looked at the hedge, the step, the wall. It was all Mrs. Ramsay's doing" (232).

In this moment, I would argue, there is a merging of the two narratives of blame in Woolf's novel. While throughout the first third of the text, the reader has been offered hints of Mrs. Ramsay's complicity in her husband's domination of her, Lily had maintained that Mr. Ramsay alone was the villain ("he wears Mrs. Ramsay to death" [43]). Now, however, Lily is willing to ascribe the fault to Mrs. Ramsay. Lily's "sudden" realization recalls a moment in Woolf's *Mrs. Dalloway*, as examined in the previous chapter. There, I looked for a possible interpretation for Clarissa Dalloway's equally sudden and unaccountable sense of guilt over Septimus' suicide, and posited an intertextual source for Clarissa's remorse. In *To the Lighthouse*, however, a very different, *contextual* resolution can be found to explicate Lily's change of heart.

As Lily stands at her canvas, Mrs. Ramsay's complicity, which has been cryptically promoted in the earlier part of the novel, now haunts Lily's thoughts. It is this haunting that produces Lily's otherwise unaccountable reassessment of blame. The passage seems to suggest that Lily, by re-reading the past, has also *re-read* the text in which she is a character. Lily's realization that Mrs. Ramsay was not perhaps "worked to death" by Mr. Ramsay, that she might instead have allowed herself to die, is thus a result of her "sudden" re-reading of the past. If the earlier chapters of the novel hint at Mrs. Ramsay's complicity in her own death, here Lily deciphers those hints, and concludes that it was "all Mrs. Ramsay's doing."

This discovery, however, is not without its price. Lily now finds herself "trembling," "unable to do a thing, standing there, playing at painting, playing at the one thing one did not play at, and it was all Mrs. Ramsay's fault" (232). Once she has surrendered to her anger at Mrs. Ramsay, it seems, Lily is forced to reassess her own failures. By doing so she is able, finally, to have sympathy for Mr. Ramsay. As she thinks soon after, "[s]he would give him what she could" (233). Now that Lily has changed the object of her blame, she sees Mr. Ramsay not as a villain, but merely as a pathetic manipulator. When Lily confronts him for the first time since her change of heart, her demeanor toward him has altered considerably. Rather than let herself be bullied by Mr. Ramsay, she deliberately ignores his obvious ploy for attention: "Instantly, with the force of some primeval gust (for really he could not restrain himself any longer), there issued from him such a groan that any other woman in the whole world would have done something" (234). As the scene continues, Mr. Ramsay's need for Lily's notice becomes increasingly forceful and grotesque: "Mr. Ramsay sighed to the full. He waited. Was she not going to say anything? Did she not see what he wanted from her? [. . .] He sighed profoundly. He sighed significantly" (234–5). Lily's newfound ability to withstand Mr. Ramsay's supplications may thus be a further result of her re-reading of the past. Earlier in the novel she had endowed him with the power of life and death, but the threat once implicit in his insatiable demands is now evacuated. "Why" Lily thinks, "at this completely inappropriate moment, when he was stooping over her shoe, should she be so tormented with sympathy for him" (238)? Although here Lily does not recognize "why" she is "tormented with sympathy" for Mr. Ramsay, the answer can be found in her new reading of the past. Lily, that is, now believes that she and Mr. Ramsay have an equal status, as both are victims of the "faults" of Mrs. Ramsay.

Like Lily Briscoe, the characters of James and his sister Cam also develop a degree of sympathy for Mr. Ramsay, their father, by the end of *To the Lighthouse*. The two have made a pact to resist Mr. Ramsay's attempts at communication: "Resist him. Fight him. [James] said so rightly; justly. For they must fight tyranny to the death" (260). Nevertheless, during the course of their journey to the lighthouse they each submit to him. This reconciliation between father and children is presented in a moving passage that may itself have informed Woolf's later, nonfictional representations of Leslie Stephen. In this scene, Cam sits looking at her father, trying to decipher his character: "And watching her father as he wrote in his study she thought (now sitting in the boat) he was most loveable; he was most wise; was not vain, nor a tyrant. [. . .] Lest this should be wrong, she looked at him reading the little book with the shiny cover mottled like a plover's egg. No; it was right. Look at him now, she wanted to say aloud to James" (291–2). As this passage concludes, then, Mr. Ramsay is no longer depicted as a tyrant in his children's eyes, but rather as a mystery: "What could he see? Cam wondered. It was all a blur to her. What was he thinking now? she wondered. What was it he sought, so fixedly, so intently, so silently?" (317).

Thus, by the end of Woolf's novel, the Ramsay children's need to understand their father outweighs their anger and resistance toward him. The three seem to have made a tenuous peace as the children silently entreat: "What do you want? they both wanted to ask. They both wanted to say, Ask us anything and we'll give it you. But he did not ask them anything" (318). Like the mountaineer he imagines himself to be, who "would not die lying down," at the close of *To the Lighthouse* Mr. Ramsay stares fixedly ahead. The last view the reader has of Mr. Ramsay is his "leaping into space" defiant (318). Unlike the pale, bleached, and withered old figure found earlier in the text, Woolf now describes Mr. Ramsay's sprightly exit: "he sprang, lightly like a young man" (318); and instead of the enfeebled philosopher who would never reach R, here we find the leader of a successful expedition: "'He must have reached it', said Lily" (318).

Mr. Ramsay's completion of the journey to the lighthouse leads Lily to muse on her earlier apportioning of blame. The novel concludes with Lily attempting to complete her painting: "With a sudden intensity, as if she saw it clear for a second, she drew a line there, in the centre. It was done; it was finished. Yes, she thought, laying down her brush in extreme fatigue, I have had my vision" (320). Introduced as a last interruption, this straight line that Lily draws is like a repetition of the final image of Mr. Ramsay, "very straight and tall" (307). It embodies both the idea of intrusion (by dividing the picture) and that of "sudden intensity."[13] Moreover, this "line," which I associate with both the "sudden" death of Mrs. Ramsay, and Mr. Ramsay's tendency to disrupt, is placed in the center of the painting, cutting it in two. Lily's "extremely fatiguing" vision, therefore, is of the collusion of Mr. and Mrs. Ramsay in the tragedies that befell their family. The line in the center splits the painting into two equal parts, thus illustrating the difficulty of such a resolution: for Lily, both partners are equal in blame. While Lily resolves her struggle with Mr. and Mrs. Ramsay by finishing her painting, Woolf's own portrait of her parents was far from complete. Although two years after finishing *To the Lighthouse,* Woolf claimed that writing the novel had "laid them" in her mind (*DVW* 3:208), this was far from true. Leslie Stephen, in particular, would be recreated by Woolf several more times in the years to come.

Orlando, "Lives of the Obscure," and other "Sketches of the Past"

After completing *To The Lighthouse,* Woolf began to plan her next long work. In her diary in February 1927, she had decided, "I shall write memoirs," and began thinking about the historical research necessary for a second installment of her project "Lives of the Obscure" (*DVW* 3:129).[14] Interestingly, this undertaking seems to stand in direct opposition to Leslie Stephen's work on the *DNB,* which recounted the lives of the "great." I wonder then if her decision to begin such a task was informed by thoughts of her father? If so, perhaps Woolf's recent re-evaluation of him in *To the Lighthouse* had not "laid" his ghost to rest as she believed, but had instead rekindled her battle with his memory. As I shall argue, Woolf's renewed interest in memoirs and biography can be read as a further negotiation of Stephen's influence. When she contemplated writing the "Lives of the Obscure," however, it was not Leslie Stephen as "father" that Woolf challenged, but rather Leslie Stephen the biographer.[15]

By October of 1927, Woolf's considerations of the "art of biography" had led her to her next project. She described this work in her diary as follows: "a biography beginning in the year 1500 & continuing to the present day, called Orlando" (*DVW* 3:161). Like the "Lives of the Obscure," *Orlando* is an alternative biography that deconstructs the kind of traditional "lives" of the great that Leslie Stephen had written. As Woolf noted, it does so by telling the history of a fictional character over a 400-year span. In the introduction to her book *Vita and Virginia,* Suzanne Raitt asserts that there is a connection between *Orlando* and Leslie Stephen's work on the *DNB.* As she suggests: "*Orlando* reached back into individual and familial traditions as well as into literary ones. In a way Woolf's task in *Orlando* paralleled her father's in the *DNB*" (Raitt, *Vita* 19). If Woolf's *Orlando* has parallels with traditional biography, it nevertheless subverts the very *idea* of biography. At the most basic level, *Orlando* defies the primary tenet of biography: Orlando was not a "real" person. From its original conception, then, Woolf's "biography" was not to privilege the same kind of "truth" that her father's *DNB* had.

Indeed, from the moment the reader opens Woolf's text and sees a portrait of "Orlando as a boy," the satirical nature of the work becomes clear. Upon reading the first sentence, moreover, one is promptly drawn to question the usual expectations a biography raises: "He," Woolf writes, "—for there could be no doubt of his sex" (*Orlando* 15). As the very gender of the text's subject is raised as a location of possible controversy, the work's deconstruction of traditional biographical forms has begun. Woolf then continues in the opening paragraph to confront and satirize the most standard ingredients of a "great man's" biography: lineage, wealth, and historic status. After Orlando's gender is made clear, for instance, the reader, perhaps expecting to be told of his ancestry or accomplishments, instead encounters a metaphoric rendering of Orlando's sense of racial superiority. Orlando is shown "slicing at the head of a Moor which swung from the rafters" (13).

Here, as Woolf hints at the racism and brutality implicit in the stories of distinguished men, she also suggests that Orlando's feeling of supremacy is itself a patriarchal legacy. Explaining the origin of the swinging head, Woolf writes "Orlando's father, or perhaps his grandfather, had struck it from the shoulders of a vast Pagan" (13). As Orlando is uncertain of the provenance of this swinging trophy, his "slicing" at it also works to destabilize his own status as subject. Woolf's mocking tone throughout the introduction, that is, points to a larger concern over biography, as it critiques the biographer's need to claim some kind of privileged status for their subject. The swinging of this head could thus be read as an indication of the biographer's unreliability, as well as the instability of Orlando's own importance: "it swung, gently, perpetually in the breeze which never ceased blowing through the rooms of the gigantic house of the lord who had slain him" (13).

If this opening paragraph contains many of the elements found in a typical biography of a "great" man (his ancestry, his wealth, and his historical status), the arrangement and presentation of this information simultaneously provides a critique of their importance. One does not expect, for example, to encounter a biographer's subject engaging in the unheroic act of slashing at a dead and shrunken head. Such an image, in fact, functions to indict the very idea of heroism as suspect. Thus, Orlando, the "great" subject of this biography, is introduced to the reader as a coward, attempting to reproduce the "bravery" of his forefathers in a pathetic and derivative form.

On October 22, 1927, Woolf noted in her diary, "I am writing Orlando half in a mock style very clear & plain" (*DVW* 3:162). It is not, however, simply the form of traditional biography that she mocks in this text. *Orlando* also satirizes the ways in which works like the *DNB* elevate and sanctify people into heroic and/or saintly status. In composing *Orlando,* then, Woolf may have finally addressed the controversy that had arisen between her and Caroline Stephen more than twenty years earlier: the question of truth-telling in biography. Throughout *Orlando,* Woolf calls attention to this dilemma in various ways. Early on in the text, for example, the reader is told that "[d]irectly we glance at Orlando standing by the window, we must admit that he had eyes like drenched violets, [. . .] Directly we glance at eyes and forehead, thus do we rhapsodise. Directly we glance at eyes and forehead, we have to admit a thousand disagreeables which it is the duty of every good biographer to ignore" (15). Interestingly, the language Woolf employs in this passage seems to echo Lytton Strachey's words in the "Introduction" to his 1918 work *Eminent Victorians.* There, Strachey argues wryly that "ignorance is the first requisite of the historian" (vii). Woolf, on the other hand, appears to refigure both Strachey's argument and his words in her own "biography." In *Orlando,* she notes that it is "the duty of every good biographer to ignore" "disagreeables." If my assumption is correct, Woolf's text may also promote another shocking suggestion Strachey makes in his "Introduction." There, Strachey asserts that the "history of the Victorian Age will never be written." As Woolf knew, that history had in fact already been written, by Leslie Stephen in the *DNB.*

Does Woolf echo Strachey in *Orlando?* Does she similarly devalue Stephen's biographical works, by retrieving and employing Strachey's argument of "ignorance" as a necessary tool for biography? The linguistic connection between these passages in *Orlando* and *Eminent Victorians* could strengthen such an argument, but it may also prompt a further consideration. In his text, Strachey defines the "ignorance" necessary to a biographer as a lack of historical knowledge. In this excerpt from *Orlando,* on the other hand, Woolf employs the word "ignore" to mean *deny:* the biographer sees Orlando's imperfections, but chooses not to relate them. This difference in emphasis, I would argue, promotes a reading of this passage in Woolf's "biography" as an intersection of her conflicting feelings toward Stephen and his work. While Woolf had once struggled with Caroline over publishing disagreeable facts about her father's character, in *Orlando* she satirizes such sanitized portraits.

Then again, another reading of this scene could be proposed: perhaps here, Woolf *denies* the importance of truth-telling. In contributing to Maitland's life of Stephen, that is, the young Virginia chose to "ignore" a range of difficult "truths" about her father. Among these were his tyrannical temper, his obsession with failure, and what Marcus calls his "emotional bullying of women" (Marcus, "Niece" 119). In *Orlando,* however, the "disagreeables" that the biographer by "duty" must "ignore" are purely superficial. Thus, by satirizing truth itself as made up of superficial and unimportant "disagreeables," Woolf could be seen to cover her own earlier avoidance of truth-telling. Woolf alludes in this passage to Strachey's dismissal of Victorian biographies, and by doing so she not only "ignores" but also *denies* her father's great legacy. For if biography itself is shown by Strachey and Woolf to be irrelevant, then it would follow that so was the great biographer, Leslie Stephen.

In composing a fictional biography of an immortal hero/heroine, then, Woolf had deconstructed and renegotiated several intertwined concerns. Historical status, gender, ancestry, biography, and truth-telling are all critiqued in *Orlando*. Another presence that Woolf could not "ignore" also surfaces here: the legacy of Leslie Stephen. This connection between Woolf's work on alternative biographies and the influence of her father is furthered by a note that she made in her journal on November 28, 1928, shortly after the successful publication of *Orlando:* "Father's birthday. He would have been 96, 96, yes, today; & could have been 96, like other people one has known; but mercifully was not. His life would have entirely ended mine" (*DVW* 3:208). As the entry continues, Woolf makes clear that despite her relief at her father's "mercifully" being dead, he is still very much a force in her life: "I used to think of him & mother daily; but writing The Lighthouse, laid them in my mind. And now he comes back sometimes, but differently. (I believe this to be true—that I was obsessed by them both, unhealthily; & writing of them was a necessary act.) He comes back now more as a contemporary" (*DVW* 3:208). Here, Woolf's claim that writing *To the Lighthouse* had laid the ghosts of her parents to rest is belied as she repeats the words: "he comes back sometimes," "[h]e comes back now." The urgency that this repetition suggests may point to Woolf's continuing "unhealthy" "obsession" with the figure of her father. While in this passage Woolf stresses that Stephen now comes back "differently" and as "more of a contemporary," she nevertheless admits that if he were still alive, her life would be "ended."

Woolf's ambivalence toward her father's influence was not resolved by writing *To the Lighthouse*. Indeed, Woolf continued to create biographical sketches of him for the rest of her life. One such portrait was a commemorative piece written on what would have been Stephen's one-hundredth birthday in 1932. Although it is meant to be a memorial to her father, Woolf's essay begins with the rather dismissive statement "[b]y the time that his children were growing up the great days of my father's life were over" ("Stephen" 76). Throughout the essay Woolf repeatedly employs this language of faded glory. She mentions, for instance, the "relics" and the "rusty alpenstocks" in his study, and concludes that Stephen's "years of activity were over" (76). As in several earlier portraits of her father, Woolf's words here depict him as old and weak. In contrast to those earlier "biographies," however, in this essay Woolf directly addresses her father as a writer. She lists the names of four of his works, and then informs the reader that when she was growing up "[h]e still wrote daily, and methodically" (76).[16]

In this piece, Woolf once again refers to Stephen's startling habit of suddenly reciting verse aloud, as well as his talent for making paper cut-outs. She also provides an example of his more frightening outbursts: "not all his mathematics together with a bank balance which he insisted must be ample in the extreme, could persuade him, when it came to signing a cheque, that the whole family was not 'shooting Niagara to ruin'" (78). The candor of these reminiscences indicates a new direction in Woolf's relation to the memory of her father. Although in *To the Lighthouse* Woolf had divulged some painful truths about her father's character, these observations were qualified and veiled by being contained in a work of fiction. In this later nonfictional essay, Woolf more explicitly confronts the darker, tyrannical side of Stephen's nature. Nevertheless, Woolf's reluctance to explore these painful truths in detail is soon made clear; her discussion of Stephen's fierce temper is quickly countered by an assertion of his relative liberality. "Even today," Woolf writes, "there may be parents who would doubt the wisdom of allowing a girl of fifteen the free run of a large and quite unexpurgated library. But my father allowed it" ("Stephen" 79). Thus, if Woolf attempts to tell the truth about her father here, this piece also suggests that "truth" itself is multifaceted and contradictory. A tight-fisted tyrant or a liberal and generous man? For Woolf, as this essay implies, Leslie Stephen was both.

By the conclusion of the article, the ambiguity of Woolf's portrait of her father leads her to question the reliability of her memories; she turns instead to offering the reader received images of him. Woolf notes, for instance that fellow writers were taken with Stephen, stating: "Meredith saw him 'as 'Phoebus Apollo' turned fasting friar'," (80) while Hardy, as Woolf recounts, remembered his "spare and desolate figure" in "The Schreckhorn" (80).[17] Next, Woolf cites a portion of Hardy's poem before leaving the reader with Lowell's assessment of her father as "the most loveable of men." Finally, she concludes that Stephen is "after all these years, unforgettable" (80). Unforgettable indeed: Woolf was to write of her father yet again.

In 1980, a previously unknown seventy-seven-page typescript by Virginia Woolf came to light and was acquired by the British Library (BL 61973). It is now published as a portion of Woolf's essay "A Sketch of the Past," in a revised edition of *Moments of Being*. In the preface to this second edition, the editor Jeanne Schulkind notes: "[w]ritten in 1940, this hitherto unknown material provides the missing link between the typescript and the manuscript which were brought together as 'A Sketch of the Past', the most substantial and significant of the autobiographical writings in *Moments of Being*" ("Preface" 6). For Schulkind, the importance of this piece is as follows:

The British Library typescript contains twenty-seven pages of entirely new material in which Woolf describes her father, Leslie Stephen, and the ambivalence of her relationship to him which her recent reading of Freud had caused her to reassess. Her mature, analytic account illuminates one of the more important influences on her development both as an individual and as a writer, and provides a valuable corrective to the earlier version which, because it is partial, is also misleading ("Preface" 6).

Here, Schulkind terms the first published version of "A Sketch of the Past" as "partial" and "misleading." One might use the same words to describe Woolf's other, earlier portraits of her father. As the final vision of Stephen that Woolf was to compose, how does this "sketch" compare with the others I have examined? This typescript was begun in June of 1940, and it seems on the whole to offer a more self-assured reading of her father than the earlier works I have looked at above. In this sketch Woolf does not offer lists of Stephen's accomplishments, as she had done in Maitland, nor does she represent him with the bitterness evident in *To the Lighthouse.* Instead Woolf claims that she wishes to portray her father truthfully, "as I think he must have been" ("Sketch" 108).

Woolf's recollection of Stephen in this piece begins "[m]y father now falls to be described, because it was during the seven years between Stella's death in 1897 and his death in 1904 that Nessa and I were fully exposed without protection to the full blast of that strange character" ("Sketch" 107). The term "full blast" that Woolf uses in this passage is itself important, for it seems to embody the very purpose of her "sketch": her project was to give a full and unexpurgated rendering of her father's "strange character." As Woolf soon admits, however, she is uncertain of her ability to deliver such a portrait with accuracy. She notes, for example, the following difficulties: "I am much nearer his age now than my own then. But do I therefore 'understand' him better than I did? Or have I only queered the angle of that immensely important relationship, so that I shall fail to describe it, either from his point of view, or my own? I see him now from round the corner; not directly in front of me" (107–8). In this reflection, I suggest, there arises a major distinction between this late portrait of Stephen and those I have examined previously. Here, for the first time, Woolf pauses to question her capacity to write her father's life. In this sketch, Woolf confesses that she sees her father from "round the corner," and feels that she may therefore be incapable of describing her "immensely important" relationship to him.

While Schulkind asserts that Woolf's recent reading of Freud had served as a "corrective," a curative in her negotiation of her father's memory, I question this interpretation of the memoir. Understanding is not resolution, and although Woolf acknowledges her conflicting feelings toward Stephen here, her portrait of him evinces little sign of forgiveness. Indeed, Woolf's own description of Freud's theory of ambivalence in this essay confirms her continuing struggle with her father: "I discovered that this violently disturbing conflict of love and hate is a common feeling; and is called ambivalence. But before I analyse our relation as father and daughter, I will try to sketch him as I think he must have been, not to me, but to the world at large" (108). Woolf's sense, then, of being in "violently disturbing conflict" with her father seems to undermine any suggestion that her feelings toward him were resolved by her reading of Freud. In Schulkind's view, this piece demonstrates that in "frankly acknowledging the vehemence of her anger against him [Woolf was] free to acknowledge the depth of her love and affection for him" ("Introduction" 13). In the passage above, however, Woolf decides to delay writing an analysis of their "relation as father and daughter," and to instead "sketch" her father as he was to the "world at large." I would argue that this change of focus should be read as an avoidance, rather than an acknowledgement as Schulkind suggests, of the "vehemence of her anger against him."

As the piece continues, moreover, it appears that although Woolf had decided to provide an unbiased portrait of her father, the very objectivity of this rendering "bores" her. The factual content of Stephen's life is, as Woolf remarks, "all so obvious that I cannot bring myself to follow it" ("Sketch" 108). She cursorily mentions Eton, Cambridge, coaching, Agnosticism, and writing, finally complaining that her father "was, so far as I can see, the very type, or mould, of so many Cambridge intellectuals. [. . .] It bores me to write of him, to try to describe him, partly because it is all so familiar" (108–9). In this passage, therefore, Woolf acknowledges her ongoing preoccupation with the details of her father's life. Having written about Stephen so frequently in the past, Woolf now confesses that she has tired of her role as his biographer. Instead, she provides a fantastic and poetical rendering of her "analysis" of their "relation as father and daughter":

> It was like being shut up in the same cage with a wild beast. Suppose I, at fifteen, was a nervous, gibbering, little monkey, always spitting or cracking a nut and shying the shells about [. . .] he was the pacing, dangerous, morose lion; a lion who was sulky and angry and injured; and suddenly ferocious, and then very humble, and then majestic; and then lying dusty and fly pestered in a corner of the cage (116).

Schulkind maintains that this "frank" portrait of Stephen indicates a working out of Woolf's ambivalence toward him. I would argue that such a reading forces a closure on this text that its own terms belie. If, that is, this portrayal of Stephen as "dusty and fly-pestered" articulates a measure of sympathy for his injuries, the explicit threat of this "caged and wild beast" is palpable nevertheless. To Woolf's "nervous little monkey," her father as lion king is clearly "ferocious," "dangerous," and "angry." Moreover, Woolf's need to render this dark image of her father as an allegory must itself confirm her continuing difficulty in confronting her memories of him. As Woolf had remarked years earlier, for her it was far less dangerous to tell the truth about a character disguised in fictional clothes.

Woolf's need to explore the past at a safe, fictionalized distance is also confirmed by the similarity between the character of Mrs. Ramsay and Woolf's rendering of her mother in "Sketch of the Past." Of Julia Stephen, Woolf writes: "It was thus that she left us the legacy of his dependence, which after her death became so harsh an imposition [. . .] for many years she made a fetish of his health; and so [. . .] she wore herself out and died at forty-nine; while he lived on, and found it very difficult, so healthy was he, to die of cancer at the age of seventy-two" ("Sketch" 133). Woolf's consideration of her mother in this memoir thus echoes Lily Briscoe's realization at the end of *To the Lighthouse:* "it was all Mrs. Ramsay's fault" (*Lighthouse* 224). Lily, as I argued, had come to terms with her difficulties with both Mr. and Mrs. Ramsay by inscribing a line down the center of her painting, thus completing her "vision." This passage in "A Sketch of the Past," however, forces me to re-examine the perhaps disturbing meaning of that "vision."

By blaming her mother for her own death, as well as for the "legacy" of her father's "dependence," Woolf, both here and in the earlier fictional portrait of her childhood in *To the Lighthouse,* privileges a patriarchal reading of her family's relations. Woolf's later censure of her mother's actions in "A Sketch of the Past" is therefore connected to Lily's "vision." In both, Woolf forces women to bear responsibility for the effects of male domination, while simultaneously disallowing them the power to change their inherited roles. Far from the closure that Lily's painting had suggested, Woolf's last memoir instead reveals that her struggle with the past was ongoing. Like Lily's "vision," it seems, Woolf's own view of her parents was one that maintained patriarchal priorities. Moreover, this constrained stance surfaces in many of Woolf's texts, as they attempt to analyze and understand the father, while blaming the mother for her own inheritance: a legacy of complicit dependence.

In an earlier moment in "A Sketch of the Past," Woolf also reproaches her mother for Stephen's "imposition" on his children. Here, she addresses not only Julia's impact on her thoughts, but, more generally, the notion of influence itself, and its connection with reading, writing, and biography:

> She was one of those invisible presences who after all play so important a part
> in every life. This influence [. . .] all those magnets which attract us this way to
> be like that, or repel us the other and make us different from that; has never

> been analysed in any of those Lives which I so much enjoy reading [. . .] if we
> cannot analyse these invisible presences, we know very little of the subject of
> the memoir; and again how futile life-writing becomes. I see myself as a fish in
> a stream; deflected; held in place; but cannot describe the stream ("Sketch" 80).

Here, Woolf denies her capacity to "describe the stream" that is comprised of the "invisible presences" around her. I would argue, however, that this inability is belied throughout her oeuvre. Indeed, in every novel, essay, memoir, and letter I have examined in these chapters, one encounters Woolf's stunning descriptions of the "magnets" that attracted her and those that "repelled" her. Fittingly, as Woolf predicts above, through my reading of these texts I have also discovered much about "the subject(s) of this memoir."

As Woolf suggests, to disregard her depictions of these influences would make "life-writing" "futile." Reading this late sketch, then, I find that as Woolf foretold in 1924, the "old V. of 1940" did see more, and see it differently than did the "young V." Woolf envisioned her diary as a source for later, as yet unimagined reflections, and the intertextual nature of Woolf's negotiations of the past is there revealed. Like Lily Briscoe, who was "suddenly" able to re-read the text she inhabits, and hear the voices that went before with a newfound understanding, Woolf herself, in novels, essays, and memoirs, sifted through the textual remnants that surrounded her. By employing these various "invisible presences" in her works, Woolf, like Lily, offered her vision: a strange and contradictory reading of the pages of her past.

Conclusion ❧

Fish in a Stream
or Spider in a Web?

But any deductions that we may draw from the comparison of one fiction
with another are futile, save as they flood us with a view of infinite possibilities, assure us that there is no bound to the horizon, and nothing forbidden
but falsity and pretence. "The proper stuff of fiction" does not exist; everything is the proper stuff of fiction; whatever one honestly thinks, whatever
one honestly feels.

—Virginia Woolf "Modern Novels"(190)

In this passage from the conclusion of Woolf's 1919 essay "Modern
Novels," she writes of the ultimate futility of comparing one fiction
with another. Although here she is specifically discussing the "immeasurable" distance she envisions between the fiction writing of Russia and
that of England, her statement feels pertinent to me on a more general, and
indeed personal, level as well. As Woolf warns of the uselessness of con-
trasting different fictions, my entire enterprise in the preceding pages is
called into question. Woolf's caution here suggests that it would be "pretence" to insist that any "deductions" that I draw from such comparisons
are, in any real sense, definitive. As Woolf makes clear, such a claim would
represent an opportunity missed: in her view the very nature of literary endeavor demands that there is "no bound to the horizon, and nothing forbidden but falsity and pretence."

As I look back over the preceding chapters, however, I am confident that
I have embraced this idea; by demonstrating that many different, and diver-
gent, contexts can be used to produce viable readings of a given text, I have,

I hope, offered "a view of infinite possibilities" of the art of fiction. In this study, I have examined a wide range of works, biographical, fictional, non-fictional, and poetic, and read them alongside a variety of critical notions. Interestingly, though, one major theme seems to reverberate throughout the cacophony of textual interpretations offered here: in every case, these readings of literary history and poetic influence have been marked with cultural and/or political inflections. Whether considering Bloom's paradigm of weak and strong poets engaged in battle, or Riffaterre's intertextual haunting of one text by another; Roland Barthes' account of the death of the author, or Kristeva's infinite circularity of meaning; Tompkin's arguments about public and private discourse, or Gilbert and Gubar's model of a feminine nurturing influence: all of these literary formulations rely on partial and specific readings of influence and indebtedness. As I posited, literary influence and the nature of literary history are enacted via far more subtle and complex mechanisms than can be accounted for by current theoretical models. These paradigms, when relied upon singularly, tend to constrain interpretations and refute conflicting possibilities when, in fact, as Woolf predicted, in the world of fiction "there is no bound to the horizon" (190).

The dynamics of textual relations and connections are labyrinthine, and if we use our Daedalus-like cunning to escape, to fly from the complexities of the intertextual maze, we will surely miss the lessons to be learned by tracing and retracing the paths of possibility. Frustrating as it may be for the curious reader who likes best to employ his or her critical skills to seek resolutions, writing emerges along myriad, circuitous routes: each time we choose to travel down just one, a hundred more remain unexplored. Moreover, this layering of literary debts and inspirations is itself a source of intrigue for readers. As each new influence is inscribed upon the texts I examine in this study, the words that came before are changed, burdened, obscured. Thus, in the widest possible sense, each of the works I have studied here is a palimpsest, contaminated by the writing that preceded it.

As Woolf points out, however, such contamination is no bad thing, as nothing should be forbidden in the realm of literature; for Woolf, "'the proper stuff of fiction' does not exist" (190). In my examination of specific authors, therefore, I have suggested the ways that these various networks of influence and indebtedness, while offering a context in which to read the possible negotiations at work in texts, raise more questions than they answer. For Leslie Stephen, Thomas Hardy, Katherine Mansfield, John Middleton Murry, and Virginia Woolf, I would argue, this would come as no surprise; each of these writers was fascinated by the difficulties and intricacies of language and meaning. Indeed, it was this intense passion for writing that drew them to read one another's works. For this reason, the relationships among these figures occurred as complex intertextual events; events that were difficult even for them to interpret. As letters, poems, stories, magazines, essays, and novels shifted among them, these five deciphered and mediated such "intersections of textual surfaces" in their lives time and time again. For them, as well as for the curious readers studying their works, their textual relations remain, for the most part, unresolved.

I began the long journey toward completing this work by examining the differing accounts of literary influence and literary history offered in the works of Virginia Woolf and Harold Bloom, and I see no reason not to return to them in my conclusion. In my opening chapter, I cited from Woolf's late essay "The Leaning Tower" (1940). As I noted, in this paper Woolf speaks explicitly about literary influence and goes on to proclaim: "We must then have a theory as to what this influence is. But let us always remember—influences are infinitely numerous; writers are infinitely sensitive; each writer has a different sensibility" (163). Here, then, Woolf's own reading of literary indebtedness insists on the infinite variety of influences upon the "infinitely sensitive" writer. In her view, moreover, it is impossible to trace such influences accurately, for, she argues "that is why literature is always changing, like the weather, like the clouds in the sky. Read a page of Scott; then of Henry James; try to work out the influences that have transformed the one page into the other. It is beyond our skill. We can only hope therefore to single out the most obvious influences" (163). With such words Virginia Woolf delivers an admonishment to the critics of literary influence who come after her: any attempt to definitively untangle and decipher the informing pressures upon her works will be, she warns, "beyond our skill." Might Woolf be right in this? Is it possible that influence study is, after all, a futile exercise?

Harold Bloom, the father of modern influence study, offers a response to Woolf's comments in "The Leaning Tower" in his "Introduction" to *Modern Critical Views: Virginia Woolf.* There, he notes: "A critic of literary influence learns to be both enchanted and wary when such a passage is encountered. Sensibility is indeed the issue, since without 'a different sensibility' no writer truly is a writer" ("Introduction" 2). In this account of his reaction to Woolf's essay, Bloom maintains that he is "both enchanted and wary" of encountering Woolf's admonishment. The content of the "Introduction" that follows, however, suggests that in Bloom's reading of Woolf, both wariness and enchantment fall away before his own powerful paradigm of influence. For no sooner has Bloom acknowledged Woolf's warning that each writer has a "different sensibility," than he rushes to fit Woolf's particular "sensibility" into his influence model. Woolf's sensibility, he argues, is inherited from the Victorian essayist Walter Pater. "[W]ithout 'a different sensibility,'" Bloom states, "no writer truly is a writer. Woolf's sensibility essentially is Paterian . . ." (2).

Critic Perry Meisel has, as Bloom points out, convincingly demonstrated Pater's influence on Woolf, and I do not take issue with Meisel's persuasive arguments here.[1] What I do find curious, however, is Bloom's apparent denial of the meaning of Woolf's warning: Woolf insists that theories of influence are dangerous and limiting, that influences are infinite, and that accurate analyses of literary debts are therefore "beyond our skill." Bloom's response to this caution, however, seems to willfully ignore Woolf's meaning, as without hesitation he associates her own sensibilities with Pater's. He does not, that is, seem interested in the possibility of other influences on this "infinitely sensitive" writer. Instead, Bloom silences Woolf's critique of the meager skills demonstrated by critics attempting to decipher influence.

Bloom is not alone, of course, in making use of strategies of limitation in his readings. As I have argued in the previous chapters, the ideas of Julia Kristeva and Roland Barthes, for example, also close certain doors of critical inquiry by ignoring the body, the person of the author. As Barthes argued, the "modern scriptor is born simultaneously with the text, is in no way equipped with a being preceding or exceeding the writing" ("The Death of the Author" 145). Like Bloom's own very different method of interpreting texts, Barthes' account of the final anonymity of authorship, as we have seen, leads once again to limited and limiting readings, and denies the existence of other possibilities.

Influence flows along circuitous routes, and the examples of Hardy, Stephen, Murry, Mansfield, and Woolf illustrate the variety of dynamics at work in the relationship between writers and the texts they read. What I have encountered in each case is not the battle to the death that Bloom's theories predict, but nor do these textual connections seem to have been able to occur without the very real and personal encounters among the writers who produced them: I have indeed found that subterfuge and anxiety, desire and ambition informed these highly textual relationships. Thus, I am led to believe that despite Barthes' arguments, the person of the author continues to be as viable a location for uncovering meaning as any other. Furthermore, in my study I have also illustrated that in each influential association, the public image and literary legacy of the writer at hand has emerged as another quarter for struggle—a site for ambitions, anxieties, and subterfuge to surface.

In my view, the purpose of intertextual readings is to articulate creative and linguistic mediations, and to propose the conscious and unconscious motives that emerge in and intersect texts. In this study, I have attempted to point to just such negotiations, by demonstrating how struggles that surface in certain intertextual moments may have been historically constructed. But, as critic Jay Clayton warns, such histories "must be acknowledged to be partial and specific—oriented to particular tasks, with particular readers in mind" ("Alphabet" 57). It seems then that I must acknowledge that my own readings are equally, and necessarily, partial and specific. That does not, however, make them any less important: the partial and specific are a gift— they allow the theorist entry into an otherwise forbidding world of possibility. I can see desire and denial, influence and indebtedness on the small scale, I can understand it, analyze it, propose its origins, predict its possible outcomes. This is why metaphor is the best tool of the poet: human beings can only comprehend the universe through association, by projecting the dynamics of microcosms onto our model of infinity.

As Bloom argues throughout *The Western Canon,* the most difficult quality for literary critics to account for or describe is originality. Thus, while I am busy associating this text with that and connecting this allusion with that historical moment, perhaps at the same time I should be wary of overlooking the uniqueness of every single text. As I work to account for the problematic passages I encounter in my reading, that is, I must remind myself that these textual dilemma are not only symptoms of difficulty, but opportunities for witnessing originality. Indeed, in such moments one may see a palimpsest for what it truly is: not just the visible legacy of the past, but the unique, unresolved, contaminated, idiosyncratic voice of the author at work.

Of all the five writers I have examined here, I find most interest in the one whose works offer the least sense of resolution: Virginia Woolf. For me, it is not the completed or resolved "vision" that Woolf achieves in any one text that is compelling, but rather the mutable and contradictory nature of her many different *visions.* Daughter of a patriarch, rebelling against male domination, her own texts also evince pride in Sir Leslie's patriarchal status; hater of "great men," Woolf's admiration of their literature is also explicitly illustrated by her retrieval of tropes and themes from those "classics" in her works; a writer searching for an original voice, Woolf relied heavily on words from the literary past. These dichotomies confirm Woolf's own argument in "The Leaning Tower." There, she maintains that such conflicting evidence: "proves that we are in the dark about writers; anybody can make a theory; the germ of a theory is almost always the wish to prove what the theorist wishes to believe" (163). As Woolf insists, we should be wary of the wishes of theorists. Cultural prejudices are insidious and obscure our reading to a great degree. It is our job as readers to acknowledge those prejudices and to admit to our partial and specific understanding. It is only by doing so that we can take charge of our readings and claim for them not definitiveness, but originality, which is, in the end, the highest human achievement.

As we saw in the previous chapter, in "A Sketch of the Past" Virginia Woolf depicted herself as controlled by outside forces; a fish "held" and "deflected" in a stream of powerful influences. In my own partial, specific view, however, Woolf was not only a powerless fish in a stream, but also a brilliant spider in the intertextual web. Many ghosts, as I have seen, haunted Woolf, but more importantly, she spun those "invisible presences" in her life into threads of prose. She was inspired by her literary ancestors, and wove and embroidered that indebtedness and influence into her works. I hope, finally, that in this study I have at least partially illumined and retraced Woolf's startling creative method. As I align and define my own developing voice against, and in sympathy with, the words of writers from the past, I also endeavor to create not only something new, but something of beauty. Such was the work of Woolf's life. It is, I believe, this interplay between Woolf's debts and her sublime workmanship that creates her unique "sensibility." Choosing here an image from Mansfield, there a trope from Hardy, piecing the whole together with strands of her own family history, Woolf worked a shimmering, contradictory, and impossibly intricate vision: both the framework for, and the intersection of, the textual surfaces of her life.

Notes

Chapter One

1. Woolf first published this essay as "Modern Novels" in *The Times Literary Supplement*, 899 (April 10, 1919):189–90. Except where noted, I cite here from this original 1919 edition of the essay. The revised essay appears under the title "Modern Fiction" and published in Woolf's first collected volume of her essays, *The Common Reader: First Series Edition*, Hogarth Press, 1925, 184–95.
2. The term "intertextuality" was coined by Julia Kristeva in her 1969 work, *Séméiotikè recherches pour un sémanalyse* (Paris: Editions du Seuil, 1969). As Jay Clayton and Eric Rothstein note, Kristeva's own development of the term "intertextuality" was "itself a complex intertextual event, one that involved both inclusion and selectivity. She initially used it in her dialogue with the texts of Mikhail Bahktin," Clayton and Rothstein, "Figures in the Corpus" 18.
3. See Clayton and Rothstein, "Figures in the Corpus."
4. See, in particular, Rosemarie Morgan's 1992 study *Cancelled Words: Rediscovering Thomas Hardy*, which comprehensively details Stephen's amendments to Hardy's *Cornhill* submissions.

Chapter Two

1. An indication of the attention given to the publication of this book can be seen by even a cursory glance at the reviews and articles that accompanied both its original release and its re-release in paperback. I list here just a sampling of those articles that exceeded 500 words. Of particular interest may be the wide range of magazines involved; from *The Economist* to the *New Republic*, from *Newsweek* to *Entertainment Weekly*—Bloom's text has certainly caught the attention of a diverse group: *Bookworld:* (Washington Post) 24 (Sept 25 1994) 1; *Chronicle of Higher Education:* 41 (Sept 7 1994) A11; *New York Times Book Review:* 99 (Oct 9 1994) 9; *Commentary:* 98 (Dec 1994) 60; *London Review of Books:* 16 (Dec 22 1994) 8; *New Republic:* 211 (Oct 10 1994) 36; *New York Review of Books:* 41 (Nov 17 1994) 4; *New York Times Late ed:* 144 (Oct 17 1994) C15.

2. See *The Western Canon,* 553.

3. The willingness of Leslie Stephen to pander to his reading public is discussed at length in F. W. Maitland's *Life and Letters of Leslie Stephen.* See for example pages 274–6.

4. Leslie Stephen had also used such alpine tropes in his essay "The Schreckhorn," which was published in Stephen's 1871 work, *The Playground of Europe.*

5. As Maitland writes in his 1906 biography: "Stephen did not see the sonnet; but Mr. Hardy [. . .] allows me to print it here" (Maitland 278).

6. Although "The Schreckhorn" was composed in 1897, it was first published in Maitland in 1906, and later collected in Hardy's *Satires of Circumstance,* 1914.

7. In Maitland, Hardy cites a portion of a letter from Stephen regarding the Schreckhorn climb. As Stephen told Hardy in this letter, during the ascent he was "frequently flattened out against the rock like a beast of ill-repute nailed to a barn" (cited in Maitland, 277).

8. The *Times* of February 23, 1904, for instance, notes in its obituary of Stephen that his family had "been notable through three generations, both at home and in the Colonies for its intellectual vigour" (10), and concludes that "as a biographer and critic, Sir Leslie came to fill the first place in the literary world of his day [. . .]" (10). See also James Bryce's introduction to Stephen's collected essays, in which he states that "Leslie Stephen came of a family originally from Aberdeenshire which had produced remarkable men during the three generations preceding his own" Bryce, "Introduction," ix.

9. Note that Hardy's poem "The Schreckhorn" was also included in both of Noel Annan's biographies of Stephen, *Leslie Stephen: His Thought and Character in Relation to his Time,* 1951, and *Leslie Stephen: The Godless Victorian,* 1984.

10. In addition to the assessments of Stephen in note 8 above, also of note for their insistence on the "greatness" of Stephen's heritage are: Maitland's *Life and Letters of Leslie Stephen;* Gillian Fenwick's *Leslie Stephen's Life in Letters;* Phyllis Grosskurth's *Leslie Stephen;* as well as Annan's revised 1984 biography *Leslie Stephen: The Godless Victorian.*

11. See for example, Stephen's letter to Hardy of early 1874, in which Stephen writes "[e]xcuse this wretched shred of concession to popular stupidity, but I am a slave" (cited in Maitland 274–5).

12. Stephen's hatred of vulgarity and his belief in the power of texts to corrupt readers is well documented (see for instance his essay "Art and Morality" in *Cornhill,* July 1875). I have not, however, discovered other complaints about his undue severity as a censor during his editorship of *Cornhill.* The various contributors to the magazine (Edmund Gosse, R. L. Stevenson, and Mrs. Oliphant among them) who also offered Maitland anecdotes, all have high praise for their former editor. One, a Mr. Sully, wrote, for example, that Stephen "seemed to me the most considerate of editors, almost too timid" (cited in Maitland 269).

13. See for instance, Mowbray Morris' review of *Tess,* "Culture and Anarchy" in the April 1892 *Quarterly Review,* and Mrs. Oliphant's on *Jude* in "The Anti-

Marriage League" in *Blackwood's* magazine, January 1896. Both are examples of the kind of moral outrage heaped upon Hardy's last novels.

14. Smith Elder, publishers of *Cornhill,* paid Hardy £400 for the serial rights alone.

15. Stephen's own view of the balance of power in this relationship is made clear in a letter to Hardy of January 1899. There Stephen notes, "I am always pleased to remember that 'Far from the Madding Crowd' came out *under my command"* (cited in Maitland 450, my emphasis).

16. See the Preamble to Rosemarie Morgan's *Cancelled Words* in which Stephen's censorship is held responsible for the lack of spontaneity in *Madding Crowd.* See also the chapter on *Madding Crowd* in Michael Millgate's 1971 *Thomas Hardy: His Career as a Novelist,* censuring Stephen's "Grundyism" (81–3).

17. As Stephen mentions here, the *Spectator* had given high praise to the first installment of *Madding Crowd,* stating that if the work were not written by George Eliot, "then there is a new light among novelists" (cited in Seymour-Smith 179).

18. Noel Annan states that Stephen was elected at Christmas 1854 to a clerical Fellowship at Cambridge, "which required the holder to take Holy Orders" (1951 28).

19. Seymour-Smith cites from Gittings' 1975 "Introduction" to *The Hand of Ethelberta,* xviii.

20. Thomas Hardy, *The Hand of Ethelberta* in *Cornhill,* July 1875–May 1876, vols. 32–3 (32:241). All further citations from this work refer to this serialized edition.

21. On January 20, 1915, Hardy wrote to Woolf: "I used to suffer gladly his grim & severe criticisms of my contributions & his long silences for the sake of sitting with him" (*CLTH* 5:76).

22. As Robert Lee Woolf writes, Braddon sustained heavy criticism after the publication of her novel *Aurora Floyd* in 1863. See R. Woolf, *Sensational Victorian: The Life and Fiction of Mary Elizabeth Braddon,* 188.

23. Mudie's was the most popular of the circulating libraries. See R. Woolf, pages 355–7 for a brief description. Hardy, like most novelists, depended in part on the revenue derived from being included on Mudie's selection list.

24. Thomas Hardy, *The Return of the Native* in *Belgravia,* January 1878–9. Vols. 34–7. All further citations from this text refer to this serialized edition (34:261).

25. For a description of Stephen's sense of "exclusion" from the orthodox religious and academic communities of his time, see Maitland 261–3.

26. G. K. Chesterton (1874–1936) had remarked that Hardy was "a village atheist brooding and blaspheming over the village idiot" in *The Victorian Age in Literature,* 1914, 15. As Richard Taylor notes, "Hardy took his revenge in an epitaph for Chesterton dictated on his deathbed in 1928" R. Taylor, 259 *n.* This epitaph ends: "And if one with him could not see/ He'd shout his choice word 'Blasphemy'" (cited in Taylor 259).

27. George Moore (1852–1933), as Taylor notes, "had angered Hardy since 1886 when in 'Confessions of a Young Man'" he had likened *Madding*

Crowd to an Eliot "miscarriage." Such vicious critiques continued, culminating in 1924, when in Moore's *Conversations on Ebury Street* he remarked on Hardy's "lack of invention and brain paralysis" (Taylor 79 *n*).

28. Seymour-Smith notes that Hardy had burned or otherwise destroyed many documents "such as Emma's diaries and the manuscripts of the Life [. . .] long before his death" (Seymour-Smith 834). His second wife burned what remained after his death, apparently at Hardy's request. Hardy also revised the prefaces and texts for the *Wessex Novels* edition of his works, published in 1895. A further twenty-volume edition, the *Wessex* edition, was begun in 1912, for which Hardy revised all his novels for the last time.

29. As Seymour-Smith notes, one Frank Hedgcock published a thesis on Hardy at the University of Paris in 1911, which contained a "biographical" section on Hardy's life. Hardy attacked this work as "impertinent personality & untrue" (cited in Seymour-Smith 721). Upon the publication in 1925 of Ernest Brennecke's "far more impertinent" biography *The Life of Thomas Hardy,* Hardy dictated his autobiography to his second wife (cited in Seymour-Smith 721).

30. Thomas Hardy, "Last Lines dictated by T.H. referring to George Moore," Private Collection, *Dorset County Museum* (cited in Taylor 259*n*).

Chapter Three

1. In *The Anxiety of Influence,* Bloom looks for example at the works of Milton, Coleridge, Wordsworth, Blake, Goethe, Stevens, Gray, Shelley, Keats, and Whitman, among others.

2. Anthony Alpers on *New Age:* "[s]o long as the writing was good it welcomed radical departures from established Edwardian ways of thought [. . .] and in consequence it had the reputation among young writers of being *the* paper to get into" (Alpers 107). For a further examination of Mansfield's relationship with Orage and *New Age,* see Alpers 106–16.

3. *In a German Pension* was praised by the *Manchester Guardian, The Athenaeum, The Daily Telegraph,* the *Times,* and the *Pall Mall Gazette,* among others. For an overview of these assessments, see Alpers 127- 9. The first edition ran into three printings.

4. Murry later recalled, "that is how we met. That I fell in love with her, and she with me would be a matter of purely private significance: were it not that this happening [. . .] had an effect on her as a writer" J. M. Murry, *Katherine Mansfield and other Literary Studies* 73.

5. For an examination of Mansfield's health problems, including her prolonged battle with both arthritis and gonorrhea, see Tomalin 69–78. Tomalin argues that Mansfield's inability to recover from her tuberculosis despite repeated medical treatment was the result of an immune system long compromised by an untreated case of gonorrhea.

6. See Hutchins 37.

7. John Middleton Murry, letter to Thomas Hardy, March 3, 1919, Private Collection, *Dorset County Museum.*

8. See *The Athenaeum*, 4640 (April 4, 1919): 1.

9. Murry's long poem, "The Critic in Judgment," was about to be published by Leonard and Virginia Woolf at the Hogarth Press, in July 1919.

10. John Middleton Murry, letter to Thomas Hardy, October 26, 1919, Private Collection, *Dorset County Museum*.

11. John Middleton Murry, "To T. H." from *Poets' Tribute*. S. Sassoon, ed. Private Collection, *Dorset County Museum*. Written in Murry's own hand, and signed "J. M. M., October 25, 1919."

12. As James Gibson notes: "the period 1919–1920 was a busy publishing time for Hardy because it saw not only the publication of the Mellstock Edition, [. . .] of the Wessex Edition of *Satires of Circumstance* and *Moments of Vision*, but also in 1919, the first edition of his collected poems" (xxvii). Hardy completed a further three volumes of verse before his death in 1928: *Late Lyrics and Earlier* (1922), *Human Shows* (1925), and *Winter Words* (1928).

13. John Middleton Murry, *The Letters of John Middleton Murry to Katherine Mansfield*, C. A. Hankin, ed. 199*n*. All further references to this work follow the abbreviated title *LJMM*.

14. Sharon Greer Cassavant similarly remarks on Murry's serial championship and renunciation of both political causes and literary idols. See her "Introduction" to *John Middleton Murry: The Critic as Moralist*.

15. Katherine Mansfield, *Journal of Katherine Mansfield: Definitive Edition*, J. M. Murry, ed. 1954, 190. All further citations from this work refer to this edition, and follow the abbreviated title *JKM*.

16. The poem in its entirety can be found in *The Collected Letters of Katherine Mansfield*, Vol. 3:136–7. Further references to this collection follow the abbreviated title *CLKM*.

17. See *JKM* 194–9.

18. Hardy's poem "The Maid of Keinton Mandeville" was a tribute to Sir Henry Bishop on the sixty-fifth anniversary of his death, April 30, 1855. It covers half of the first sheet of the April 30 issue of *The Athenaeum*, 4696 (1920): 1.

19. Hardy contributed another poem to *The Athenaeum* in December of 1920. Murry used the poem "At the Entering of the New Year" to cover half of the first sheet of the magazine, Murry's last as editor: 4731 (December 31, 1920): 1.

20. Murry confessed his "affair" with Bibesco in a letter to Mansfield of December 10, 1920. See *Letters Between Katherine Mansfield and John Middleton Murry*. C. A. Hankin, ed. 334. See also Alpers 323–4, 332–3.

21. Katherine Mansfield, *Katherine Mansfield's Letters to John Middleton Murry: 1913–1922*. J. M. Murry, ed. 618–9. Further references to this work follow the abbreviated title *LKM*.

22. In January 1921 Murry accepted the amalgamation of *The Nation* and *The Athenaeum*, and joined Katherine in Menton at the end of February.

23. "The Daughters of The Late Colonel" was first published in the *London Mercury* in May of 1921.

24. Hardy's first wife Emma had died in November 1912. For an examination of their relationship, see Seymour-Smith's *Hardy*, 205–9, 395–425, 476–506, 710–66.

25. See *Adelphi* 1: no. 11 (April 1924).

26. For further reading on Murry's marriage to Le Maistre, who also died from tuberculosis, see Katherine Middleton Murry's biography of her father, *Beloved Quixote* 44–62.

27. Katherine Mansfield, letter to J. M. Murry, August 7, 1922, MS Papers 4000:40 ATL, cited in Boddy 11.

28. *The Will of Katherine Mansfield*, August 14, 1922, Public Record Office, London, cited in Boddy 11.

29. For a fuller examination of Murry's editorship of Mansfield's papers, see Boddy 9–22, and Ian Gordon's earlier study "The Editing of Katherine Mansfield's *Journal* and *Scrapbook*" 9.

30. Although Leslie Stephen had produced an account of his life after his wife's death in 1895, this so-called Mausoleum Book was a private work intended, as Stephen told F. W. Maitland, "entirely for her children" (letter to Maitland May 31, 1895, *Maitland papers*, Cambridge University Library). The work was not published in full until 1977.

31. As Boddy notes, Lytton Strachey, D. H. Lawrence, and Virginia Woolf, among others were horrified by Murry's publication of the journals. See Boddy 9–12.

Chapter Four

1. Strachey wrote to Virginia on July 17, 1916: "[Mansfield] was decidedly an interesting creature, I thought—very amusing and sufficiently mysterious. She spoke with great enthusiasm about the Voyage Out, and said she wanted to make your acquaintance more than anyone else's." See *Virginia Woolf and Lytton Strachey*, L. Woolf and J. Strachey eds. 56.

2. Anthony Alpers notes that Woolf and Mansfield first met on about November 1–5, 1916 (Alpers 410).

3. Peter Alexander describes the beginnings of the Hogarth Press as follows: "Virginia had been talking since 1915 of doing her own printing and Leonard took her seriously. Their purchase of a hand printing press, in March 1916 [. . .] was not initially a serious attempt to earn money [. . .] more likely it was an attempt on Leonard's part to interest Virginia in something therapeutic and practical" (Alexander 99).

4. Sydney Janet Kaplan argues that Mansfield's original inspiration for the story also included her relationships with D. H. Lawrence and his wife Frieda, and her affair with Francis Carco. See Kaplan 104.

5. For a fuller examination of the evolution of *The Aloe* into "Prelude," see Kaplan 103–17.

6. Katherine Mansfield, "Prelude," 1918, in *Collected Stories of Katherine Mansfield*, 1945, 24. All further citations from "Prelude" refer to this edition.

7. Leonard Woolf cites Virginia as complaining of Mansfield's "cheap scent and cheap sentimentality." *Beginning Again* 205.

8. See, for example, *DVW* 1:226 (December 10, 1918), in which Woolf notes "[o]n Monday I paid what has now become my weekly visit to Katherine."

9. Leonard Woolf attributed Woolf's breakdowns to Virginia's "almost pathological hypersensitiveness to criticism." See *Beginning Again* 76–82, 149.

10. As Murry had already asked Lytton Strachey, but not Virginia, to write for the magazine, her "vanity" appears to have been insulted until this invitation. See *DVW* 1:243 and 243*n*.

11. For an overview of the essays that Woolf contributed to *The Athenaeum* during the period of Murry's editorship, see Edward Bishop, *A Virginia Woolf Chronology,* 49–51.

12. Woolf's essay "Modern Novels" was published in *The Times Literary Supplement,* April 10, 1919.

13. Alpers suggests that Mansfield had "inspired" Woolf to write "Kew Gardens." See Alpers, Appendix "Chronology," August 12, 1917, and 119–22.

14. See *The Times Literary Supplement,* October 30, 1919, 607.

15. In fact, Woolf, contributed a review to the very issue of *The Athenaeum* that contained Mansfield's critique of *Night and Day.* See Woolf's "Maturity and Immaturity" 1220.

16. See *DVW* 2:28*n*. J. W. N. Sullivan had compared Mansfield's work to Checkhov and Dostoyevsky in the April 2, 1920, issue of *The Athenaeum.*

17. Woolf noted: "I have plucked out my jealousy of Katherine by writing her an insincere/sincere letter" (*DVW* 2:80).

18. See *DVW* 2:91, February 16, 1921.

19. As Woolf noted in the following February, her work in 1921 seemed to her to be of little value: "I can only hope that like dead leaves they may fertilise my brain. Otherwise, what a 12 months it has been for writing—& I at the prime of my life" (*DVW* 2:161).

20. See *DVW* 2:86.

21. Woolf's brother Thoby Stephen died of typhoid fever on November 20, 1906.

22. Mansfield wrote the following "note" to Leslie after his death: "I now know what the last chapter is. It is your birth—your coming in the autumn" (*JKM* 89).

23. See Mansfield's letter to Woolf, August 1917, in which the postscript reads: "Do let us meet in the nearest future darling Virginia & don't quite forget Katherine" (*CLKM* 1:324).

Chapter Five

1. There is some disagreement about the precise dating of the original manuscript. See Heine 399–432.

2. Virginia Woolf, *The Voyage Out: Definitive Edition* (1990) 74–5. All further citations from this work refer to this edition. *The Voyage Out* was first published in 1915.

3. In Woolf's earlier, April 1919 version of the essay, she chose to single out *Jude the Obscure* rather than *The Mayor of Casterbridge* as Hardy's highest achievement ("Modern Novels" 189). This may demonstrate Woolf's growing fascination with *Mayor* during the period (1924–5) she was revising "Modern Novels" and writing *Mrs. Dalloway.*

4. Woolf wrote "Modern Novels" criticizing traditional novels during the same period in which she was completing *Night and Day,* considered by Mansfield and many later critics as Woolf's most "traditional" novel.

5. See also the following references to Hardy: *DVW* 1:291 (July 12, 1919), *LVW* 2:440 (letter to Roger Fry, August 1920), *DVW* 2: 104, (March 1921), *DVW* 2: 126 (August 1921), *DVW* 2:150 (December 1921), *DVW* 2:204 (October 1922), in each of which Woolf remarks on the Hardy "obituary."

6. Virginia Woolf, "How it Strikes a Contemporary." *The Times Literary Supplement,* 1107:221. All further references cite from this original edition.

7. Soon after the amalgamation of *The Nation and Athenaeum* in 1923, Leonard Woolf became the magazine's literary editor. See Leonard Woolf, *Downhill All the Way* 94 and 128.

8. Although Woolf's diary entries exemplify the emphasis she had placed on the design of *Mrs. Dalloway,* she later denied the importance of her "method" to the reader: "The reader it is hoped will not give a thought to the book's method or to the book's lack of method." See Virginia Woolf, "Introduction" to *Mrs. Dalloway* (Modern Library Edition 1928). Reproduced in *The Shakespeare Head Press Edition of Virginia Woolf: Mrs. Dalloway.* Ed. M. Beja. Oxford: Blackwell, 1996, 197–9. All further references cite from this source.

9. In his 1924 book *Conversations on Ebury Street,* novelist George Moore openly abused Hardy's work. See Seymour-Smith, *Hardy* 471–5.

10. Thomas Hardy, "Preface" to *The Mayor of Casterbridge.* First included in the 1895 edition of the novel. Cited here from the New Wessex edition, 1990, 25.

11. See *DVW* 3:101.

12. Woolf noted that she attended Hardy's funeral at Westminster Abbey on January 6, 1928. See *DVW* 3:173 and 173*n.*

13. Max Beerbohm had written a letter to Woolf in which he praised the *Common Reader* as "above any modern book of criticism." A note in *The Diary of Virginia Woolf* states that "Woolf had agreed to speak to the Newnham Arts Society in May." See *DVW* 3:173 and *n.*

Chapter Six

1. Woolf noted in this entry: "Anyhow, I feel that I have exorcised the spell wh. Murry & others said I had laid myself under after Jacob's Room" (*DVW* 2:317).

2. Woolf often used the term "The Old Man" to refer to her father. See for example *DVW* 3:3.

3. Leslie Stephen, cited in *New Dictionary of National Biography: Notes for Contributors* (1994) 1.

4. Quentin Bell's biography of Woolf explains that *The Hyde Park Gate News* appeared weekly from February 9, 1891, to April 1895. See Bell 1:28–32.

5. Maitland states that "Stephen contributed to all volumes except three and wrote 378 articles" (457 *n*). Women subjects made up less than 4 percent of the articles in the *DNB*.

6. Leslie Stephen, letter to Julia Stephen, *Berg Collection,* New York Public Library, Astor Lenox and Tilden foundations, cited in L. Gordon 15.

7. Frederic Maitland was married to Florence Fisher, Julia Stephen's niece, and had often been a guest at the Stephen's home. Maitland had been hand-picked by Stephen to be his biographer. Stephen left the following instructions: "The only living person who could say anything to the purpose at present would be F. W. Maitland. He as I always feel understands me, and I have explained my views on the subject to him." L. Stephen, *Sir Leslie Stephen's Mausoleum Book* (1977) 4 *n.*

8. Caroline Emelia Stephen wrote several mystical and religious texts including *The Light Arising: Thoughts on the Central Radiance, Quaker Strongholds,* and *The Vision of Faith.* See Marcus, "Niece" in *Languages of Patriarchy* 115–35.

9. This article, a review of *The First Duke and Duchess of Newcastle-upon-Tyne,* by Thomas Longueville (Longmans, Green & Co., London, 1910), first appeared in *The Times Literary Supplement* on February 2, 1911, 40.

10. *Hours in a Library, First Series,* a collection of essays of Leslie Stephen, was published in 1874 by Smith, Elder and Co.; *Second Series,* 1876; *Third Series,* 1879.

11. Due to his failing health, Stephen gave up the editorship of the dictionary in April 1891. See Fenwick, *Leslie Stephen's Life in Letters: A Bibliographical Study* for a bibliography of Stephen's contributions to the *Dictionary of National Biography.*

12. For clarity, I use here the passage as corrected by Woolf for the American edition of *To the Lighthouse* published by Harcourt Brace. *To the Lighthouse* (American Edition). New York: Harcourt Brace, 1927, 194. This passage appears in the original Hogarth Press Edition as follows: "[Mr. Ramsay stumbling along a passage stretched his arms out one dark morning, but, Mrs. Ramsay having died rather suddenly the night before, he stretched his arms out. They remained empty.]" (120) For further details on differences between the two editions see J. A. Lavin 85–211.

13. As Suzanne Raitt suggests, this "line" may be a further indication of the closeness of this novel to autobiography, and more specifically, of Lily's connection to Woolf: "Woolf drew a line down the centre of her last passage of the manuscript [of *To the Lighthouse*], as Lily does down her painting." Raitt 34.

14. Woolf had written two "Lives of the Obscure," now collected in the *Common Reader, First Series:* "Taylor's and Edgeworths" and "Laetitia Pilkington."

15. In addition to Stephen's contributions to the *DNB* he also wrote several full-length biographies, a four-volume work entitled *Studies of a Biographer,* and a series of shorter works for the "English Men of Letters" series. See Maitland 498–9 for a full listing.

16. Woolf writes that by this time "he had written the *History of English Thought in the Eighteenth Century,* which is said by some to be his masterpiece," and refers to Stephen's *The Science of Ethics* and *The Playground of Europe.* Woolf, "Stephen" 76. Woolf makes no mention, however, of Stephen's biographical works.

17. In Meredith's *The Egoist,* the character of Vernon Whitford (who was based upon Leslie Stephen) is described with the phrase "Phoebus Apollo turned fasting Friar" (12). First published in 1879.

Conclusion

1. See Perry Meisel, *The Absent Father: Virginia Woolf and Walter Pater* 1980.

Works Cited

Alexander, Peter. *Leonard and Virginia Woolf: A Literary Partnership.* London: Harvester Wheatsheaf, 1992.

Alpers, Anthony. *The Life of Katherine Mansfield.* Oxford: Oxford Press, 1982.

Annan, Noel G. *Leslie Stephen: The Godless Victorian.* London: Weidenfeld and Nicolson, 1984.

———. *Leslie Stephen: His Thought and Character in Relation to his Time.* London: MacGibbon & Kee, 1951.

Barthes, Roland. "The Death of the Author." *Image-Music-Text.* Trans. Stephen Heath. New York: Hill and Wang, 1977. 142–8.

———. "From Work to Text." *Image-Music-Text.* Trans. Stephen Heath. New York: Hill and Wang, 1977. 155–64.

Bell, Quentin. *Virginia Woolf: A Biography.* 2 Vols. New York: Harcourt Brace, 1972.

Belsey, C. and J. Moore eds. *The Feminist Reader: Essays in Gender and the Politics of Literary Criticism.* London: Macmillan, 1989.

Bishop, Edward. *A Virginia Woolf Chronology.* New York: MacMillan, 1989.

Bloom, Harold. *The Anxiety of Influence.* London, Oxford, New York: The Oxford University Press, 1973.

———. "Introduction." *Modern Critical Views: Virginia Woolf.* Ed. H. Bloom. New York: Chelsea House Publishers, 1986. 1–6.

———. *A Map of Misreading.* London, Oxford, New York: The Oxford University Press, 1975.

———. *The Poetics of Influence.* London, Oxford, New York: The Oxford University Press,1988.

———. *The Strong Light of the Canonical.* London, Oxford, New York: The Oxford University Press, 1987.

———. *The Western Canon.* London: MacMillan, 1994.

Boddy, Gillian. "Leaving 'All fair'? Working Towards a New Edition of Katherine Mansfield's Notebooks." *Worlds of Katherine Mansfield.* Ed. H. Ricketts. Auckland: Nagare Press, 1991. 9–22.

Bowlby, Rachel. *Virginia Woolf: Feminist Destinations.* Oxford: Basil Blackwell Ltd., 1988.

Bryce, James. "Leslie Stephen and His Works." L. Stephen, *Essays on Freethinking and Plainspeaking.* London: Smith, Elder and Co., 1907. ix–xxiii.

Burgan, Mary. *Illness, Gender and Writing: the Case of Katherine Mansfield.* Baltimore and London: The Johns Hopkins University Press, 1994.

Burke, Carolyn. "Report from Paris." *Women's Writing and the Women's Movement: Signs* 3 (Summer 1978): 843–55.

Casagrande, Peter J. *Hardy's Influence on the Modern Novel.* London: MacMillan, 1987.

Cassavant, Sharon Greer. *John Middleton Murry: The Critic as Moralist.* University, Alabama: University of Alabama Press, 1982.

Chase, M. E. *Thomas Hardy from Serial to Novel.* New York: Russell & Russell, 1964.

Chesterton, G. K. *The Victorian Age in Literature.* London: Williams and Norgate, 1914.

Clayton, Jay. "The Alphabet of Suffering: Effie Deans, Tess Durbeyfield, Martha Ray and Hetty Sorrel." Clayton and Rothstein, *Influence and Intertextuality* 37–60.

———. and Eric Rothstein. "Figures in the Corpus: Theories of Influence and Intertextuality." Clayton and Rothstein, *Influence and Intertextuality* 3–36.

———. and Eric Rothstein eds. *Influence and Intertextuality in Literary History.* Madison: The University of Wisconsin Press, 1991.

Cox, R. G. ed. *Thomas Hardy: The Critical Heritage.* London: Routledge and Kegan Paul, 1970.

de Bolla, Peter. *Harold Bloom.* New York and London: Routledge, 1988.

Dick, Susan. *Virginia Woolf.* London, New York, Melbourne, Auckland: Edward Arnold, 1989.

Eagleton, Mary ed. *Feminist Theory: A Reader.* Oxford: Basil Blackwell, 1986.

Fenwick, Gillian. *Leslie Stephen's Life in Letters: A Bibliographical Study.* Aldershot, England: Scolar Press, 1993.

Freud, Sigmund. *The Complete Psychological Works of Freud.* (Standard Edition). Trans. J. Strachey. Vols. 4 – 10, 17, 21. London: Hogarth Press, 1955–58.

Friedman, Susan Stanford. "Weavings: Intertextuality and the (Re)Birth of the Author." Clayton and Rothstein, *Influence and Intertextuality* 146–180.

Fulbrook, Kate: *Katherine Mansfield.* London: Harvester Press, Ltd., 1986.

Gibson, James. "Introduction." *The Complete Poems of Thomas Hardy.* Ed. J. Gibson. London: MacMillan, 1976. xix-xxxii.

Gilbert, Sandra M. "What do Feminist Critics Want? A Postcard from the Volcano." *The New Feminist Criticism.* Ed. E. Showalter. London: Virago, 1985. 29–45.

———. and Gubar, Susan. *The Madwoman in the Attic: The Woman Writer and the 19th Century Literary Imagination.* New Haven: Yale University Press, 1979.

Gittings, Robert. "Introduction." T. Hardy, *The Hand of Ethelberta.* London: MacMillan, 1975. xi-xxii.

Gordon, Ian. "The Editing of Katherine Mansfield's *Journal* and *Scrapbook.*" *Landfall* (Christchurch) 13 (March 1959) 1:62–9.

Gordon, Lyndall. *Virginia Woolf: A Writer's Life.* Oxford: Oxford University Press, 1984.

Grosskurth, Phyllis. *Leslie Stephen.* Harlow, Essex: Longmans, Green & Co. Ltd, 1968.

Hankin, Cherry ed. *Katherine Mansfield and Her Confessional Stories.* London: MacMillan, 1983.

———. ed. *Letters Between Katherine Mansfield and John Middleton Murry.* London: Virago Press, 1988.

————. ed. *The Letters of John Middleton Murry to Katherine Mansfield*. London: Constable, 1983.

Hanson, Clare ed. *The Critical Writings of Katherine Mansfield*. London: MacMillan, 1987.

Hardy, Florence Emily. *The Life of Thomas Hardy*. London: MacMillan, 1962.

Hardy, Thomas. "According to the Mighty Working." *The Athenaeum* 4640 (April 4, 1919). 129.

————. "At The Entering of the New Year." *The Athenaeum* 4731 (December 31, 1920). 881.

————. *The Collected Letters of Thomas Hardy* (*CLTH*), 6 Vols. Eds. R. Purdy and M. Millgate. Oxford: Clarendon Press, 1978–1988.

————. *The Complete Poems of Thomas Hardy*. Ed. J. Gibson. London: MacMillan, 1976.

————. *Desperate Remedies*. London: William Tinsley's, 1871.

————. *Far From the Madding Crowd*. *Cornhill* 29–30 (Jan-Dec 1874). 29:1–661 30:1–673.

————. *The Hand of Ethelberta*. *Cornhill* 32–33 (Jul 1875–May 1876). 32: 1–760 33: 1–640.

————. *The Hand of Ethelberta. Introduction by Robert Gittings*. London: Macmillan, 1975.

————. *Human Shows*. London: Macmillan, 1925.

————. *Jude the Obscure*. London: Macmillan, 1896.

————. *A Laodicean*. London: Harper Bros., 1881.

————. *Late Lyrics and Earlier*. London: Macmillan, 1922.

————. "The Maid of Keinton-Mandeville." *The Athenaeum* 4696 (April 30, 1920). 565.

————. *The Mayor of Casterbridge*. The New Wessex Edition. London: Macmillan, 1990. First published 1886.

————. *A Pair of Blue Eyes*. London: William Tinsley's, 1873.

————. *The Return of the Native*. *Belgravia*, 34–7 (January 1878–9). 34: 257–508 35: 1–508 36: 1–508 37: 1–256.

————. *Satires of Circumstance*. London: Macmillan, 1914.

————. *Tess of the D'Urbervilles*. London: Osgood McIlvaine, 1891.

————. *The Trumpet Major*. London: Smith, Elder and Co.,1880.

————. *Under the Greenwood Tree*. London: William Tinsley's, 1872.

————. *Winter Words*. London: Macmillan, 1928.

Hawkes, Ellen. "Woolf's Magical Garden of Women." *New Feminist Essays on Virginia Woolf*. Ed. J. Marcus. 31- 60.

Heine, Elizabeth. "Virginia Woolf's Revisions to *The Voyage Out*." V. Woolf, *The Voyage Out: Definitive Edition*. London: Hogarth Press, 1990. 399–452.

Homans, Margaret ed. *Virginia Woolf: A Collection of Critical Essays*. New Jersey: Prentice-Hall, Inc., 1993.

Hutchins, Patricia. "Thomas Hardy and Some Younger Writers." *Journal of Modern Literature* 3, No. 1 (Feb. 1973). 35–44.

Huxley, Aldous. *Two or Three Graces and Other Stories*. London: Chatto and Windus, 1926.

Jacobus, Mary. "The Difference of View." Belsey and Moore 66–76.

———ed. *Women Writing and Writing about Women.* London: Croom Helm, 1979.

Kaplan, Sydney Janet. *Katherine Mansfield and the Origins of Modernist Fiction.* Ithaca and London: Cornell University Press, 1991.

Kiely, Robert. *"Jacob's Room:* A Study in Still Life." *Modern Critical Views: Virginia Woolf.* Ed. H. Bloom. New York: Chelsea House Publishers, 1988. 207–14.

Kolodny, Annette. "A Map for Rereading." *The New Feminist Criticism.* Ed. E. Showalter. 46–62.

Kristeva, Julia. *Desire in Language: A Semiotic Approach to Literature and Art.* Ed. L. S. Roudiez. Trans. T. Gora, et al., New York: Columbia University Press, 1980.

———. *Séméiotikè: Recherches pour un Sémanalyse.* Paris: Edition du Seuil, 1969.

———. "Women's Time." Belsey and Moore 201–16.

Laurence, Patricia Ondek. *The Reading of Silence: Virginia Woolf in the English Tradition.* Stanford, California: Stanford University Press, 1991.

Lavin, J. A. "The first editions of *To the Lighthouse." Proof* 2 (1972). 185–211.

Lea, Frank A. *John Middleton Murry.* New York: Oxford University Press, 1960.

Lee, Sydney. "Leslie Stephen." *Dictionary of National Biography: Supplement, 1901–1911.* Ed. Sir S. Lee. London: Smith, Elder and Co, 1912. 398–405.

Longueville, Thomas. *The First Duke and Duchess of Newcastle-Upon-Tyne.* London: Longmans Green & Co., 1910.

Love, Jean O. *Virginia Woolf: Sources of Madness and Art.* Berkeley: University of California Press, 1977.

Maitland, F. W. *The Life and Letters of Leslie Stephen.* London: Smith Elder and Co, 1906.

Majumadar Robin, and Allan McLaurin eds. *Virginia Woolf: The Critical Heritage.* Boston and London: Routledge & Kegan Paul, 1975.

Mansfield, Katherine. *The Collected Stories.* (repr. from 1945 ed.)London: Constable and Co. 1962.

———. "A Ship Comes into the Harbour." *The Athenaeum* 4673 (November 21, 1919). 1227.

———. "A Short Story." *The Athenaeum* 4650 (June 13, 1919). 459.

———. *Bliss and Other Stories.* London: Constable, 1920.

———. *The Collected Letters of Katherine Mansfield (CLKM).* 3 Vols. Eds. V. O'Sullivan and M. Scott. Oxford: Clarendon Press, 1984.

———. *The Dove's Nest and Other Stories.* Ed. J. M. Murry. London: Constable, 1923.

———. *The Garden Party and Other Stories.* London: Constable, 1922.

———. *In a German Pension.* London: Stephen Swift, 1911.

———. *Journal of Katherine Mansfield (JKM).* Ed. J. M. Murry. London: Constable and Company, 1927.

———. *Journal of Katherine Mansfield: Definitive Edition.* Ed. J. M. Murry. London: Constable and Company, 1954.

———. *Katherine Mansfield's Letters to John Middleton Murry, 1913–1922.* Ed. J. M. Murry. London: Constable and Company, 1951.

————. "Prelude." *The Collected Stories* (repr. from 1945 ed.) London: Constable and Co. 1962. 11–60.

————. *The Scrapbook of Katherine Mansfield.* Ed. J. M. Murry. London: Constable and Company, 1939.

————. *Something Childish and Other Stories.* Ed. J. M. Murry. London: Constable, 1924.

Marcus, Jane. "Art and Anger." *Feminist Studies* 4, No 1 (Feb 1978). 68–98.

————. "Liberty, Sorority, Misogyny." *Virginia Woolf and the Languages of Patriarchy.* Ed. J. Marcus. 75–95.

————ed. *New Feminist Essays on Virginia Woolf.* Lincoln: University of Nebraska Press, 1981.

————. "Niece of a Nun: Virginia Woolf, Caroline Stephen and the Cloistered Imagination." *Virginia Woolf and the Languages of Patriarchy.* Ed. J. Marcus. 115–35.

————. "Thinking Back through our Mothers." *New Feminist Essays on Virginia Woolf.* Ed. J. Marcus. 1–30.

————ed. *Virginia Woolf and the Languages of Patriarchy.* Bloomington: Indiana University Press, 1987.

Meisel, Perry. *The Absent Father: Virginia Woolf and Walter Pater.* New Haven and London: Yale University Press, 1980.

Meredith, George. *The Egoist.* (repr. from revised 1897 ed.)London: The Bodley Head, 1972.

Miller, Nancy K. ed. *The Poetics of Gender.* New York: Columbia University Press, 1986.

Millgate, Michael. *Testamentary Acts: Browning, Tennyson, James, Hardy.* Oxford: Clarendon Press, 1992.

————. *Thomas Hardy: His Career as a Novelist.* London: Bodeley Head, 1971.

Morgan, Rosemarie. *Cancelled Words: Rediscovering Thomas Hardy.* London and New York: Routledge, 1992.

————. *Women and Sexuality in the Novels of Thomas Hardy.* London and New York: Routledge, 1988.

Moore, George. *Conversations on Ebury Street.* London: Heinemann, 1924.

Murry, John Middleton. *Aspects of Literature.* London: Collins, 1920.

————. *Between Two Worlds.* London: Johnathan Cape Ltd., 1935.

————. *The Critic in Judgement.* London: Hogarth Press, 1919.

————. *Defending Romanticism: Selected Essays of John Middleton Murry.* Ed. M. Woodfield. Bristol: Bristol Press, 1989.

————. *The Evolution of an Intellectual.* London: Cobden Sanderson, 1920.

————. *Katherine Mansfield and other Literary Studies.* London: Constable, 1959.

————. *The Letters of John Middleton Murry to Katherine Mansfield (LJMM).* Ed. C. A. Hankin. London: Constable, 1983.

————. *Poems 1917–1918.* London: Hampstead, 1918.

————. "The Poetry of Mr. Hardy." *The Athenaeum* 4671 (November 7, 1919). 1147–9.

———. "The Supremacy of Thomas Hardy." *Defending Romanticism: Selected Essays of John Middleton Murry.* Ed. M. Woodfield. Bristol: Bristol Press, 1989. 207–13.

———. "Thomas Hardy." *Defending Romanticism: Selected Essays of John Middleton Murry.* Ed. M. Woodfield. Bristol: Bristol Press, 1989. 297–308.

———. "To T.H." *Poet's Tribute.* Ed. S. Sassoon. Private collection *Dorset County Museum.* (1918).

———ed. *Journal of Katherine Mansfield.* London: Constable and Company, 1927.

———ed. *Journal of Katherine Mansfield: Definitive Edition.* London: Constable and Company, 1954.

———ed. *Katherine Mansfield's letters to John Middleton Murry, 1913–1922.* London: Constable and Company, 1951.

———ed. *The Scrapbook of Katherine Mansfield.* London: Constable and Company, 1939.

Murry, Katherine Middleton. *Beloved Quixote: the Unknown Life of John Middleton Murry.* London: Souvenir Press, 1986.

Oliphant E. "The Anti-Marriage League." *Blackwood's Magazine* 159 (January, 1896). 135–49.

Paul, Janis, M. *The Victorian Heritage of Virginia Woolf.* Norman, Oklahoma: Pilgrim Books, 1987.

Paulin, Tom. *Thomas Hardy: The Poetry of Perception.* Totowa, New Jersey: Rowman and Littlefield, 1975.

Pinion, F. B. *Thomas Hardy: His Life and Friends.* London: MacMillan, 1992.

Raitt, Suzanne. *Virginia Woolf's To the Lighthouse.* London: Harvester Wheatsheaf, 1990.

———. *Vita and Virginia.* Oxford: Clarendon Press, 1993.

Ricketts, Harry ed. *Worlds of Katherine Mansfield.* Wellington: Nagare Press, 1991.

Riffaterre, Michael. "Interpretation and Undecidability." *New Literary History* 12:2 (1981). 227–242.

Rose, Phyllis. *Woman of Letters: A Life of Virginia Woolf.* London: Pandora Press, 1986.

Rushdie, Salman. "Imaginary Homelands." *Imaginary Homelands: Essays and Criticism, 1981–1991.* London: Granta Books, 1991. 9–21.

Schulkind, Jeanne. "Introduction." V. Woolf, *Moments of Being.*(2nd. ed.) London: Hogarth Press, 1985. 11–24.

———. "Preface." V. Woolf, *Moments of Being.*(2nd. ed.) London: Hogarth Press, 1985. 6.

Seymour-Smith, Martin. *Hardy.* London: Bloomsbury, 1994.

Showalter, Elaine. *A Literature of Their Own: British Women Novelists from Bronte to Lessing.* New Revised ed. London: Virago, 1984.

———. ed. *The New Feminist Criticism.* London: Virago, 1985.

Stephen, Caroline. *The Light Arising: Thoughts on the Central Radiance.* Cambridge: Heffer, 1908.

———. *Quaker Strongholds.* London: Headley Brothers, 1890.

———. *The Vision of Faith.* London: Heffer and Sons, 1911.

Stephen, James Fitzjames. *Liberty, Equality, Fraternity.* 1873. New Edition, by R. J. White. Cambridge: Cambridge University Press, 1967.

Stephen, Sir Leslie. *An Agnostic's Apology and other Essays.* 2nd Edition. London: Smith, Elder and Co., Duckworth and Co., 1903.

———. "Are We Christians?" *Essays on Freethinking and Plainspeaking.* London: Smith, Elder and Co. Duckworth and Co., 1907. 126–76.

———. "Art and Morality." *Cornhill* 32 (July 1875). 91–101.

———. "A Bad Five Minutes in the Alps." *Essays on Freethinking and Plainspeaking.* London: Smith, Elder and Co. Duckworth and Co., 1907 177–225.

———. *History of English Thought in the Eighteenth Century,* 2 Vols. London: Smith Elder and Co., 1876.

———. *Hours in a Library.* London: Smith Elder and Co. First Series, 1874, Second Series, 1876, Third Series, 1879.

———. *Letters.* (Unpublished letters to Julia Stephen).*Berg Collection,* New York Public Library, Astor, Lenox, and Tilden Foundations.

———. *Sir Leslie Stephen's Mausoleum Book.* Ed. A. Bell. Oxford: Clarendon Press, 1977.

———. *The Playground of Europe.* London: Longmans, 1871.

———. *The Science of Ethics.* London: Smith Elder and Co., 1882.

———. *Studies of a Biographer.* London: Duckworth and Co., Vols 1 and 2 (1899), Vols. 3 and 4 (1902).

Strachey, Lytton. *Eminent Victorians.* London: Harcourt Brace Jovanovich, 1918.

Taylor, Richard H. ed. *The Personal Notebooks of Thomas Hardy.* London: MacMillan, 1978.

Tomalin, Clare. *Katherine Mansfield: A Secret Life.* London: Viking, 1987.

Tompkins, Jane. "Me and My Shadow." *Gender and Theory.* Ed. L. Kauffmann. Oxford: Basil Blackwell Ltd. 1989. 121–39.

Woodfield, Malcolm. "Introduction." *Defending Romanticism: Selected Essays of John Middleton Murry.* Ed. M. Woodfield. Bristol: Bristol Press, 1989. 1–52.

Woolf, Leonard. *Beginning Again.* London: Hogarth Press, 1964.

———. *Downhill all the Way.* London: Hogarth Press, 1967.

———and J. Strachey eds. *Virginia Woolf and Lytton Strachey.* London: Hogarth Press, 1956.

Woolf, Robert Lee. *Sensational Victorian: The Life and Fiction of Mary Elizabeth Braddon.* New York: Garland Publishers, 1979.

Woolf, Virginia. *Collected Essays by Virginia Woolf (CEVW),* 4 Vols. Ed. L. Woolf. London: Hogarth Press, 1966–67.

———. *The Common Reader.* First Series edition. London: Hogarth Press, 1925.

———. *The Common Reader.* Second Series edition. London: Hogarth Press, 1932.

———. *The Complete Shorter Fiction of Virginia Woolf.* Ed. S. Dick. New York: Harcourt Brace Jovanovich, 1986.

———. *The Diary of Virginia Woolf (DVW),* 5 Vols. Ed. A. O. Bell. London: Hogarth Press, 1977–1984.

———. "The Duke and Duchess of Newcastle-Upon-Tyne." *Tht Times Literary Supplement* 473 (February 2, 1911). 40.

———. "How it Strikes a Contemporary." *The Times Literary Supplement* 1107 (April 5, 1923). 221–2.

————. "Hours in a Library." *The Times Literary Supplement* 776 (November 30, 1916). 565–6.

————. "Introduction." (*Mrs. Dalloway*). *The Shakespeare Head Press Edition of Virginia Woolf: Mrs. Dalloway.* Ed. M. Beja. Oxford: Blackwell, 1996. 197–9. First published: *Mrs. Dalloway* (Modern Library Edition) New York: Random House, 1928.

————. *Jacob's Room.* (New ed. 1929)London: Hogarth Press, 1929. First published in 1922.

————. "The Leaning Tower." *Collected Essays by Virginia Woolf,* 4 Vols. Ed. L. Woolf. London: Hogarth Press, 1966–7. 2: 162–181.

————. "Leslie Stephen." *Collected Essays by Virginia Woolf,* 4 Vols. Ed. L. Woolf. London: Hogarth Press, 1966–7. 4: 76–80.

————. *The Letters of Virginia Woolf (LVW),* 6 Vols. Eds. N. Nicholson and J. Trautmann. London: Chatto, 1975–80.

————. "Maturity and Immaturity." *The Athenaeum* 4673 (Nov 21, 1919). 1220.

————. "Modern Novels." *The Times Literary Supplement* 899 (April 10, 1919). 189–90.

————. "Modern Fiction." *The Common Reader,* First Series edition. London: Hogarth Press, 1925. 184–195.

————. *Moments of Being.* (2nd ed.) Ed. J. Schulkind. London: Hogarth Press, 1985.

————. *Mrs. Dalloway.* London: Hogarth Press, 1925.

————. *Mrs. Dalloway.* (The Modern Library Edition). New York: Random House, 1928.

————. *Mrs. Dalloway's Party.* Ed. S. McNichol. New York: Harcourt Brace Jovanovich, 1973.

————. *Night and Day.* London: Duckworth, 1919.

————. *Orlando: A Biography.* (12th imp. 1978) London: Hogarth Press, 1928.

————. *Roger Fry: A Biography.* London: Hogarth Press, 1940.

————. *A Room of One's Own.* London: Hogarth Press, 1928.

————. "A Sketch of the Past." *Moments of Being.* London: Hogarth Press, 1985. 64-159.

————. "Sterne." *Collected Essays by Virginia Woolf,* 4 Vols. Ed. L. Woolf. London: Hogarth Press, 1966–67. 3: 86–93.

————. "A Talk About Memoirs." *Collected Essays by Virginia Woolf,* 4 Vols. Ed. L. Woolf. London: Hogarth Press, 1966–67. 4: 216–220.

————. *Three Guineas.* London: Hogarth Press, 1938.

————. *To the Lighthouse.* (New ed. 1930)London: Hogarth Press, 1927.

————. *To The Lighthouse* (American Edition).New York: Harcourt Brace, 1927.

————. *The Voyage Out.* London: Duckworth and Co., 1915.

————. *The Voyage Out,* The Definitive Edition. Ed. E. Heine. London: Hogarth Press, 1990.

————. *Women and Writing,* Ed. M. Barrett. London: Women's Press, 1979.

Woolmer, Howard J. *A Checklist of the Hogarth Press.* Revere, Pennsylvania: Woolmer/Brotherson Ltd.,1986.

Index